Solitary Travelers

Solitary Travelers

Nineteenth-Century Women's Travel Narratives and the Scientific Vocation

Lila Marz Harper

Madison • Teaneck
Fairleigh Dickinson University Press
London: Associated University Presses

Associated University Presses
440 Forsgate Drive
Cranbury, NJ 08512

Associated University Presses
16 Barter Street
London WC1A 2AH, England

Associated University Presses
P.O. Box 338, Port Credit
Mississauga, Ontario
Canada L5G 4L8

The paper used in this publication meets the requirements of the American National Standard for Permanence of Paper for Printed Library Materials Z39.48-1984.

Library of Congress Cataloging-in-Publication Data

Harper, Lila Marz, 1955–
    Solitary travelers : nineteenth-century women's travel narratives and the scientific vocation / Lila Marz Harper.
        p.   cm.
    Includes bibliographical references and index.
    ISBN 0-8386-3860-0 (alk. paper)
        1. Travelers' writings, English—History and criticism.   2. Literature and science—Great Britain—History—19th century.   3. English prose literature—Women authors—History and criticism.   4. English prose literature—19th century—History and criticism.   5. British—Travel—Foreign countries—History—19th century.   6. Bird, Isabella L. (Isabella Lucy), 1831–1904—Journeys.   7. Kingsley, Mary Henrietta, 1862–1900—Journeys.   8. Wollstonecraft, Mary, 1759–1797—Journeys.   9. Martineau, Harriet, 1802–1876—Journeys.   10. Women travelers—History—19th century.   11. Science in literature.   I. Title.

PR788.T72 H37   2001
820.9'355—dc21   00–050409

Contents

Acknowledgments   7

1. New Opportunities: Women, Science, and Travel   11
2. Mary Wollstonecraft: "A New Genus"   36
3. Harriet Martineau: An Investigative Observer   82
4. Isabella Bird Bishop: An RGS Fellow   133
5. Mary H. Kingsley: In Pursuit of Fish and Fetish   175
6. Conclusion   222

Notes   233
Works Cited   260
Index   271

Acknowledgments

SOLITARY TRAVELERS DEVELOPED OUT OF MY INTEREST IN EXPLOR-
ing the interactions between literature and science, an interest
which resulted in my specializing in the Victorian era, a time when
literature and science were richly interwoven and, having had a
childhood centered on natural history with its early ecological sensitivity and drive to understand the individual organism on its own
terms, such themes in literature caught my attention. I benefited
from Dr. William Rossi's graduate seminar on nineteenth-century
science and literature at the University of Oregon and Dr. Richard
Stein's suggestion to look at women's travel narratives when beginning my dissertation work at the University of Oregon. In my research, I found unexpected clarification of and insight into my own
family's work on the margins of science and better understanding
of the history behind my mother's botanical work and my father's
biology and geology teaching.

Writing the dissertation and revising the manuscript was a long
process done in absentia and I owe much to the patience of Dr.
Rossi whose sensitive reading of the chapters' drafts taught me
much about writing and how to respond to writing. Additionally, I
thank the members of my dissertation committee, Dr. Stein, Dr.
Richard Stevenson, and Dr. Frances Cogan, for their patience in the
process. I would also like to thank the editors and readers at Fairleigh Dickinson University Press for their encouragement and detailed responses to this work. As I have done all my own typing and
proofreading, the errors are all my own.

Working in isolation, away from a major research library, was
difficult and I was dependent on the help of Becky Smith and the
Interlibrary Loan staff at Central Washington University Library for
running material down and the combined wisdom of Victoria discussion list for answering many queries and just keeping me sane
and in contact with current scholarship.

I am indebted to the Central Washington University graduate
school and College of Arts and Humanities for conference travel
support and my colleagues in the department of English for their

7

moral support and encouragement. Particularly, I cannot sufficiently express my deep gratitude to the current and past members of the adjunct faculty for their loyal support and solidarity in difficult times over the past eleven years. Thank you, Patricia Garrison, Ruthi Erdman, Virginia Mack, and Karen Gookin. You know what we have been through.

My thanks to Indiana University Press for permission to quote from Doris and Paul Beik's translation of Flora Tristan's essay in *Flora Tristan, Utopian Feminist,* Elizabeth Hagglund for sending me material on Mary Kingsley, and Dr. Anka Ryall for sharing her research on Wollstonecraft and natural history. And additional thanks to the fellows at the University of Oregon's Graphic Arts and Media Services, Tony Michaels and Cristian Boboia, for helping me obtain an engraving of Harriet Martineau on short notice.

To my husband, James Harper, a slightly bewildered mathematician, and my son Artemus Harper, for whom this project must have seemed never ending—it finally ended. I cannot thank you enough for your support through all of this and for holding my hand through numerous computer upgrades. And for Sara Katherine Harper, who was born during the last stages, I hope you will find the work readable someday.

And, finally, this is for my parents, Sally and Harold G. Marz, who introduced me to the natural world and taught me how to observe, who have always had bird feeders up, seeds germinating, and compost maturing, and who have worried over the numbers of bees, butterflies, migrating birds, and the future of other species.

Solitary Travelers

1
New Opportunities:
Women, Science, and Travel

IN MAY 1896, A THIRTY-YEAR-OLD BEATRIX POTTER, ACCOMPA-
nied by her uncle, Sir Henry Roscoe, went to Kew Gardens to meet
the director, William T. Thiselton-Dyer, and George Massee, assistant director, former president and founder of the British Mycological Society and the Kew's chief mycologist. Potter had informally
studied mycology with Charles McIntosh, a self-educated and
highly respected Scottish naturalist, for about four years and had
produced a series of beautifully detailed macroscopic and microscopic studies of fungus.[1] She also had been successful in mastering
the difficult process of germinating spores. Additionally, her uncle
was a highly regarded chemist and Vice-Chancellor of the University of London. This connection got her entrance into Kew; but
when she attempted to submit her work, she was met with disbelief.
With her uncle's support, she prepared a paper to present to the
Linnean Society of London. There is every indication from her
drawings and journals that she had succeeded in germinating spores
where others had failed; additionally, she was drawing very fruitful
conclusions about the symbiotic relationship between fungi and
algae in lichen. Her paper, "On the Germination of the Spores of
Agaricinea" was listed in the *Proceedings* as having been presented
on 1 April 1897. It was read by a male member of the society, and
she was not allowed to attend the meeting. No encouragement apparently followed. While her interest continued, Potter did not continue to pursue her attempts to gain professional recognition.[2] She
eventually found her financial independence in writing and illustrating children's literature.

Potter was a scientific genius in a time when the term "genius"
was only applicable to men. It may be said that science lost a good
botanist and the rest of society gained Peter Rabbit, but Potter also
very early recognized the need to preserve open land and, influenced by Canon Hardwicke Rawnsley and Octavia Hill, she used

11

the proceeds from the sales of her children's books to set aside land in the Lake District for the National Trust, conserving thousands of acres.[3] Additionally, her art was informed by her scientific training. While her interests in natural history remained, they had to be redirected and Potter's experience was not unique. Others may not have been as determined nor had the proper family connections, but more than a century before Potter, many scientifically-oriented women attempted to gain a place in science with varying degrees of success and these attempts were made before the word "scientist" became a household word. What is particularly striking about Potter's experiences with the director of Kew Gardens and the Linnean Society is that they mark a subtle but still important shift in women's relationship with the study of natural history and, thus, with their future in the development of the sort of professionalized science we are familiar with today. Potter's experience signals the closing of a door into new professions which women had seen as being temptingly cracked during a period roughly dating from the 1790s to the 1890s.

"Science" has come to mean in modern times a certainty of knowledge, a form of linear thinking that has become particularly male-identified. This has been so accepted that until relatively recently it was commonly believed that women were new to the field. Because of these modern preconceptions, it is difficult to form an understanding of "science" as it would be understood in the shape of natural philosophy or natural history. To a certain extent, as science developed into the modern sense of the word, a professional history was created which acknowledged and selected who would represent and make developments in the field and, thus, be acknowledged for their efforts.

Scientific biography has focused on individuals who made discoveries, developed theories, or were engaged in developing breakthrough experiments. The absence of women in these biographical accounts indicates the role of various social forces in obscuring their involvement and also shows how the various roles made by contributing collectors, field observers, and science popularizers in the development of observational, theoretical, and experimental science tend to be obscured by the standard biographical focus.

There was, for one, the tendency to ignore the contributions of women who contributed to their families', often husband's, work as collectors, catalogers, and illustrators. These women were unacknowledged partners in the botanical studies of J. S. Henslow, Dawson Turner, J. D. Hooker and W. J. Hooker.[4] Quite a few women active in science during the eighteenth and nineteenth centuries are discussed in *Uneasy Careers and Intimate Lives: Women in Science 1789–1979*, edited by Pnina G. Abir-am and Dorinda Outram, a collection of case studies of women who made science a career. This study examines the process by which science was removed from its domestic base and became an activity separate from and at odds with family life. Ann B. Shteir's "Botany in the Breakfast Room: Women and Early Nineteenth-Century British Plant Study" mentions that Elizabeth Linné, daughter of Linneaus, published botanical observations.[5] Mary Turner provided drawings for her husband, Dawson Turner, for his work on British seaweeds.[6] Jane Loudon worked with her husband, John Claudius Loudon, on his many botanical publications before writing her own after his death.[7] Additionally, Marilyn Baily Ogilvie discusses how Margaret Murray Huggins collaborated with her husband, William Huggins, and provided the photographic expertise for their astronomical spectroscopy work.[8] Debra Lindsay points particularly to the American scientific marriages of Mary Churchill who provided transcription, editing, and translation work for her husband Spencer Baird, first assistant secretary for natural history at the Smithsonian; Mary Howard, collaborator and literary agent for the early Native American ethnologist, Henry Rowe Schoolcraft; and Elizabeth Cary, who took field notes and kept journals for Louis Agassiz.[9]

Recent scholarship in the history of science has, however, asked the question of where were the women or perhaps what became of the women. Such overviews as Margaret Alic's *Hypatia's Heritage* and *Women of Science: Righting the Record* (edited by G. Kass-Simon and Patricia Farnes), highlight the accomplishments of women in science, accomplishments which most histories of science until recently tended to overlook. Londa Schiebinger's *The Mind Has No Sex?: Women in the Origins of Modern Science* examines the development of the association of science with masculinity. Studies of nineteenth-century pre-professional science have indicated that women were more involved in the development of natural history studies than has been previously suspected. And occasional individuals have been unearthed who, despite all odds, did participate in various scientific disciplines. For the most part, many such as Jane Marcet and Mary Somerville were accepted in their lifetime as textbook writers. However, many others worked anonymously on projects headed by male family members or as working class collectors such as Mary Anning (1799–1847), discoverer of early specimens of *Ichthyosaurus* and *Plesiosaurus* fossils in Lyme, which so inflamed the Victorian imagination.[10] (She also figured out that coprolites were fossilized dinosaur "faeces" and found specimens showing coprolites inside the fossilized animals.)[11] More often than not though, such women were unacknowledged.

My study here addresses the problems women faced in their attempts to be acknowledged by examining natural history travel narratives; it reveals the difficult and vexing issues of authority that women encountered as natural history and natural philosophy became absorbed into the professional sciences. The difficult authorial context which women faced is strikingly apparent in women's natural history travel narratives, particularly and most interestingly in those narratives in which the authors assume a "solitary" posture. I position texts where these rhetorical tensions are apparent against the illuminating recent scholarship devoted to nineteenth century women writers as popularizers of science, synthesizing these insights into women's struggles to gain professional recognition and applying them to detailed studies of four significant authors working in the period from the 1790s to the 1890s, the period when modern science was really being defined.

In order to bring to light and explore what appears to be a lost tradition in women's intellectual history, I need to bring together threads from several discrete areas of scholarship, and ask questions about women writers' professional lives and, most importantly, to take these writers' professional ambitions seriously, to see them as engaged in an effort to create opportunities for themselves despite the social and educational restrictions posed by their gender. The benefits of such a coalescence of scholarship on women's travel writing, history of science, and women's vocations are that we are able to better see how, for a period of time, the travel narrative served as the means by which women could gain a foothold in a traditionally masculine-dominated field, even as that field became increasing more restrictive. And as the expectations for scientific authority changed in nature, the writer's context and her responding rhetorical strategies to meet those changes also modified. Notably, the scientist-as-explorer identity is adapted by each writer's hand to make carefully targeted inroads into the concept of what constituted scientific authority, recasting the popular sense of what is identified as an explorer. Additionally, I am going to evoke a different definition of what scientific activities involve. While the modern concept of "scientific" brings to mind the laboratory of the chemist or physicist, nineteenth-century science was less limited; it included elements of both hobby and mental discipline; it was a way of observing the world. Initially, eighteenth- and nineteenth-century science presented itself not as an area of study so much as a method which related observation to the forming of hypotheses, a method which could be applied to human activities as well as to the natural world. The natural history tradition was based on close and careful observations and made less distinction between the natural world and the people living in that world; thus, sociology, anthropology, ethnology, and archeology, as well as botany and geology, are scientific.

The writers I deal with here all combine comparative social and economic observations with natural science and geographical studies in their narratives. As such, these narratives are part of the history of science, although they are seldom recognized as science. It is not that women have not been involved with the development of modern science, rather that modern terminology and classification of what is really science and who is really a scientist have obscured their participation. As Barbara T. Gates and Ann B. Shteir, the editors of the anthology *Natural Eloquence: Women Reinscribe Science,* make clear, in order to more fully understand the role women have played in scientific work, it is essential that we closely examine just what constitutes "science" and realize the inherent exclusionary force such a term can have in essentially shutting out women from the history of science. Particularly in the Victorian and Edwardian period, women's participation in scientific endeavors was expressed in more popular texts. These texts performed the auxiliary purpose of explaining scientific research to the general population and, in the process, obtained popular and governmental support for scientific research while also educating future scientific investigators during a time when such training was not yet formally available from universities.

The role of popularization in science has generally been dismissed. Only in the1990s has there been a scholarly effort to treat popularization of science as an important part of our understanding of the social and cultural contexts of nineteenth-century (especially Victorian) science.[12] During the 1870s and 1880s, professional scientists claimed to be the only ones with the license to comment on new research as they attempted to remove views of nature generally associated with popular accounts, those Bernard Lightman identifies as "anthropomorphic, anthropocentric, teleological, and ethical views of nature."[13] The public was essentially told they should support scientific research for utilitarian reasons, but this was not enough. There was a public need to draw moral and ethical lessons from science and this made the more accessible discussions of natural history successful.

Such works as *Natural Eloquence* and Gates's recent *Kindred Nature: Victorian and Edwardian Women Embrace the Living*

World have done much to sketch out the ways women engaged in and expressed their involvement in natural history study through activities which have been viewed as being on the margins of scientific discourse: pedagogical narratives, identification guides, conservation polemics, children's fiction, and travel narratives—the concentration of this study.

Among the forms of popular prose available to writers with an interest in science, travel writing is more flexible in that it responds to a spectrum of audiences and, thus, a skilled writer can twitch and refocus material to fairly precisely aim the writing to different degrees of background and expertise among intended readers. By the 1840s, travel narratives were playing an important role in scientific popularization.[14] Some travel writers aimed their prose to children, some to women's magazines with a missionary bent, and a few wrote with a sense of an audience intrigued by the economic success of British imperialism, along with those scientific groups which had piggybacked their professional growth to this economic success. We can see this careful movement from general to more sophisticated audiences in the careers of Isabella Bird Bishop and Harriet Martineau as they explored the professional futures for women in geographic (in the case of Bird Bishop) or sociological research (in the case of Martineau). By describing the world beyond Britain, and emphasizing their ability to observe, women travel writers were able to write from a position of authority, a narrative stance which was very difficult to obtain in the eighteenth and nineteenth centuries. While others, particularly Maria Frawley, have studied women's travel writing and observed that such writing has been used to establish inroads into professions, here I focus more specifically on the more gendered areas of science as the targeted profession. I argue that in order to understand the sort of rhetorical convolutions and delicate maneuvering women had to accomplish, attention should be focused on the travel narrative, particularly those written in the solitary voice, for this form of narration allows the woman writer to establish a voice of authority in ways unavailable in any other genre. Focusing on the travel narratives of Mary Wollstonecraft, Harriet Martineau, Isabella Bird Bishop, and Mary Kingsley, I examine their rhetorical strategies against the background of women's involvement in scientific activities as natural philosophy and natural history give way to the early developing professional sciences.

The methodology which undergrids the following chapters is biographical, but my approach is informed by the history of science. I approach the biographical details asking such questions as where did these writers' scientific interests take them? What did they hope to accomplish? What obstacles did they face? Often, I look at attempted goals and in doing so, seek insight into the complex relationship between women's lives and careers, one which positions women in the history of science. In order to better see the problems women faced, I single out women who share goals and rhetorical approaches, but who also are self-supporting, dependent on their own production for their livelihood. In a sense, here, I follow the old scientific adage to control the variables when performing a study. My biographical treatment is concerned with producing a sympathetic understanding of career obstacles and a heightened awareness of what it took to write professionally in a non-supportive atmosphere.

My rhetorical focus is on the solitary narrative position, a position which offers an unusual authoritative voice for women but one which, at the same time, places her in a personally vulnerable role within her writing. Realistically, for women traveling alone, travel has always been and still is difficult, and to present oneself as essentially being alone invites questions about the traveler's morals. Some of these issues are alluded to by the outspoken traveler, feminist, and social reformer, Flora Tristan, who outlined the conditions she had to face in 1835 while traveling without an escort in Europe and the New World. In a pamphlet entitled *Nécessité de faire un bon accueil aux étrangères*, she speaks of the anguish a woman traveler feels when alone and among strangers in Paris confronted with the assumption that she is engaged in prostitution. Upon arrival, she explains, the traveler quickly feels a sense of doom:

> Some kind of misfortune seems already to be threatening. She feels a lump in her throat, her eyes fill with tears, and she says to herself, "My God! What will become of me! I am *alone*, all alone in this big city in which I am a stranger!" That is the effect of Paris on the woman who arrives there for the first time alone and without any references. . . . [S]he will be received at the celebrated Hôtel d'Angleterre with a certain air that we cannot give a name to. You may be sure that they will start by saying to her: "Madame is *alone*" (emphasizing the word *alone*); and after her affirmative reply they will tell the servant boy or maid to take her to the worst chamber in the house. She will be waited upon only after everyone else, and God knows how! Nevertheless she will be made to pay ten francs more for her poor room than a *man* would be charged.[15]

Tristan continues to report that if a male visitor comes to her room, it would be seen as proof that the traveler has "evil intentions."

While the travelers in this study do not explicitly mention this cultural bias (speaking of it would further implicate the writer as it
would indicate knowledge she should not name), it is an evident
concern, always buried between the lines of the narrative, an in-
grained cultural lesson all women learn, so that to take on the role
of a solitary explorer means something very different for a woman
writer than a man. Speaking from a solitary position means balancing the advantages of the authoritative rhetorical power gained
against the potential loss of moral standing as the author is made
vulnerable to charges of immoral behavior. In fact, admitting to
traveling alone becomes easier to do when the woman traveler is
further from European populated areas. Distance brings with it a
sense of anonymity and fewer restrictions, and this is a lesson that
women travelers eventually learn.

WOMEN IN SCIENCE

I start my study in the Enlightenment period, which was compar-
atively more open to women's participation in naturalist and philosophical studies than the situation a century later. During this time
such women as Jane Marcet produced introductory textbooks which
were well respected and heavily used as they allowed the working
class the means to teach themselves this new knowledge and way
of seeing, one which seemed particularly egalitarian and open to
new revolutionary ideas. It is against this background that I examine the travel narrative of Mary Wollstonecraft, the well-known
feminist and self-employed writer/philosopher whose natural history interests and expertise have generally been overlooked. Her intellectual sphere of influence was entangled with that of such earlier
radical natural philosophers as Erasmus Darwin and the social reforms of the British Jacobins. For these groups, the study of science
was aligned with social revolution.

Wollstonecraft was an important figure for later nineteenth-century women writers, as she has been for twentieth-century feminists, but she was a figure who could not be openly acknowledged.
Although not directly cited by later travelers, her travels in Norway,
Denmark, and Sweden formed a major influence on other women
travel writers; but admittedly, it is difficult to pin this down as we
follow the genre into the mid-Victorian period. It is possible to
show influential links between Wollstonecraft and Martineau based
on passages from Martineau's autobiography and her earlier writings. Additionally, Anna Jameson's writings show Wollstonecraft's

influence. However, for the other writers I examine, the connections are more speculative, but still intriguing.

Wollstonecraft was particularly interested in the potential of science as a profession for women because during the Enlightenment, books and periodicals invited women as well as men to consider the scientific finds of the day. *The Ladies' Diary* encouraged mathematical recreation in the early eighteenth century and scientific topics were featured in Eliza Haywood's *The Female Spectator*, a magazine oriented toward a female audience in the 1740s. This magazine particularly featured natural history and natural philosophy as appropriate recreation for women,[16] and this tradition of magazines providing scientific explanations for women was continued into the nineteenth century in Jane Loudon's *The Ladies' Companion at Home and Abroad*.[17] If a distinction can be made between how scientific issues were presented to men as opposed to women, it would be that women were steered to observation, rather than experimentation, towards what was viewed as less weighty areas of science. Observation, though, should not be discounted. The development of biology, anthropology and most of the life sciences depended more heavily on field observation than experimentation until the rise of cellular biology and genetics in the modern age.

In the eighteenth and early nineteenth centuries, there was a general call for everyone to participate in observation and collecting, answering the urgings of Linneaus to catalog the natural world. Rousseau also declared that nature was the source of a moral clarity that had been lost in the artificial social world and that the natural world should be observed to remedy social faults. An additional influence was Buffon, who suggested a more ecological, intertwined view of the natural world than Linneaus's delineated catalogs. Influenced strongly by Rousseau and having reviewed an English translation of Buffon, Wollstonecraft's travel accounts were shaped by the natural history concerns of this time. Then, at the turn of the eighteenth century, William Paley's *Natural Theology* established natural history observation as a religious duty, thus encouraging the involvement of Anglican ministers, missionary societies and, particularly, women in a mass discovery of the natural world leading to waves of various collecting manias—wild flowers, ferns, shells, mosses, marine life—which attracted the attention of hobbyists (and nearly depleted the fauna and flora of Britain).

The natural history fashion which reached its high point in Britain and, to a lesser extent, in the United States from 1820 to 1870, combined with Britain's growing imperialism, stimulated popular interest in exotic life forms, thus providing jobs in the collecting of

natural materials along with the writing and publication of guides
and periodicals. David Elliston Allen's *The Naturalist in Britain: A
Social History* and Lynn Barber's *The Heyday of Natural History:
1820–1870* verify that some women were indeed earning a living
from the popularity of natural history. Lynn L. Merrill's *The Romance of Victorian Natural History* emphasizes that natural history
studies were an important part of science and literature and challenges the tendency of most science histories to award some scholars with the title "scientist" and stigmatize others as hobbyists, a
practice which effectively removes most women from consideration
and continues the rhetorical strategy Richard R. Yeo notes as typical
of the later professionalized scientific community. The history of
botany particularly shows attempts to divest the professional ranks
of women as they had been especially active in the field after being
encouraged to develop such interests in the eighteenth and early
nineteenth centuries. Shteir mentions the particular case of John
Lindley, the first professor of botany at London University, who in
his lectures and publications attempted to make firm demarcations
between botany as "an amusement for ladies" and that botany
which was "an occupation for the serious thoughts of man."[18]
Many women provided the field identification manuals needed in
these endeavors and provided expert guidance, some under their
own names, others under the names of their husbands. Anna Atkins
published *British Algae* (1843), the first guide to make use of early
photographic techniques.[19] Margaret Gatty wrote the authoritative
British Seaweeds (1862).[20] Sarah Bowdich Lee attempted to capture the appearance of live fish in her *Fresh Water Fishes of Great
Britain* (1828). And Jemima Blackburn wrote the widely hailed
Birds from Moidart and Elsewhere (1895).[21] Philip Gosse's much
admired illustrations for *The Aquarium* (1854), which popularized
the hobby, were done by his wife, Emily Bowes Gosse.[22] Similarly,
Elizabeth Gould was the unacknowledged illustrator for John
Gould's *Birds of Australia* (1840–48).[23] All of these writers and illustrators of nature guides worked directly from nature and took
painstaking care with the accuracy of their work; they were field
naturalists.

Whereas during the early 1900s, Paley was a major force driving
the understanding of the natural world, and one that women writers
adhered to longer than male writers, in the period just prior to the
Darwinian, Chambers's initially anonymous *Vestiges of the Natural
History of Creation* and Charles Lyell's *Principles of Geology* were
sources that informed early Victorian naturalists. Harriet Martineau, like Wollstonecraft, was a self-supporting writer who had

challenged many restrictions to women's intellectual achievement. She traveled in the U. S. from 1834–36 and the Mideast in 1846, and was optimistic about the future role of women in the sciences. During her U. S. travels, she argued for a scientifically investigative approach to social sciences, writing a very early textbook on sociological methodology in route, then practicing her systematic observation techniques during her travels. Her American travels are more constrained when compared to her Mideast travels; this reflects the influence of Chambers's *Vestiges*, which encouraged the general public to engaged in speculation on questions involving the natural world. There would be another pendulum shift in attitudes toward such open involvement in scientific issues after Chambers's work as the Darwinian period brought a concerted effort to control such speculation through professionalization.

Patricia Phillips's *The Scientific Lady: A Social History of Women's Scientific Interests 1520–1918* indicates that by the 1850s organized efforts to improve women's educational opportunities focused on providing science training for the women of the laboring and middle classes. While educational opportunities were limited, the few women's schools which did exist, following Erasmus Darwin's recommendations for women's education, focused on science and modern languages rather than the traditional Classics.

While this general involvement of the population in the study of science gave developing professional societies support in the form of income from ticket sales to lectures (and the British Association for the Advancement of Science [BAAS] particularly depended on ticket sales to women), after the mid-1800s it was feared that government support for the sciences would be eroded if women were allowed to continue their inroads into professional scientific organizations. Many societies in the later half of the nineteenth century attempted to edge the women out of their societies. Such exclusion of women from full membership in organizations has been noted as being part of a general tendency of middle-class men, once they obtained commercial and professional power.[24] The Royal Geographical Society allowed a few women membership in 1892–93, then prohibited future membership for women. Similar responses came from Anthropological Institute and the Royal Asiatic Society.

Throughout the eighteenth and nineteenth centuries, natural history had been seen as an uplifting national pastime for both the genteel and working classes. Simultaneously, on a pre-professional level, there was a struggle to incorporate the study into the universities, obtain public funding and establish organizations and journals. The struggles over professional membership formed the background of Isabella Bird Bishop's multiple travel books as Bird Bishop attempted to redefine and redirect her travel narratives toward a more professional audience. She gained the prestigious membership to the Royal Geographical Society but found resistance from scientific societies in granting her support for her travels. Although restraining from public declarations of her dissatisfaction, she was increasingly annoyed that less experienced men were granted the travel and research support that she was denied.

Additionally, the post-Darwinian understanding of evolution became increasingly essentialist in its emphasis on eugenics and social Darwinism. After 1860 with an evolutionary understanding of human origins, "science became an increasingly confident and imperial ideology, laying claims to fields of human behavior previously thought closed to it."[25] This included dictating what was the "natural" role of women. As science gained an authoritative voice in regards to social structure, women's roles in science by the turn of the nineteenth century became very restrictive as women were forced to reinterpret and/or subtly undercut a scientific culture which sought to limit women to nurturing domestic roles more intensely than before Darwin. We can see the resulting balancing act this created in the 1897 travel narratives of Mary Kingsley as she both praises science and the domestic role of women even as she undermines it. Presenting herself as a loyal student of science, she collected specimens and made anthropological observations, became involved in colonial policy, had fish named after her and was quoted in Frazer's *Golden Bough*. But it was only after her martyr-like death that her friends were able to establish a professional scientific society in her honor.

Finally, Phillips ironically concludes that, at a critical juncture, when British women's opportunities in the sciences might have improved, women's schools turned away from their earlier strengths in the sciences to emphasize the traditional Classics curriculum at a time when men's training was de-emphasizing the classics, leading to the demise of science as a female vocation.

THE TRAVEL NARRATIVE

It would be mistaken to view women as serving in strictly auxiliary positions in natural history without feeling some stirring of professional ambition. Choosing the travel narrative as a way of involving themselves in the study of natural history does not in itself indicate a retreat from more rigorous study. Rather, such a choice among men often indicated the beginning development of a career. During the Enlightenment and up until the early part of the Victorian era, the division between the activities of the collecting-minded naturalist and the theoretically-focused researcher was not as firm nor as rigid as it would later become. Thus, Charles Darwin in 1837 could make his career based on his travel experiences, which formed the basis of his later study of natural selection. Among nineteenth-century scientists, Darwin was not alone in traveling and writing about travel experiences. His co-discover of natural selection, Alfred Russel Wallace, is also known for his influential travel account, *The Malay Archipelago.*

So travel accounts which are concerned with natural history should be examined more carefully for indications of how individual scientific careers were advanced, especially that of women travelers. Scientific histories have often presented scientific studies as being motivated by a commitment to knowledge for its own sake, a mode of rhetoric similar to that used to rationalize exploration and "discovery" of new lands, as if the natural resources and trade potential were an afterthought. However, as Janet Browne notes, many expeditions which today we view as having been essentially scientific in nature "were invariably drawn up to fulfill complex administrative and national purposes in which geographical exploration and the rhetoric of discovery were only parts—albeit essential parts—of the developing infrastructure of empire."[26] In the 1770s, the overriding purpose of Cook's voyages was to claim Australia for Britain and Joseph Banks' botanical studies showed the feasibility of future settlement. In Darwin's case, the *Beagle*'s voyage was part of a project by the British Admiralty to chart Latin America for future naval and commercial operations in competition with France, which had their own naturalists working in the area.[27] In addition to funding explorations, government offices such as the Admiralty furnished financial aid for publication and Darwin gained some public funding for publishing his voyages, as did many of the major British natural history texts.[28] Women naturalists, however, did not have easy access to these opportunities and support, and generally functioned with smaller-scaled operations while attempting to justify the usefulness of their work so that they could gain similar government support.

This study examines the rhetorical methods used in women's travel accounts written in the nineteenth century, particularly accounts written by women who approached their travels as a vocation and source of income, and who justified their activities in terms of a commitment to the pursuit of natural history-related knowl-

edge, be it geographical, anthropological, sociological, or biological. Thus, the focus here is on women's interest and involvement
in late-eighteenth- and nineteenth-century natural history and the
vocational opportunities this field offered women as shown in the
travel writings of Mary Wollstonecraft, Harriet Martineau, Isabella
Bird Bishop, and Mary Kingsley. These travel accounts reflect
complex responses to the increasing efforts in British culture to dis-
courage women's involvement or influence in determining the future direction of professional societies and to restrict them to the
domestic sphere. Most studies of women's travels narratives have
been of a general nature, introducing several writers, organized by
geographic area or (as in the case of Maria Frawley's study) by discipline orientation. As Pnina Abir-am and Dorinda Outram, editors
of *Uneasy Careers and Intimate Lives*, have pointed out, there is a
need, however, for more detailed studies of women and science in
an historical context and particularly for "an approach that [will]
enable us to discover if, in fact, there are continuities in female experience, or whether such experience can be liberated from a mythi-
cal 'eternal feminine' and seen to be as dependent as masculine
experience on particular historical circumstances."[29] This study of
four women who made the opening opportunities to travel and participate in natural history studies into a vocation, is a move in that
direction. However, these individual sorties into scientific vocations
were, of necessity, partial and qualified successes. There are not
tales of bold advances, but of attempts and limited achievement,
probably more true of women's nineteenth-century experiences in
general than the easier to understand uncluttered tales of heroic accomplishment.

While many earlier, more popular, historical treatments of
women travelers tend to dismiss them as amusing dilettantes, it
should be noted that the reports of these women were not only popular, but the information they provided was taken seriously by their
contemporaries. There were sufficient numbers of women involved
in exploration that professional societies were continually pressured
and, later in the century, increasingly declined to admit them as
members.

Beneath their ostensive rationales for travel, however, there is
often a more personal subtext. Unlike similar accounts from male
writers, women's travel narratives contain descriptions of the often
contradictory feelings of despair, elation, and anxiety connected to
the writer's personal pursuit of individual freedom away from the
restricted and stifling home culture. But while I am seeking an understanding of motivations, my methodology is more strongly

rooted in an understanding of social pressures, opportunities, and restrictions that women faced when they attempted to become more actively involved in natural history. The two genders do face different social and cultural expectations, and my use of biography elicits the type of career obstacles which very much directed these women's lives, and in the recognition of those social/cultural restrictions, find a greater appreciation for what was accomplished.

By studying women who traveled alone, or at least presented themselves in their narratives as traveling independently, it is possible to examine the rhetoric used in comparable situations where the woman's independence must be acknowledged and the presence of others in the traveling party do not become, either in fact or rhetorically, the motivating influence or guidance for the travel. This is a particularly difficult rhetorical position for women writers to maintain, and recognizing the advantages and trade-offs of this rhetorical choice makes these texts particularly interesting. When we compare the writing of Kingsley or Bird Bishop with Florence Dixie or Anna Forbes, those who traveled with family members, the different tensions in their narratives become apparent. Additionally, I have made an effort to choose working women, women who depended upon their travel writing for their livelihood, not those who, such as Marianne North, were independently wealthy and had family connections which gave them a certain amount of freedom in pursuing their interests and, thus, could remain aloof from public response. For such writers, at least, the threat of public censure did not have the power it could have for a person who might be a manuscript away from destitution.[30] While the generalization has been made that most women were at least middle class with the means to travel,[31] closer examination of Bird Bishop and Kingsley suggest less secure economic positions and Wollstonecraft and Martineau's financial struggles are well known. Unlike most other studies in this area, then, here the rationale for choosing these particular authors is focused on the social and economic position of the traveler and her intellectual ambition, not the geographic area in which she is traveling. Accordingly, the focus will be more on the narrator's professional goals and the rhetorical strategies she uses to work toward those goals, than on what she observes.[32] As such, my approach is more closely aligned with material feminism theory.

My title, *Solitary Travelers*, reflects this focus on the independence of the traveler and the major obstacles she had to maneuver her way around, since in both travel and life she sought independence and solitude in a culture where such behavior was both highly suspect and difficult to obtain. Describing Martineau's search for solitude in her Mideast travel book, Gillian Thomas notes,

> it is important to recognize that the daily experience of the Victorians with regard to solitude and privacy was very different from our own. Their world was, in general, physically quieter than ours, but was frequently very much less private. Compared with her modern counterpart, an unmarried middle-class woman . . . would have had relatively few opportunities to be completely alone in a household that typically included numerous servants and relatives.[33]

Accompanying such drives for independence and isolation in very conformist cultures are expressions of alienation, bordering on despair. My title also suggests the ties between the women's travel narrative and the Romantic tradition, starting with Mary Wollstonecraft's travels. When Wollstonecraft encountered a similar term from Rousseau's late work, *Reveries of the Solitary Walker,* she developed the image of a solitary walker in her private correspondence to describe her own personal feelings of despair. This tradition of feminism, personal confession, and travel is common to all the travelers of this study. Indeed, for later women writers it also became a source of tension as they acknowledged Wollstonecraft's call for women's vocations while trying simultaneously to distance themselves from her outcast status.

Some further questions which guide this study are: From Wollstonecraft onwards, what happened to women's involvement in those disciplines which grew out of natural history? Considering the masculine metaphor of sexual conquest used to describe exploration and study, what metaphors did women travelers use? Or perhaps, how did they modify their male predecessor's metaphors? How did the women narrators rationalize their abandonment of the domestic sphere? What sort of rhetorical techniques did women use to avoid directly challenging the status quo, while yet testing the social limits for female behavior? Can the travel narrative offer insights into the problem of women's vocations in ways the novel cannot? How do the travelers reshape their own conception of themselves in alien cultures?

Noting the problems associated with past thematic and topical models, my approach involves case studies of the rhetoric of solitary women travelers over approximately a century.[34] The study includes: Mary Wollstonecraft's *A Short Residence in Sweden, Norway and Denmark* (1796), Harriet Martineau's *Retrospect of Western Travel* (1838) and *Eastern Life* (1846), Isabella Bird Bishop's *A Lady's Life in the Rocky Mountains* (1879), *Among the Ti-betans* (1894), *Journeys in Persia and Kurdistan* (1891), and Mary Kingsley's *Travels in West Africa* (1897) and *West African Studies* (1899). Biographical and historical background information are important since these authors experienced similar cultural constraints and pressures as spinsters who tried to maintain a genteel class standing. In the cases of Martineau, Bird Bishop and Kingsley, such pressures were sufficient to cause psychosomatic illnesses.

A review of the scholarship on travel writing and natural science requires an examination of three areas that are brought together in this study: the travel narrative as a literary genre; Victorian women writers and these women's search for vocation; and the relationship between and the process by which the older and accessible study of natural history was supplanted by a more exclusive and professionalized natural science. These three areas can helpfully be visualized as a Venn diagram of overlapping circles, with each circle representing one of the above areas of study. My focus in this study lies on the terrain formed within the intersection of these overlapping fields. By juxtaposing these areas of study, it is possible to gain an understanding of how the travel narrative, as it became an instrument for the accumulation of natural history observation, presented an apparent opportunity for some women to engage in professionally recognized field work and to gain a foothold in the evolving scientific societies, only to be moved out of those positions when government funding opportunities connected to the growing British empire required a more socially prestigious, all male, membership.

From a modern perception, Victorian travel narratives seem quite interdisciplinary. However, whether we term the writers biologists, economists, social scientists, geographers, or amateurs, we must remember that disciplinary boundaries were not as strictly delineated in the nineteenth century as in the present. All travelers who took their ventures seriously were expected to engage in a widespread collection of observations and measurements of both the natural world and human societies according to a procedure initiated by Linnaeus, with the expectation that theorists would later generalize and codify the data. But while travel accounts were an important source of information for the developing sciences, that does not remove them from literary considerations. Until quite recently, travel narratives, unlike the closely related genre, autobiography, have received little serious study; they have, for the most part, been ignored or dismissed as a form of writing which is outside the realm of literary scholarship, belonging to the factual-based province of geographers and historians.[35]

The scarcity of scholarly work on women travelers is not the consequence of a historical lack of women travelers. After all, our earliest example of an autobiographical narrative written in the vernacular is that of Margery Kempe, writing circa 1436–38, and her account is essentially a travel narrative. The nineteenth century saw the access to travel open up and, as a result, by the 1870s, many women were traveling and writing about their experiences for an eager public. By 1892 there were sufficient numbers of women involved in serious exploration that the Royal Geographical Society admitted fifteen women to membership, then another seven in 1893.[36]

Considering the number of women involved in writing travel narratives, it is surprising that scholarly studies have only focused on this area in the last twenty years, but this situation is being quickly remedied. Most scholars start with Dorothy Middleton's *Victorian Lady Travellers* which gives accounts taken from books and letters of the lives of seven Victorian women who wrote about their travels. But Middleton's accounts are biographical, focusing on the travelers' lives rather than their writing. Nevertheless, through her selection of writers, she constructs a field of study (all the works on women travelers that follow refer to this work and to this list of writers). And the basic research she has done enables her to make two important observations: these women tended to be middle-aged spinsters who traveled alone with much smaller expeditions than similar male travelers, and there is a connection between the passive role women played at home and the contrasting freedom promised in travel. Additionally, Middleton takes note of the painstaking measurements that appear in these texts, taken as if somehow to justify their travels, and the strange illnesses suffered by many of the travelers, illnesses which apparently disappeared as soon as they set foot on foreign land.

While there has been a tendency to find these travelers to be disappointing role models politically, Mary Louise Pratt's "Fieldwork in Common Places" draws very different conclusions and opens this body of work to readings which emphasize how they go against established colonial discourses.[37] Pratt argues that the personal narrative is an important part of anthropological writing, one which incorporates the observer in the writing and allows anthropologists to become aware of the context of their own positions as observers, seeing themselves "writing inside as well as outside the discursive traditions that precede them; inside as well as outside the histories of contact on which they follow."[38] Such observations may be generalized to other types of scientific observations.

Susan Morgan's "Victorian Women, Wisdom, and Southeast Asia," while limited to women's writings about Southeast Asia, makes several generalizations that apply to travel writings about other parts of the world and which are helpful to this study. Approaching women's travel accounts as an aspect of the Victorian tradition of the sage, as defined by John Holloway, Morgan points out that women's accounts placed value on personal lived experience and this validated the writers' voice and accomplishments. Morgan's conclusion is a little vague, but I believe she is arguing that travel accounts written by men tended to reaffirm British ethnocentricity rather than the understanding of another culture. In contrast, women's writing, which is more concerned with an observation of and contact with the material of life, tends to be more closely linked with such scientific travel accounts as those of Darwin, Wallace, and Hooker, which is not surprising when the importance of women's vocation in natural history is considered.[39] Additionally, according to Morgan, the women's accounts show more awareness of cultural relativity, and they are more likely to show identification with other people. Such tendencies, again, are not surprising when the position of women in nineteenth century Britain is considered. Being in the position of having little political power would increase the likelihood that women observers would have more sympathy with colonized subjects of other countries. Consequently, in their travels these women were often led to compare British institutions with foreign ones and to use their travel experience to meditate on different approaches to such concerns as slavery and women's rights.

Morgan has developed her study of women travelers in Southeast Asia in *Place Matters: Gendered Geography in Victorian Women's Travel Books about Southeast Asia.*[40] Putting aside questions of what "gendered geography" actually means, Morgan has beautifully illustrated how historical particularity greatly complicates our understanding of place, bringing insight into the rhetoric of travel accounts. I share Morgan's concerns with generalizations made of Victorian women's writing, but rather than focusing on a particular place, my approach brings together the travels of women who were engaged in a common quest for the professional recognition which seemed to be promised within a territory marked "natural philosophy," "natural history," and, finally, "science." Indeed the first few chapters of Morgan's work do situate some writers within a scientific context. Anna Forbes, Marianne North, and Isabella Bird Bishop were all impacted in some way by natural history and colonial interactions in Malay. Of these, Bird Bishop falls within my study's concerns, although I focus on other works by her than those written on Southeast Asia. The other writers are outside my area of study.[41]

Pratt has continued her study of travel writing in her now well-established *Imperial Eyes: Travel Writing and Transculturation*, where she makes use of the recent body of research in post-colonial studies. Pratt's text, along with Sara Mills's *Discourses of Difference: An Analysis of Women's Travel Writing and Colonialism*, provide much needed theoretical support for studies in women's travel writing.

Using the perspective of post-colonial travelers of the 1960s and 1980s, Pratt's study, *Imperial Eyes,* analyzes European travel writing in the context of European economic and political expansion from approximately 1750–1900. This larger historical scope makes possible a study of the relationship between travel narratives and the development of the Romantic tradition in literature, showing connections between the discourse of natural history and sentimental discourse which challenge the traditional divisions between factual and literary writings. Of particular interest here is Pratt's discussion of eighteenth-century European travel writing and the way Enlightenment natural history produced a "Eurocentered form of global . . . consciousness" as the older survival travel literature was displaced by scientific and sentimental travel writing.[42]

A major focus of Pratt's is her development of the concept of a "contact zone," a term she uses for "social spaces where disparate cultures meet, clash, and grapple with each other, often in highly asymmetrical relations of domination and subordination. . . ."[43] Pratt uses the ethnographic term "transculturation" to describe the process by which cultures in this contact zone select, modify, and absorb concepts and images from colonizing cultures. In this way, she expands the focus of colonial study, showing links between the construction of European agricultural peoples and colonialized groups of people in South America. She also suggests that there may be a less passive response from colonized groups: a movement of ideas in both directions, not just from Europe to colonies but also from colonized cultures to Europe. Thus, she argues that concepts from indigenous South American cultures were elements in the formation of a world view which we call Romanticism. This transmission of ideas would make travel literature an important linkage in an intellectual nexus of natural history and the rise of Romanticism.

In contrast, Mills limits her analysis of women's travel writing to the period from the mid-nineteenth century to early twentieth, the height of British imperialism. My study overlaps with Mills's with

my chapter on Kingsley's work, which Mills found the most problematic. While the focus on the period of high imperialism is understandable, I believe that women's travel writing needs to be traced
further back to Wollstonecraft and Romanticism in order to gain a
fuller understanding of the vocational motivation of such writings
in the light of European expansion. Despite some problems with
her limited historical range, Mills's analysis does helpfully point to
some theoretical problems, ones with which this study has grap-
pled.

Mills makes use of feminist theory to identify the effect of patriarchy on women writers through various discourses of femininity,
along with "the power of colonialism which acted upon them in
relation to the people of the countries they describe in their
books."[44] She sees in the "convergence and conflict of these two
power systems" forces that affect the rhetoric of women's travel
writing.[45] While such theoretical approaches are helpful as far as
they go, my analysis complicates this situation still further by considering the effect of vocation and professional discourse on these
same writings, considerations which will also clarify some problems Mills encountered in applying her analysis to case studies.

According to Mills, initially women's travel accounts have been
naively read as "examples of strong, exceptional women who
somehow managed to escape the structures of patriarchy." Thus the
travel narratives are read in a realist sense, as a "simple presentation of positive role models" with no question of their truth status
or the effects of the pressure of textual production.[46] Confusion and
a certain amount of antagonism then erupts when closer investigations of writers' lives reveal exaggeration, racism or anti-feminist
beliefs in their narrations. This is a common problem with many
biographically-focused studies which fail to consider the social
pressure and economic market factors to which women were particularly sensitive and this problem is especially apparent when we
examine the past biographical treatments of such feminist figures
as Wollstonecraft and Kingsley, who present particularly good case
studies of the problems inherent in feminist biographical treatments.

Another problem in feminist reading is evident when, in an effort
to trace a separate women's tradition of writing, "shared elements
within the texts by women [are emphasized] in order to foreground
their difference to men's writing."[47] This, then, causes one text to
blend into another, the analysis becomes simplified and essentially,
as Mills points out, the work is reduced in an effort to organize similar features, and elements are omitted in the process of presenting

a unified reading.[48] Thus, particularly when working with women's writing, it is vital that critics consider carefully the pressures of the marketplace on an author and also strive not to lose the individual writer's voice in order to fit that author within a theoretical framework. And it is in consideration of such concerns as these, in an effort to both emphasize differences in each writer's rhetorical situation and to maintain a sense of the writer as a distinct individual, that I chose to structure this book as a series of case studies.

Mills also points out that it has been assumed that women did not play a role in the colonialism process and that they were consistently antagonistic to imperialism. This assumption "risks falling into the trap of accepting the discursive stereotypes of women's superior moral position over men."[49] Additionally, such assumptions overly simplify the complexities of colonial policies that often required that women adopt conflicting rhetorical stances, as we will see most evidently in the writings of Kingsley. Mills's foregrounding of women's participation in colonial discourse and her implicit challenge to Pratt's study is symbolized by the two authors' choice of dust cover illustrations. While Pratt's *Imperial Eyes* emphasizes the oppression of European colonialism with an etching of a barefooted Andean native climbing up a rocky slope in the rain, with a European man seated in a chair strapped to his back, Mills's cover features a similar scene with a European seated in a boat-like structure hitched to an Ugandan bearer, but here the burdensome whiteman is a woman.[50]

Such discussions of how responsible British women were in their engagement with British imperialism, however, risk becoming a process of building up myths of heroines, only to bring them down again. Rather, I would suggest the women, in some ways, can be seen as colonized peoples. From this perspective, it seems particularly interesting to examine the rhetorical techniques women writers bring into play when they, as a marginalized group within their own society, construct narratives dealing with groups of people who are similarly in recognizably inferior positions—bearing in mind that in order to produce such texts, the writers must simultaneously work within and against the constraints of feminine discourse.

From the study of travel writing as a genre, it is possible to then move to the questions of how such writing functioned as a vocation for women and of the relation of women's vocations to the newly developing professions in the nineteenth century. Up to now, studies of Victorian women and the problem of vocation have centered primarily on the Victorian novel, especially the novels of George Eliot and the question of the failure of her female characters to obtain a vocation.[51]

Julia Swindells's study, *Victorian Writing and Working Women*, is one of the few that attempt to compare gender, class and labor relations in the nineteenth century novel (especially in the works of Dickens, Eliot, Gaskell, and Thackeray), with autobiographies by working women. Swindells states that the novel is crucial to the construction of gender attitudes and sexual ideology, yet there is "something missing by and of and about women" in Victorian fiction.[52] While novel writing may be seen as the vocation at which women, as a group, were the most successful or the area in which individual women were able to achieve prominence, nineteenth-century women did attempt to and, for a short time, succeeded, in entering other professions. Swindells's study focuses on the struggles of women to enter into the medical profession and compares this with the tensions within the writing profession as the dichotomy of the work terms professional/amateur become interwoven with the gender terms of masculine/feminine. These linguistic dichotomies are very important because women, along with other practitioners of the older natural history, were essentially written out of professional science as part of an effort to create a united authoritative consensus among separate professional societies and to achieve a higher social status for scientific disciplines.

To understand why science would have a special appeal for women concerned with vocational issues, as well as the tension that would result from later qualifications of how the scientific method works, it is necessary to understand how scientific organizations initially presented their activities to the general public. Richard R. Yeo's "Scientific Method and the Rhetoric of Science in Britain, 1830–1917" examines how the public rhetoric of science served to define and redefine just what "science" meant and what its purpose was to order to advance particular professional interests. Yeo identifies three assumptions which were made about the scientific methodology in order to legitimize it and to defend it from religious attack, assumptions which I believe made science particularly attractive to intellectually oriented women. As Yeo shows, in the 1830s the scientific method was presented as accessible, unified, and transferable: it was accessible in that participation was open to everyone and involvement in science was possible without specialized training or talents. Thus, women who did not have access to the university, who lacked classical and mathematical training, could still actively participate. That the same method could be used in all branches of science, suggested that this practice was above controversy and was a neutral instrument which would not place its practitioner in a vulnerable social position. Thus, a woman could practice this vocation without becoming an outcast. Finally, as a transferable method, science promised to be applicable to the social sphere, with the potential to serve as a tool for nonviolent social change, change which would not cause social division.

The clash between such a rhetoric of accessibility and professionalizing forces later in the century is examined in Evelleen Richards's "Huxley and Woman's Place in Science: The 'Woman Question' and the Control of Victorian Anthropology." This study focuses on a situation where the initial popular message of science's accessibility conflicted with the later emphasis on the importance of the professional specialist in science. Against the background of a changing rhetoric of science, Richards examines the significance of women's membership in professional societies in the 1860s conflict between T. H. Huxley's Ethnological Society and James Hunt's Anthropological Society of London. While Hunt has been perceived as anti-feminist and Huxley has been viewed as holding more enlightened views on the "woman's question," Richards calls this conclusion into question with her close scrutiny of Huxley's role in the exclusion of women from scientific societies, particularly their exclusion from the Ethnological Society. She then relates the politics surrounding the question of admitting women to professional meetings to Eliza Lynn Linton's petition to Huxley to allow women access to these meetings. Lynn Linton's role is particularly interesting since, although she was a successful journalist, she also was an influential opponent of the women's movement and a committed Darwinist.[53]

However, Lynn Linton's position in regard to her vocation, her interest in science, and her social and political conservatism were not unique. Indeed, Kingsley's rhetorical position in her travels bear some resemblance to Lynn Linton's, as Kingsley also, at least publicly, distanced herself from the women's movement as it seemed to contradict what evolutionary science was propounding. Richards points out that, among others in the newly developing vocation of science, Huxley at first seemed to offer ideological support to feminists in the name of liberalism. But those women who did commit themselves deeply to Darwinism found that the later sociobiological interpretations of Darwinism, which gave a naturalistic, scientific basis to the sexual inequality of Victorian society, required that women relinquish earlier egalitarian claims. Richards's study suggests that within the scientific circle, there was a movement towards increasing conservatism, a stance which placed many women who sought a vocation in the sciences in the position where they felt the need to support the general discouragement of women leaving the domestic sphere, even though they, themselves, continued in their own independent activity.[54]

Finally, although he does not address science writing precisely, it should be noted that in a section on American women's nature writing in "American Pastoral Ideology Reappraised," Lawrence Buell shows how nature writing could function "as a vehicle of empowerment for women writers," allowing women to show themselves as independent and capable of behavior beyond the socially defined limits.[55] Since nature was considered as an appropriate area of study for women, nature observation could be used assertively to further vocational ambitions and, through the descriptions of women acting independently in the wilderness, challenge those restrictions which limited the authors in their social roles. As we will see, Buell's observations about women's pastoral writing also apply to women's travel narrative; as a metaphor for self-transformation, travel could also be a vehicle by which social limits could be tested while avoiding overt challenges to the status quo.

Thus, through the nineteenth century, women realized that travel could offer an access to new scientific vocations and allow them to engage in activities that would not otherwise be possible without loss of social position. At the same time, their travel narratives would allow them to challenge their restrictive domestic sphere at home indirectly through the presentation of themselves in an active controlling narrative position. Yet, these implicit challenges would also need to be carefully moderated in response to the shifting expectations made for scientific authoritative writing and even the scientific definition of the proper place of women.

2
Mary Wollstonecraft: "A New Genus"

Mary wollstonecraft's account of her travels in scandinavia is an important text for understanding the appeal of the travel
narratives for nineteenth-century women who were looking for new
vocations that would be open to them. The book established the
travel genre as a form women could use to present themselves authoritatively in a narration and within a vocation. In essence, Wollstonecraft's writing offered an invitation for women to also
participate in a narration of exploration, one very different from the
traditional narration that required that the woman hold a fixed position and wait for experience to come to her. Instead, as Mary Morris
indicates in her collection of women's travels, *Maiden Voyages,*
travel narratives allow a woman to "be the stranger who comes to
town."[1] At the same time, the public interpretation of Wollstonecraft's life, an unusually public life for her time, provided warning
signs for later women of the boundaries for behavior which they
could not ignore if they wished to maintain a level of social acceptance. Wollstonecraft's own reception and reputation, the narration
which others made of her life, delineated and established the
boundaries of nineteenth-century women's discourse as it formed
an example of a woman who was too radical for an increasingly
more conservative Victorian culture to take seriously.

Natural History and European Expansion

To understand the natural history elements of Wollstonecraft's
Scandinavian travels, it is necessary to place it in the context of
eighteenth-century natural history and the European expansion
which forms the background of what has generally been seen as a
personal, meditative account. As Pratt has pointed out with other
travel texts, it is not possible to reduce a study of this text to a simple coherent narrative. Understanding how the travel genre was

used in the 1790s and Wollstonecraft's particular goals and constraints in producing *Short Residence* also requires an understanding of the political, cultural, and economic context of her travel and
the sort of conflicts between intellectual idealism, science, and
commercial exploitation Wollstonecraft was witnessing on the
Scandinavian frontier.

In order to make the connections between Wollstonecraft, natural
philosophy themes in eighteenth-century texts, and later "natural
history" and "science," an effort must be made to rethink and see
these works in a more loose and more broadly encomposing manner. Writers of travel descriptions at this time would have a particular awareness of the possible use of their narratives in the
systematic identification of native flora and fauna. There is evidence that Wollstonecraft saw herself in some small way as part of
this classification endeavor, especially since she was traveling in
Sweden, the originating locale of Linnaeus's collecting. Additionally, the observation and identification of the natural world promised Wollstonecraft a means of both emotional control and
establishment of intellectual dignity.[2]

Hand-in-hand with this perception of natural history activities as
both rational and abstracted from the process of commercial expansion and political motivations, there was the actual use of science
and exploration to chart, control, and exploit new natural resources.
In *Imperial Eyes,* Pratt marks the year 1735 in particular as a point
when a general consciousness of the world outside Europe expanded with both the publication of Linnaeus's *Systema Naturae
(The System of Nature)* and reports from a failed expedition to
South America that established a market for exploration travel accounts.[3] The later half of the eighteenth century was then marked
by intense public, commercial, and governmental interest in exploration, and Linnaeus's classification system was the tool by which
what had been perceived as chaotic could be reduced to order. New
plant species could be identified, transported to new ecosystems
and used to establish new commercial markets for European interests (as was done in the tea and sugar trade). While today Linnaeus
is remembered for a classification system which seems disengaged
from capitalistic ventures, in eighteenth-century Sweden he was
considered an economist and was ennobled in 1762, not for his
classification system, but for his attempts during the 1740s to accli-
matize tropical plants in the hope that they would grow in Sweden.
Lisbet Koerner explains that Linnaeus "proposed a self-sufficient
national economy making use of up-to-date production technolo-
gies and natural sciences and governed by a rational state bureau-

cracy."[4] In a 1746 fundraising letter to the Swedish Academy of Science, he explained that, "Nature has arranged itself in such a way that each country produces something especially useful; the task of economics is to collect from other places and cultivate such things that don't want to grow [at home] but can grow [here]."[5] He attempted, for example, to grow such important cash crops as tea, cacao, coffee, sugar cane, ginger, pistachio, banana, olive trees, and mulberry (needed in the silk industry) in Sweden.[6]

Later works of Linnaeus (*Philosophia Botanica* [1751] and *Species Plantarum* [1753]) established the binomial nomenclature, an elegant and simple system of identification which was very accessible; and the joint project of reassembling nature into organized categories began as Linnaeus's students set out from their base in Sweden to record the world. Natural history collections and the process of collecting became serious endeavors throughout Europe. Thus, this global classificatory project gave natural history a role in any travel account and the figure of the naturalist made his, and often her, appearance. In contrast to modern science, natural history did not require a formal period of training nor an apprenticeship in practice, and women, who were already steered toward decorative areas of study, such as painting, music, and flower cultivation, were permitted to play their role in the immense classifying project. Study in natural history could be more than a pastime. It was an immense project becoming an industry in its own right, requiring preserving processes and materials to collect, transport and care for specimens; new developments in illustrations, needing consultants and caretakers, instrument makers, writers, catalogers. All these new occupations were publicized by travel accounts that kept scientific and exploration issues in the public eye,[7] but which avoided discussion of commercial and government applications.

While government support for scientific pursuits offered new opportunities for women, the use of science for the eventual exploitation of populations and resources ran counter to ideas of individual freedom endorsed by Wollstonecraft and other radicals of her circle. They saw science as a humanistic endeavor. In contrast to the hierarchical dualisms generally associated with late-eighteenth-century developing science,[8] Wollstonecraft believed that the pursuit of science developed the contemplative mind and was closely linked to aesthetics and morality.[9] Wollstonecraft made the point in the *Female Reader* (1789) that

> [t]he examples of Lord Bacon, Mr. Locke, and Sir Isaac Newton, among many other first names in philosophy, are a sufficient evidence that reli-

gious belief is perfectly compatible with the clearest and most enlarged understanding.[10]

While others used the pursuit of science to rationalize the development of new profitable capitalist economies, Wollstonecraft held to a belief that the promotion of science involved more than the gathering of facts. She felt that beyond the utilitarian usefulness of scientific exploration to aid in the development of economies and colonization, such study led to individual moral development and eventual human progress. In a 1789 review she wrote:

It is not necessary here to descant on the sublime pursuit, to which physical enquiries naturally lend the contemplative mind, when it is not rendered so purblind by microscopic observations, as to overlook a grand cause in minute effects. The utility of collecting a number of facts, and prying into the properties of matter, cannot be contested. To see the harmony which subsists in the revolution of the heavenly bodies simply stated, and silently to mark how light and darkness, subsiding as we proceed, enables us to view the fair form of things, calms the mind by cultivating latent seeds of order and taste. We trace in this manner, the footsteps of the Creator, and a kind of elevated humanity draws to the pure source of goodness and perfection, for all knowledge rises into importance, as it unites itself to morality.[11]

In her own travel account, Wollstonecraft attempted to find the grand causes beyond the minute effects, both to calm herself and to propose a better way to observe, one which led to improved societies, not just wealth. In this sense, her view of science is closely associated with the later alignment of natural history studies in Britain with natural theology, where the study of nature was justified because it led to greater knowledge of the creator's works.[12] In her review, Wollstonecraft concludes that

[e]very attempt therefore to investigate the human mind, in order to regulate its complicated movements, deserves praise; and the experience of a sagacious individual, will ever throw new light on a subject, intimately connected with the happiness of mankind, and the progress of moral movement.[13]

Such faith in scientific pursuits, however, later became tested in Scandinavia as she became more aware of how trade and science could be used to centralize state control and distance itself from moral responsibility for the welfare of its people and environment.

By the 1790s, travel writing tended to be either primarily scientific or sentimental and reviewers were divided over how the accounts should be formed. Scientific accounts were valued, yet they were also found to be tedious, without the human drama and sensibility of the more narrator-focused sentimental account.[14] While writing primarily in the sentimental mode, Wollstonecraft does try to merge natural history narration into *Short Residence.*

WOLLSTONECRAFT AND NATURAL HISTORY

Since the role of women in science history has only recently been recognized, it is not surprising that Wollstonecraft's texts have not been viewed as incorporating a scientific viewpoint. However, Wollstonecraft was quite aware of the natural history movement and knew people associated with the development of scientific societies in Britain.[15] She believed that through education and rational thought, women could control that sensibility which Rousseau considered to be sexually innate but which Wollstonecraft believed to be the result of social expectation and lack of education.

Wollstonecraft is primarily known today for the early feminist work *A Vindication of the Rights of Woman* (1792), written after her *A Vindication of the Rights of Man* (1790).[16] Although *Vindication* is the major work in Wollstonecraft's canon, her later travel writing, *A Short Residence in Sweden* (1796),[17] is an important text as it provides interesting insights into *Vindication* as Wollstonecraft continued developing her ideas on the status of women's work while observing Scandinavian society. Additionally, as the final completed work in Wollstonecraft's canon, *Short Residence* shows Wollstonecraft's innovative use of natural description, which places her within the early Romantic literary and natural history tradition, as well as her continuing struggle to form a rhetoric which could address both a male and female audience.

Although most current scholarship on Wollstonecraft has focused on her fiction, she was well aware of the scientific discussions of her time, writing several reviews of natural history texts for the *Analytical Review.* She was especially familiar, as were most educated people, with Buffon's *Natural History.* Anka Ryall's close study of the structure of *Short Residence*, its references to environmental determinism, and Wollstonecraft's characterization of Scandinavian people reveals Wollstonecraft's commitment to Buffon's more ecological, less taxonomic (or Linnaean) view of the interaction between organisms and their environment.[18] Additionally, questions about human progress were entwined with speculations over the effect of a particular region on human development. The idea that the nature of the place determines the nature of the people and government was common at this time and linked to physiocratic political economy.[19] As Wollstonecraft traveled, she observed the landscape as a shaping influence on its people.

Viewed from the perspective of later nineteenth century developments in the natural sciences, *Short Residence* offers intriguing glimpses of eighteenth-century ideas and speculations which Charles Darwin would pull together in his 1859 work on natural selection. *Short Residence* was published just before Thomas Malthus's *Essay* of 1798, yet like Malthus, Wollstonecraft also meditates on the effect of overpopulation and food shortage, reflecting a general eighteenth-century concern with famine. In Letter 11, she describes a moment when, traveling by sea, she looks out on Risør, a town consisting of two hundred houses on the coast, crowded under a high rock, inaccessible by any means other than by the sea. Seeing this claustrophobic settlement, she extrapolates

> . . . so far as to advance a million or two of years to the moment when the earth would perhaps be so perfectly cultivated, and so completely peopled, as to render it necessary to inhabit every spot. . . . (130)

Going further, she pictures "the state of man when the earth could no longer support him" and asks "[w]here was he to fly to from universal famine?" (130). From Wollstonecraft to Malthus is a route that can only be speculated on. Not much is known of Malthus's readings prior to his *Essay* of 1798, but he did, as Richard Holmes editorially notes, visit Scandinavia in 1799 and wrote *Scandinavian Diary.*[20] Sylvia Bowerbank has written a short comparison of Malthus and Wollstonecraft's description of the Scandinavian landscape. She argues that the two writers "anticipate two alternative strains in modern ecological thought," noting that unlike Malthus, while Wollstonecraft predicts limits to human progress, she does so with greater compassion.[21] Bowerbank also indicates that Wollstonecraft's contribution to ecological thought "is yet to be assessed."[22]

Wollstonecraft brings a sharp questioning element to her travel descriptions, trying to incorporate a scientific objectivity with her meditative contemplation. She is critical of what she cannot verify. She inquires among Norwegian captains whether they had seen any sea monsters, a subject of current speculation, but found no eyewitnesses and thus concluded they don't exist. Although we might dismiss such an issue as obvious, it should be noted that the naturalist

Philip Henry Gosse was postulating the existence of sea monsters as late as 1860.

This same pragmatic element in her character makes her, unlike her contemporary Charlotte Smith, and later, George Eliot, critical of such fads as Lavater's concept of phrenology (or what he called "physiognomy") to determine character from facial features. After meeting with the Danish foreign minister, Wollstonecraft sardonically mentions that Lavater had seen him two years ago and probably "found lines in his face to prove him a statesman of the first order" since "he has a knack at seeing a great character in the countenances of men in exalted stations, who have noticed him, or his works" (*Short* 179). Having translated Lavater's book on the subject into English, she was very familiar with his argument and it did not escape her notice that wealthy, important people tended to be evaluated or read as having a noble physiognomy.[23] Mesmerism was similarly dismissed as "hocus pocus tricks" in *Vindication,* one of the "instances of folly which the ignorance of women generates" (302).

Rather Darwinian language also appears later on in Letter 22 as Wollstonecraft contemplates the deathly toll of war and the fragility of individual life. While quite depressed near the trip's end in Germany, Wollstonecraft comes across a group of German soldiers training and thinking of their likely death, she reflects on

> . . . an old opinion of mine, that it is the preservation of the species, not of individuals, which appears to be the design of the Deity throughout the whole of nature. Blossoms come forth only to be blighted; fish lay their spawn where it will be devoured; and what a large portion of the human race are born merely to be swept prematurely away. Does not this waste of budding life emphatically assert, that it is not men, but man, whose preservation is so necessary to the completion of the grand plan of the universe? Children peep into existence, suffer, and die; men play like moths about a candle, and sink into the flame: war, and "the thousand ills which flesh is heir to," mow them down in shoals, whilst the more cruel prejudices of society palsies existence, introducing not less sure, though slower decay. (185–86)

Here the modern reader can hear echoes of Tennyson's *In Memoriam* (1850) lines: "So careful of the type she seems, so careless of the single life" (stanza 55). This is not to say that such ideas, despite her reference to "an old opinion of mine," are necessarily original to Wollstonecraft. A possible precursor might be the comment buried in volume 13 of Buffon's *Histoire Naturelle Générale* (written in 1765) that:

An individual, of whatever species it be, is nothing in the universe; a hundred, a thousand individuals are nothing. Species are the only entities of nature [les seuls etres de la nature]—perduring entities, as ancient, as permanent, as Nature herself.[24]

However, originality is not of interest here so much as the fact that in this one account are evidences of close natural observation, speculation on the effect of increasing population, and a focus on the fate of the species as a whole rather than the individual, important pieces of the natural selection puzzle Charles Darwin would later assemble in *Origin of Species*. Combined with these observations, which are clearly shaped by eighteenth-century scientific inquiry, are additional questionings of the effect of mining and deforestation on the environment, questions which expanding colonial drives have pushed aside until quite recently. The placement of all these elements should grant this text a place in the history of the development of scientific ideas.

While it may be tempting to try to trace a line of influence directly from Wollstonecraft to Charles Darwin, admitedly, such attempts are subject to defeat simply because Darwin was a voracious reader, especially of travel accounts, and many evolutionary type ideas were "in the air" as Milton Millhauser puts it.[25] Wollstonecraft's influences on Darwin would more likely come via her influence on those Romantic poets Darwin read in his youth. Although the rash of studies on possible influences on Darwin has died down, it should be noted that Darwin did read Godwin's "Life of Woolstonecraft [*sic*] & Rights of Woman" and records it on 18 August 1848, the same month he read *Jane Eyre*, a Trollope novel, and Coleridge's "Friend & Aids of Reflection." 1 October 1848 records "Mary Woolstonecraft [*sic*] Tour in Sweden," which, like Coleridge's book, he rated "poor" (Darwin 477). [26] Despite this rating though, *A Short Residence* may have influenced Darwin.

In her own emotional distress Wollstonecraft looked to scientific observation—not measurements, but a thoughtful consideration of cause and effect—to help discipline and control her own emotional state. While initially it seems that Wollstonecraft saw lists and measurements, "the utility of collecting a number of facts," as naturally leading to a perception of harmony and moral uplift, by the end of *Short Residence* it is apparent that she has distanced herself from this initial assumption.

This change is expressed in the treatment accorded her own appendix that contains the expected lists of commercial-oriented figures: types of taxes, exports, and militia strength. Here she apologizes to her reader for not obtaining more information about the countries she has visited because "[p]rivate business and cares have frequently so absorbed me," but she ends emphasizing her personal qualifications for evaluation of the state of Sweden and Denmark, that she has considered "the grand causes"; in contrast to the women travelers she describes in *Vindication*, she has not focused only on the "incidental occurrences," but has considered underlying principles and philosophical generalizations. This appendix, then, when viewed in contrast to her growing criticism of imperialistic commerce in *Short Residence*, creates tension, placing personal observation against the factual objectivity valued as an aid to commerce. After reading her responses to her travel, such information seems minor, nearly meaningless. These few figures are simply tagged on at the end, placed in such a way to indicate that despite being a woman, Wollstonecraft is conscious of these facts but does not really consider them to be as important as her personal evaluation and response. Thus the presence of these figures becomes an indirect, perhaps subversive, comment on the need or expectation of such economic and militaristic ways of understanding the land.

Rather than "collecting a number of facts," Wollstonecraft, as do other natural history writers, offers the results of close observation and interaction with the natural world. This is most apparent in an observation she made during a three-week stay in Tønsberg. As Kingsley would do nearly a century later, Wollstonecraft taught herself to row and enjoyed this access to a form of transportation over which she had independent control. Here her eye was caught by "innumerable young star fish."

> They look like thickened water, with a white edge; and four purple circles, of different forms, were in the middle, over an incredible number of fibres, or white lines. Touching them, the cloudy substance would turn or close, first on one side, then on the other, very gracefully; but when I took one of them up in the ladle with which I heaved the water out of the boat, it appeared only a colourless jelly. (112)

This observation of a jellyfish (or perhaps the juvenile form of an echinoderm) shows Wollstonecraft's awareness and curiosity about the world around her, her eye for immediate detail and appreciation for natural history.[27] It also points to an interest running through the eighteenth and nineteenth centuries in the lower invertebrates. On one level in the nineteenth century, this is shown in Darwin's work on barnacles in the 1840s and Johannes Japetus Steenstrup's work on the alternation of juvenile and adult forms in the life cycles of polyps and jellyfish.[28] On a more popular level, this interest is apparent in Philip Henry Gosse's work on tidepool life in the 1850s, which led to the aquarium keeping and shore-collecting fad.[29] At the same time, this observation points to a major weakness in a study of nature that is limited to the results of measurement and collection. The glob of colorless jelly in Wollstonecraft's ladle bears no resemblance to the graceful moving creature in the water. Only subjective and immediate observation could provide such information.

Her interest in natural history and the larger questions to which such observations gave rise led Wollstonecraft to consider issues of cause and effect, issues which left her unable to hold to earlier beliefs in progress. By the end of the eighteenth century, European imperialism faced a moral crisis. Pratt notes that "after the French Revolution, contradictions between egalitarian, democratic ideologies at home and ruthless structures of domination and extermination abroad became more acute."[30] It was no longer possible to equate progress with commercial development. Yet the desire for commerce and expansion did not disappear. In *Short Residence*, Wollstonecraft is trying to work through this crisis for herself, creating contradictions as she simultaneously favors the movement of settlements into the forests, all the while observing with distress the ecological damage such development entails.

While Wollstonecraft was capable of close observation of the natural world, such observations tend to fade into the background as she attempts to harmonize descriptions of the minute with those grand causes with which she was trying to come to terms. In her response to evidences of economic development, Wollstonecraft brings in an uneasy questioning of the assumed advantages of increasing development as a means of bringing progress and individual liberty to the world, and these questions lie submerged beneath a previous surety and optimism. While she approves of tree cutting and increasing populations, she is also aware of the length of time needed for the development of a forest and something of the complexity of a forest ecosystem. She mentions the ecological succession of forests, that pines "after some revolving ages" prepare the land for firs (142). She also notes the results of erosion, that after a fire has destroyed trees, the soil will wash away without the roots to hold it and that even uprooted trees are important in that they also provide shelter for young saplings and other new growth. Unlike most European writers, who made aesthetic judgments about forests according to classical standards (the pastoral ideal required a

mixed-type forest), she does not see a virgin conifer forest as a vast
uniform daunting obstacle devoid of aesthetic value, but rather sees
variety in the pine and firs and is fascinated by the "cobweb-like
appearance of the aged pines," which she finds a better image of
decay than deciduous tree leaves.

As Wollstonecraft travels through areas of mining and logging
activities in Norway, she begins to identify more intensely with the
wilderness and becomes more critical of its destruction. From her
ecological understanding of how a forest develops, the sight of the
regeneration of the forest leads her to contemplate the nature of
death:

> I cannot tell why—but death, under every form, appears to me like
> something getting free—to expand in I know not what element; nay I
> feel that this conscious being must be as unfettered, have the wings of
> thought, before it can be happy. (152)

The description does not end here as she pursues her meditation to
yet another level of transcendence. Reaching the cascade she had
set out to visit, she sympathetically extends herself into the falls:
"my soul was hurried by the falls into a new train of reflections"
(152). Her thoughts feel as if they darted like "the torrent from the
dark cavities which mocked the exploring eye" (152), and she asks,
"why I was chained to life and its misery?" (153). Whereas previously in her descriptions, Wollstonecraft has resisted the emotional involvement associated with a response to the sublime, here
in sympathy with the unfettered waters, she feels release.

> Still the tumultuous emotions this sublime object excited, were pleasur-
> able; and viewing it, my soul rose, with renewed dignity, above its
> cares—grasping at immortality—it seemed as impossible to stop the
> current of my thoughts, as of the always varying, still the same, torrent
> before me—I stretched out my hand to eternity, bounding over the dark
> speck of life to come. (153)

In this vision, which seems close to the writings of Wordsworth and
Coleridge, is a modified sense of the sublime in which (as we will
see later), everything in nature connects and she feels a part of it,
so that the sawmills close by the falls now seem almost a desecra-
tion, as did a previously noticed alum mining operation, which
stained the ground red.

The further she journeyed, the harder it became for Wollstonecraft to hold onto her formerly morally idealistic views of science,
progress, and government reformation. These contradictions be-

tween ideology and application also carry over into a critique of the assumptions of sentimental discourse even as Wollstonecraft writes within that discourse, evidencing Pratt's observation that "women protagonists tend to produce ironic reversals."[31] Thus, while Wollstonecraft is writing a Rousseauian sentimental discourse, she is also writing against Rousseau's "noble savage" and anti-urban rhetoric. Her position in regard to Rousseau had been established in *Vindication,* and (while influenced by Rousseau) *Short Residence* continues that argument. In addition, *Short Residence* is a direct response to Gilbert Imlay's Rousseau-inspired celebration of American innocence in his travel account, *A Topographical Description of the Western Territory of North America.* Submitting Imlay's version to rational scrutiny, Wollstonecraft uses her Scandinavian experience as a parallel case to challenge Imlay's professed American expertise.

As she contemplates the landscape and the people around her, Wollstonecraft is conscious of Rousseau's and others' discussion of the influence of climate on civilization.[32] Imlay, in his travel account, discusses the possible relationship between climate and human nature. He reflects:

> It naturally struck me there must be something in climate that debased or elevated the human soul; and that chill penury which a steril country and damp cold produces, in accumulating the wants of men, had increased their dependence, which at once saps the first principles of man. I conceived, in the infancy of the world, that men in temperate climates had retained their freedom longest. Thus in England you have enjoyed a considerable share of liberty, while almost all Europe have suffered under the fetters of an odious despotism. (29)

This idea that perhaps civilization began in a temperate climate and that a cold climate would produce a culture with few liberties and a people with little spirit stayed with Wollstonecraft in her travels in the north and she responded to it.

Wollstonecraft argued against the idea of a temperate Garden of Eden. She visualized the world where humans first lived as a cold place, such as Norway, where the sun would not be taken for granted:

> . . . for this worship, which probably preceded that of demons or demigods, certainly never began in a southern climate, where the continual presence of the sun prevented its being considered as a good; or rather the want of it never being felt, this glorious luminary would carelessly have diffused its blessings without being hailed as a benefactor. Man

must therefore have been placed in the north, to tempt him to run after
the sun, in order that the different parts of the earth might be peopled.
(*Short* 89–90)

Her argument considers more closely the process of reaction; cause
and effect is carefully studied, as she bases her philosophy on the
effect of environment in shaping human character and the power of
government in shaping the environment. She calls for more sympathetic observation, believing also that the pressures and hardships
people endure must be considered when bringing judgment to bear.

Wollstonecraft feels that too often writers' ethnocentric responses, rather than opening discussion, "grid the human mind
round with imaginary circles, like the paper globe which represents
the one he inhabits" (93). Inquiry, she hopes, will eventually de-
stroy the belief in innate national character and the mental rigidity
such categorizations encourage. This viewpoint, which stresses the
effect of environment on shaping character, is strikingly different
from the sort of discursive practices generally associated with colonial discourse. While Wollstonecraft does present the women of the
lands she is traveling in (especially the women of Sweden) as dull,
limited creatures in contrast to herself, she does not associate such
qualities with inherent national character, but rather represents
them as the results of the limited opportunities with which all
women are presented. In terms of the history of science, Wollstonecraft's emphasis on the interactions of people and environment
were unusual for her time and progressive in the sense that such an
awareness helped form evoluntionary and ecological theories.

Past modern disregard of *Short Residence* has been the result of
two trends in Wollstonecraft scholarship: critical confusion over the
function of its epistolary form and a general pattern of neglect that
has accompanied the travel genre. Even when Wollstonecraft is discussed in relationship to eighteenth-century science and women, as
with Marina Benjamin's "Elbow Room: Women Writers on Science, 1790–1840," reference is only made to *Vindication* and *Short
Residence* is ignored. When *Short Residence* has been treated critically, there has been difficulty seeing the work as a whole as it has
been treated as either a source for biographical material or as early
feminism. Looking at past treatments of these travels, Mitzi Myers
concludes that "[t]o grant primacy to either social criticism or personal revelation—or to see the two as disjunct—does a disservice
to [the text's] organic integrity. . . ."[33]

The complex integration in *Short Residence* of public and private
worlds, together with the distortion of past readings, has proved to

be a major organizational challenge in this chapter. In order to establish Wollstonecraft in the tradition of women travelers, I will now approach her work in two discrete stages. After first examining the issue of past treatments of Wollstonecraft while summarizing important elements of her biography, I will proceed to analyze the rhetorical strategies in *Short Residence* that develop from her goals and purposes for writing the book: her private need to reshape her life and her public need to reestablish her authority. The relationship between travel accounts, imperialism and natural history as well as the later association of women, natural history, and radicalism needs to be emphasized in order to understand how Wollstonecraft is making use of the travel genre to establish a professional identity. Finally, we will see how Wollstonecraft uses her personal relationship with the American Gilbert Imlay to move the narrative into a public sphere while raising troubling questions about the linkages between revolutionary and technological progress, war-profiteering, and ecological destruction.

DIFFICULTIES WITH PAST BIOGRAPHICAL EMPHASES

Since Wollstonecraft's writings are a reflection of the tremulous times she lived in and her own intellectual and emotional intensity, it is difficult to discuss and understand her work without a biographical framework, particularly because her work contains much autobiographical material. However, at the same time, the privileging of biographical elements has, in the past, produced distorted readings of Wollstonecraft's writings because her life has been read as a moral of what went wrong with the radicalization of women's roles or as an eerie prophecy of what would happen to her daughter, Mary Godwin Shelley. In essence, these readings have distracted readers from a critical analysis of her rhetoric, leaving a theoretically challenging discourse unexplored. In the following I will attempt to both acknowledge the importance and yet resist the pull of Wollstonecraft's life in my own study of her work.[34]

Rather than using biographical material to better understand and gain insight into her writings, past studies of Wollstonecraft's writing have focused on her life as revealed through her writings. The difference in emphasis is important. An emphasis on a writer's life raises the temptation to make that person a personality, exaggerating particular characteristics or foibles; in this way, an individual may be reduced to a symbol of outdated thought or behavior. A focus on an author's writing, however, may acknowledge her ideas

Mary Wollstonecraft. An engraving based on a painting by John Opie and published by Joseph Johnson in 1798. From *Mary Wollstonecraft: Letters to Imlay,* **edited by C. Kegan Paul (London, 1879).**

and creations as part of an historical continuity, adding to a deepening understanding of the human condition. A major problem in feminist criticism in general (and the biographical treatment of Wollstonecraft is a striking example of this) is that too much critical weight can be placed on the author's life. When this happens, often the analysis of her work is slighted as the drama of an interesting life takes center stage and becomes a narrative or exemplum of a particular condition.[35]

Studies of women writers have particularly tended toward "this subversion of theory by biography."[36] Once attention is directed to their sex, the emphasis continues in an ad hominem manner, privileging life over work, a treatment not usually used in the same way with male writers. While biographical studies do have their purpose, with women writers the results can be detrimental in that as a life is narrated to answer such questions as whether or not the author suffered for her nonconformity to social expectations, her work, as a result, becomes subordinate to her personal life and, thus, tangential to recorded history. When we are looking at the history of such a gendered profession as science, the problem is multiplied. Such foregrounding helps to explain why Wollstonecraft's travels have received so little critical attention and also supports the response of later women travel writers to her work. Wollstonecraft is an important figure in her own right, but she also establishes for later writers (such as Martineau) an example of an independent woman who did pursue a writing profession successfully; yet at the same time, in the later public outcry and notoriety after publication of Godwin's biography of his late wife, Wollstonecraft's life became a warning to later women writers that their public would not grant them the same separation of private life and vocation that they would men. For women who wished to work in an intellectual territory which was becoming more and more male-dominated, this warning was taken seriously.

In Wollstonecraft's case, the critic's impetus towards biography arises from several sources. Since the Victorians' intense obsession with the personal lives of the Romantic poets was nearly equivalent to that revolving around a modern pop star, Wollstonecraft's nineteenth-century literary reputation suffered because she was both Percy Shelley's mother-in-law and the self-acknowledged inspiration of the poet's work (and of his fascination with Wollstonecraft's second daughter, Mary). This curious identification with the lives of such poets as Shelley and Byron is exemplified, for example, in the behavior of the fictional narrator of Henry James's *The Aspern Papers* (1888).

Attention was additionally brought to Wollstonecraft's personal problems by William Godwin's biography of his wife written within a year after Wollstonecraft's death in childbirth. His *Memoirs of the Author of "A Vindication of the Rights of Woman"* (1798), which was published along with an edition of her correspondence, was generally felt to be unnecessarily revealing, especially in the increasingly conservative climate of Britain after the French Revolution. Adding to this distortion of Wollstonecraft's reputation, *Vindication* went out of print for over a hundred years until it was reissued in 1890 with an introduction by Millicent Fawcett. Thus activists in the women's rights movement were often aware of Wollstonecraft's work only through secondary sources. This combination of factors left the Victorian reputation of Wollstonecraft dependent on the *Memoirs* and *Letters to Imlay*, which, according to Eleanor Flexner, created an image of "a passionate and tragic figure outside the pale of conventional society, more significant for her transgressions and suffering than for any contribution she made to social progress. . . ."[37] This may be why Wollstonecraft is confused in people's minds with her daughter, Mary Shelley,[38] so much so "that many people think the mother wrote *Frankenstein*."[39] Attempts to salvage her reputation, such as that made by Charles Kegan Paul in 1879 to save Wollstonecraft from the charge of atheism, probably added to the confusion. His preface to her collected correspondence painted her as a wronged woman deserving of sympathy, misdirected yet devout.

> The name of Mary Wollstonecraft has long been a mark for obloquy and scorn. Living and dying as a Christian, she has been called an atheist. . . . She ran counter to the customs of society, yet not wantonly or lightly, but with forethought, in order to carry out a moral theory gravely and religously adopted. Her opinions, save on one point, were those which most cultivated women now hold. Mary Wollstonecraft loved much and suffered much; she had the real enthusiasm of humanity before the word were known which designate a feeling still far from common . . . she has been one of the martyrs of society.[40]

This presentation only diverted attention away from her anti-patriarchal stance, and sublimated her rhetoric into a more socially acceptable form. Additionally, a 1908 edition of her letters to Imlay was unfortunately entitled *The Love Letters of Mary Wollstonecraft to Gilbert Imlay* (ed. Roger Ingpen), a title which strongly suggests that public interest after the turn of the century remained focused on scandal.

In the modern era, Wollstonecraft was rediscovered as an icon of feminist thought, but her personal life failed to satisfy the heroic needs of 1970s feminist biographers. At times, these biographers failed to withhold judgment and allowed personal disappointment in Wollstonecraft's emotional failings to color accounts of her life and writing, a disappointment that has had a divisive effect even among feminists of such different political orientations as those of Claire Tomalin and Flexner. Janet Todd, in a reminiscence of 1970s feminist criticism, notes that past studies of Mary Wollstonecraft downgraded her resourcefulness to favor a reading that highlighted personal flaws. At the same time, there tended to be a resistance to viewing such a feminist icon critically, a response Todd acknowledges in her own view at the time.[41] Wollstonecraft's name was often mentioned, but her work seldom read as she attracted the stigma of whatever was most feared in feminist political action—free love, atheism, family instability, etc. Her contributions to natural philosophy were generally overlooked and only fairly recently are scholars looking at Wollstonecraft's entire opus of work.

A NEED FOR A VOCATION

Wollstonecraft shared with many successful women writers, especially those of the nineteenth century, a perilously fragile and tenuous claim to gentility. From what can be gathered from her modern biographers,[42] an enterprising capitalist grandfather took advantage of the industrialization of the weaving trade to move from the working class into the rank of gentleman; the family, however, was not able to move any further up the social ladder and the family money became concentrated in the hands of Wollstonecraft's older brother Ned, leaving Wollstonecraft and her sisters few options for livelihood outside marriage. Wollstonecraft spent her life pursuing some way of survival outside her brother's home through teaching, governessing, and finally writing.

Wollstonecraft's life shows a series of determined attempts to establish herself as an independent professional woman, and writing *Short Residence* was part of those endeavors. She attempted to set up a school with her sisters Eliza and Everina and friend Fanny Blood in Newington Green where she met Richard Price, a Rational Dissenter (Unitarian) and was subsequently influenced by Unitarian skepticism and its focus on rational argument. Her first publication, *Thoughts on the Education of Daughters* (1786), an educational manual written, ironically, after the failure of a school/lodging house run by Wollstonecraft, was one of the first documents to voice what would in the Victorian period become an increasingly major concern—the question of women's vocations. Wollstonecraft observed that for women "few are the modes of earning a subsistence, and those very humiliating."[43] She also observed that the situation was becoming worse in her time as the few trades practiced by women were being taken over by men. It was very apparent to her that women had to develop new professions in new fields and, as a teacher, Wollstonecraft would have been adept at the study of natural history then encouraged among girls. Shortly after the failure of her school though, Wollstonecraft was forced to enter one of the few options then open to her and became a governess to Lord Kingsborough near Cork, Ireland.

This post required knowledge of French and (in efforts not unlike that of the later Brontë sisters who were similarly motivated by hopes of improving their job options), she feverishly learned enough of the language to claim she could teach it. When that position fell through, she managed, through her connection with Price and on the strength of her teaching manual, to acquire a position with her publisher, Joseph Johnson, as an in-house translator, reviewer, and writer.

Johnson published much of the literature for Dissenting societies and, just before Wollstonecraft's arrival, he had decided to publish a monthly magazine, the *Analytical Review,* which reviewed literary and scientific works and was an early influence in encouraging the growth of Romanticism. As a book reviewer of several subjects, including natural history and travel, Wollstonecraft gained familiarity with the writings and ideas of people involved with these early scientific societies.[44] As a reflection both of her scientific interests and her awareness of the unusual nature of her new position with Johnson's publishing house, she described herself as "the first of a new genus" in a 1787 letter to her sister, Everina;[45] the taxonomic term indicated that she fully realized that she was making an major movement into a way of life quite different from the general roles which circumscribed the female "species."

In her position as a self-supporting woman writer, she wrote her response to Burke's *Reflections on the Revolution in France* (1790), *A Vindication of the Rights of Man* (1790), and then *A Vindication of the Rights of Woman* (1792).[46] In 1792, Wollstonecraft went to Paris on her own to study the progress of the French Revolution. The situation in France became dangerous and the bloodshed Wollstonecraft witnessed disturbed her. On December 26 in a letter to Johnson, she wrote of needing to sleep with her candle burning after witnessing Louis XVI being led to trial for treason, so haunted was she by his image.[47] While she was in France, war was declared with England (on February 1), she met Imlay and became pregnant with his daughter.

Understanding Wollstonecraft's relationship with Imlay is important in order to understand what motivated the travels described in *Short Residence* and the difficult rhetorical position she was placed in as she wrote. Additionally, Imlay came to symbolize the use of radical progressive rhetoric in order to justify ecological destruction. When he met Wollstonecraft, Imlay was the author of a descriptive account of the Kentucky region and a novel, *The Emigrants*, a polemic for more flexible divorce laws. He registered Wollstonecraft as his wife so she could claim protection from the U.S. embassy and would not be deported by the French. Her relationship with Imlay then had a quasi-legal status. But she avoided traditional marriage which would entail the loss of her own independence, and indeed, her legal status as an individual under British laws, laws which she declared "make an absurd unit of a man and his wife" and which "by the easy transition of only considering him as responsible, [reduces her] to a mere cipher."[48] However, Wollstonecraft's attempt to develop a new model for domestic relationships was not well understood by either her contemporaries or those around her. Her relationship with Imlay confused and shocked British society, largely because she could not be easily pegged as either wife or mistress, the major distinction required to classify a woman's position and one which gave guidance to how people should respond to her. She had indeed moved outside the socially understood classifications of late-eighteenth-century British women and into a new genus.

At this point, Wollstonecraft experienced a series of emotional traumas that cannot be overlooked in understanding her final work, especially since her behavior has been read as evidence of a character flaw. Essentially, Imlay either abandoned Wollstonecraft and his child or tried to gradually sever the relationship. Imlay's motives are unclear. Depending on what stance one takes, he was either an adventurer or an entrepreneur, entangled in several schemes, involving land development and opportunistic smuggling, skirting various national laws, and leaving a trail of bad debts behind. The details are sketchy and biographers are divided in how to respond to Imlay's behavior; some, such as Tomalin, going so far as to blame Wollstonecraft for bad judgment in men. A more sympathetic approach to understanding Wollstonecraft's (and other Romantics') emotional entanglements is Holmes's *Footsteps: Adventures of a*

Romantic Biographer. Here, he makes useful comparisons between the optimistic feelings centered around the French Revolution, his own personal sense of the "heady excitements of 1968" in France, and the cynicism which followed both movements.[49] It is easy to berate such misjudgments as those Wollstonecraft made, but it should be remembered that revolution is a great promiser of transformation, both social and personal, and Wollstonecraft's life must be understood in the context of her time. And these were difficult times. As Penelope J. Corfield noted, "in 1789, it was chic in Britain to be radical, by 1794 it was *de rigueur* to be conservative."[50] As *Short Residence* was written in 1795, this shift in national politics should be carefully considered when assessing Wollstonecraft's writing. To state, as does Tomalin in her biography, that Wollstonecraft could not conceal her emotions and "could never wear a mask or keep a weapon in reserve,"[51] is to make unwarranted generalizations based only on Wollstonecraft's personal correspondence. Both Wollstonecraft's *Vindication* and *Short Residence* show her ability to clearly understand her rhetorical situation and to adapt her voice to fit the needs of that situation.[52]

Wollstonecraft herself never seems to have understood the reasons for Imlay's mistreatment. Apparently, she was unaware of the details of Imlay's life in America, which he could easily have hidden when he met her in France. She alternated between forgiveness and rage, blame and rationalization for his behavior, all to no avail. Imlay would waver, not wanting to directly hurt her, but also not remaining loyal. Eventually, as she learned more details about some of the war-profiteering business tactics used by Imlay and those he dealt with, she attributed blame for his coldness partly to his interaction with the commerce of the day and transferred her anger to imperialistic capitalism.

During her pregnancy, Wollstonecraft wrote *A Historical and Moral View of the French Revolution.* Her daughter Fanny was born in May 1794 and Imlay returned to London alone, leaving Wollstonecraft in Paris during winter with a food and fuel shortage. Wollstonecraft's letters to him (his replies do not survive) suggest that Imlay's correspondence was scant and distant in tone and that she, in response, became uneasy. She finally returned to London, verified her fears about Imlay's faithlessness and made her first suicide attempt. During her recovery, possibly from a laudanum overdose, Imlay made the curious suggestion that she make a business trip to Sweden for him.

This then sets the stage for Wollstonecraft's travel to Sweden in the summer of 1795 and the subsequent writing of *Short Residence.*

She left for her trip in June while still in poor emotional health, desperate to regain full control of her life and to improve her financial situation so she could provide full support for her daughter without depending on Imlay's help. At the same time, she was also clinging to some hope that Imlay would return to her, that he still cared and he would meet her at the journey's end in Germany. *Short Residence,* then, is her exploration of her emotional state and an attempt to regain some faith in herself, enough self-integrity to allow herself and her child to survive. The actual details as to the purpose and activities involved are not mentioned in her text, although it is apparent that her goal is to retrieve Imlay's lost investments. Per Nyström's research into the early shipping records of Gothenburg suggests that Wollstonecraft was negotiating in Scandinavian courts for the return of a load of silver which Imlay had attempted to smuggle into wartime France past British blockades under the guise of neutral Danish registry, only to have the ship stolen by the Norwegian captain. It was this case of thievery among thieves that Wollstonecraft had to redress. As support for this hypothesis, Holmes points out that the itinerary of Wollstonecraft's Scandinavian trip corresponds to the residences of the members of the Board of Inquiry who were appointed to examine the matter.[53] But while Wollstonecraft was helping Imlay, the trip also presented a chance for her to publish a book in a popular genre with which she could gain some public sympathy for her plight as well as financial support as she attempted to regain control of her life, a control which also meant providing for her daughter. As travel proved more difficult in time of war and as accounts of other lands provided fuel for speculation about the "natural" human state, there would be ready market for such travel accounts as Wollstonecraft's.

CRITICAL MISUNDERSTANDINGS OF THE EPISTOLARY FORM

Mary Wollstonecraft's *Short Residence* poses some difficult problems for the reader. The correspondent and his relationship with the narrator is not clarified, the purpose of the travel is only referred to in the vaguest of terms and no reason is given for the trip's itinerary. Such absences of expected information in a travel account could lead a reader to assume that the text was a collection of personal papers, not intended for publication. However, these sketches, arranged as letters, were intended for publication by Wollstonecraft, as indicated by her "advertisement" or short preface. Wollstonecraft's explanation, or perhaps defense, for the personal nature of the accounts is that while she struggled with eliminating the introspective elements of the letters, the resulting manuscript was too "stiff and affected" (62). She writes of trying to avoid the first person, which makes the author "the little hero of each tale," but finally concludes that she could not produce a "just description" of her observations except by relating the immediate impressions they made on her mind and emotions.[54] Holmes points out, however, that while the original manuscript has not survived, there is little repetition between *Short Residence* and her letters to Imlay from the same period. He concludes (and I would agree) that this text was originally a journal written in the epistolary form, not letters which were actually mailed.[55] While I do not wish to belabor this point, the form Wollstonecraft selected has caused confusion among scholars and possibly contributed to this work being overlooked. For if, as another natural history travel writer, Mary Kingsley, remarked, "No one expects literature in a book of travel,"[56] then certainly less will be expected of travel letters. As mentioned earlier, perhaps because there was so much focus on Wollstonecraft's personal life from both nineteenth- and twentieth-century commentators, there has been a tendency to assume that anything called "letters" was actual correspondence, even though the epistolary form was quite common in the eighteenth century.

This confusion over the use of epistolary form can be traced back to Charles Kegan Paul's 1879 memoir which indicated that Wollstonecraft's letters to Imlay "were afterwards divested of all that was personal and private, and published under the title *Letters written during a short Residence in Sweden, Norway, and Denmark* [*sic*] and are a thoroughly picturesque and graceful description of a summer tour." [57] This assumption that *Short Residence* is a collection of letters and thus not deserving of serious literary consideration has continued to the present.[58] Recently, Pratt has categorized Wollstonecraft's travel writing as being written in the form of "occasional" letters in contrast to autobiographical narrative.[59] Pratt suggests that they were thus less accessible, less permanent, and perhaps not well thought out, although this was a common form for both men and women during this time period.[60]

Closer analysis, however, suggests that *Short Residence* should be treated as an account written in the epistolary form for public reading rather than as actual letters written to a particular person. The structure of many of the entries is more sophisticated and the tone more controlled when compared to Wollstonecraft's private correspondence. And, remembering how the careful planning behind Coleridge's proclamation of immediacy in his writing was unraveled in John Lowes's *The Road to Xanadu,* it is wise, especially with a text designed by its author for publication, to assume that a process of conscious shaping took place, even if the author claims the impressions are immediate and spontaneous.

Moreover, it seems that while *Short Residence* may have been prepared by Wollstonecraft to shame an unfaithful lover with evidence of her love and suffering, it was also intended to communicate her views and her position to the general public. The results were then not strictly a travel account nor a memoir but a merging of the two by which Wollstonecraft tries to come to grips with her feelings through recording her impressions of a northern landscape while, at the same time, finding a way to present her situation to her audience.[61]

Indeed, the influences of *Short Residence* may be more wide ranging than has generally been acknowledged. While one can only speculate, it is difficult to read Wollstonecraft's account today without hearing strong echoes of later language in both Romantic and Victorian literature and natural philosophy. Here, for example, is an early use of the Aeolian harp (Letter 6), best known for its use as an analogy for the mind of the poet in Shelley's "Defence of Poetry." Wollstonecraft writes:

> Nature is the nurse of sentiment,—the true source of taste;—yet what misery, as well as rapture, is produced by a quick perception of the beautiful and sublime . . . and the harmonized soul sinks into melancholy, or rises to extasy, just as the chords are touched, like the aeolian harp agitated by the changing wind. (*Short Residence* 99)

Similarly, in Letter 8, she recalls the "reveries of childhood," which in a proto-Wordsworthian passage leads her to a sense of her creator (111).[62]

If the assumption can be made that *Short Residence* was shaped by Wollstonecraft for public discourse, then the structure of the work may be seen in terms of rhetorical strategies. From the preceding biographical discussion, it is apparent that Wollstonecraft needed to elicit sympathy from her reading public while simultaneously reestablishing her intellectual status in a post-French Revolution anti-Jacobin Britain. To do this, she modeled her "letters" or short essays on the method used in Rousseau's last work, *Reveries of the Solitary Walker,* which reflects his interest in botany in his later life.

Following Catherine Macaulay's lead, Wollstonecraft had many sharp criticisms of Rousseau's presentation of women. (Chapter 5 of *Vindication* is primarily devoted to the subject.) But, the emotional honesty Rousseau exhibited in his writings also attracted her. Wollstonecraft first read Rousseau's *Emile* in 1787 and Mary Poovey, referring to her letters from this time period, suggests that Wollstonecraft's identification with the emotions in the book "helped her to define the distress she had felt for so long" while not giving in to it.[63] Similarly, when facing an emotional crisis over Imlay, she looked to Rousseau's *Reveries* to help her identify and thus gain control over her depressed state through observations and study of the natural world. So closely did Wollstonecraft associate *Reveries* with her own periods of depression that she and her later husband, William Godwin, referred to her depressive state as becoming a "Solitary Walker."[64] Published in 1782, four years after Rousseau's death, *Reveries* was written in a dark period of his life during which Rousseau felt abandoned, yet it also shows he had reached a point of calmness through study of the local flora, a state Wollstonecraft also hoped to reach during her travels.

In addition to offering a model for emotional control through natural history studies, Rousseau's motives for writing *Reveries* are similar to Wollstonecraft's. In this book, Rousseau attempts "to give an account of the successive variations of my soul" through a series of walks, yet at the same time he is using the opportunity to try again to justify himself to a public whom he feels has turned away. Most of Rousseau's walks are concerned with a particular topic, yet the movement of each little walk or essay is seldom methodical, but appears as a train of thought, a meditation inspired by what he observes during his strolls around Paris. It is not difficult to understand the appeal Rousseau's last work had for Wollstonecraft, who called him a writer "whose opinions I shall often have occasion to cite."[65] In it, she encountered passages that voice some of the troubled feelings in the undercurrent of *Short Residence*:

> All the time when, untroubled in my ignorance, I imagined that men felt nothing but benevolence and respect towards me and opened my frank and trusting heart to my friends and brothers, the traitors were silently ensnaring me in traps forged in the depths of hell. Taken unawares by this most unforeseen of misfortunes, the most terrible there is for a proud soul, trampled in the mire without knowing why or by whom, dragged into a pit of ignominy, enveloped in a horrible darkness through which I could make out nothing but sinister apparitions, I was overwhelmed by the first shock, and I should never have recovered from the prostration into which I was cast by the unexpectedness of this catastrophe, if I had not previously prepared the support I needed to struggle to my feet again.[66]

Although there are some elements in Rousseau's writing which verge on paranoia, such passages seem to voice Wollstonecraft's own anguish of betrayal, betrayal personally by Imlay and betrayal socially as she became an outcast. Yet while writing such emotional outpourings would be tempting for Wollstonecraft, the self-revelation of Rousseau's writing was for women a luxury which could not be indulged if they wished to be taken seriously and maintain a professional status in their society. Although Wollstonecraft did write that she was "the first of a new genus," she followed that brave statement with the confession that, "I tremble at the attempt yet if I fail."[67] Her position and her authority were neither assured nor evident, and she was quite aware of the vulnerability of her position. As with later women writing in the sciences (and reflecting on the title of Abir-am and Outram's collection of essays on women in science), she was uneasy in her career and the intimacy of her life. While she was of a new "genus," she could not be a "genius." For behind that missing "i/I," the use of the personal pronoun, lay many assumptions of power and authority not readily available to women writers and for which they had to apologize. Thus, Wollstonecraft, while moved by Rousseau, was restricted by the conventions of feminine discourse and had to show emotion more circumspectly in her own writings.

Like Rousseau's *Reveries*, Wollstonecraft's *Short Residence* is a series of short essays which appear to move from observation of the natural world to meditation in an elusive manner—in the process, showing her state of mind, evoking sympathy, and illustrating her sensitivity to the natural world. It is as if she expects to find in the contemplation and consideration of how the natural world works a way of gaining emotional control. The first letter's observations of the landscape lead her through a progression of emotions as the natural scenery at first awakens painful memories, then moves her toward a sense of healing, resolution, and finally reaffirmation of her own ability to survive. Looking over the sea to check on the progress of the boat returning to the ship after her landing, for example, she sees a clump of heart's ease (*Viola tricolor*) reminding her of her correspondent's abandonment, and, in a display of self-mockery, she quotes from *A Midsummer's Night's Dream* where (as Holmes notes) this plant is used in a potion to cause Titania to fall in love with the ass-headed Bottom.[68] Wollstonecraft's attentions are returned to the present, however, by her child's discovery of wild strawberries (67), which serve as a reminder of the positive fruit of her union with Imlay and establishes her use of landscape as a conduit to emotional health.

From this reverie, Wollstonecraft's moves the focus of her gaze yet again. Viewing the patches of vegetation of the bay among the forbidding yet sheltering rocks, gives her a sense of peace, suggesting as they do the ability of natural life to survive and flourish in a very rough and difficult environment. The scene seems to serve as a reassurance that she also will survive. While Wollstonecraft makes reference to the sublime in her nature descriptions, she does not dwell on scenes of vast, disordered, sweeping, overwhelming natural forces; rather she moves her observations to the beautiful in nature which evoke feelings of calmness and quiet pleasure. Even in her response to the cascade in Norway, the "tumultuous emotions" are "pleasurable" (153). She explains her preference when she reflects that "the sublime often gave place imperceptibly to the beautiful, dilating the emotions which were painfully concentrated" (68). As Poovey points out, in *Vindication* Wollstonecraft uses rhetoric to control her own emotions, not just to control the emotions of the audience (67). Trying to project a sense of restraint and self-discipline while seeking in the smaller observations, the "still little patches of earth" (67), a relief to the "horrors I had witnessed in France" (68), Wollstonecraft avoids an aesthetic in which she would be swept away by emotions.[69] As in *Vindication*, she is aware of "the danger of indulged feelings and the danger of inviting the charge of 'feminine hysteria.' "[70]

Combined with this movement toward a more controlled emotional response to nature is a sense of melancholia and a feeling of disjointedness as she follows these observations of the landscape with the statement, "I have then considered myself as a particle broken off from the grand mass of mankind" (69), a remark which reverberates about a century later in Kingsley's reference to herself as "an agitated ant left alone in a dead universe."[71] For Wollstonecraft, her purpose in life seems isolated from the present and is focused on "futurity," as she lives for the hope of future change, despairing of the present. This approach to nature, one which combines the power of the natural world to calm along with a sense of emotional abstraction or isolation from others, seems very close to what, in later works of Victorian and Edwardian women's natural history narration, Gates identifies as the "Victorian female sublime." Gates defines this sublime as substantially different than the Burkean male-identified sublime in that "the Victorian female sublime emphasized not power *over* nature but the power *of* nature in a given place, and not a rhetoric of presence so much as a rhetoric based in absence, especially absence of the self."[72]

As Poovey notes, by combining the travel narrative form with a letter format, Wollstonecraft is able to create a tension between, on one hand, a process of personal revelation and self-discovery, and, on the other, the necessary objectivity and control she needs to deal with potentially overwhelming emotion.[73] The narrative voice of *Short Residence* is shaped by this conflicting need to elicit sympathy through revelation of suffering while simultaneously avoiding the stigma of emotion associated with feminine discourse. Because women suffered more from public disclosure of scandal than men, Wollstonecraft needed to reveal just enough to gain a reader's empathy while not explicitly admitting to having overstepped social constraints.

Thus, Wollstonecraft is able to modulate her revelation of emotion as she seeks calmness through contemplation of the natural world and, at the same time, rhetorical control and structure by taking on the mantle of a respondent's objectivity, a narrative pose available in the epistolary form. This was a common rhetorical technique at the time Wollstonecraft was writing. It allows Wollstonecraft to claim she is writing only because her unnamed correspondent commands her to report on what she sees. A similar respondent's pose, one which allows an authoritative address without sounding presumptuous, can be seen in action in the 1782 *Letters from an American Farmer* by the very non-American, aristocratic St. John de Crèvecoeur. This was a very popular book in Europe and Wollstonecraft and her circle were familiar with it. Here the narrator, identified as a second generation Pennsylvania farmer, describes the natural history and society of British North America by claiming a European friend (Abbé Raynal, F. R. S.) commands him to write in the interest of furthering scientific knowledge. Later natural history travel writers such as Martineau and Kingsley will substitute a more abstracted science for the commanding correspondent to create tension between the subjective and objective response to nature.

In addition to allowing Wollstonecraft to maintain emotional control, the epistolary format also solved two problems she had to deal with in her writing: sense of audience and control of readers' response. In *Vindication* she had difficulty visualizing her audience. While conscious that most of her readership would probably be men, Wollstonecraft hoped that women would also be among her readers; this dual audience anticipation complicated her task and undercut the force of her arguments. Consequently, *Vindication* has been faulted for an unevenness resulting from its need to address a primarily male audience, who held the power to effect change, while periodically redirecting the arguments to a female audience who needed to be convinced that such change would be for their benefit.[74] The establishment of an unnamed correspondent in *Short Residence* may well have allowed Wollstonecraft to remove the oversensitive, self-conscious concern over the gender of her audience with which she had previously struggled.

While the epistolary structure allowed the writer to speak to her reader in a more direct manner than would be acceptable in a form intended for public discourse, it also allowed her to control how much specific detail was revealed. Addressing an unnamed correspondent while on a journey, the letters thus have a very personal and intimate tone. By keeping the motives for the travel mysterious, and by not identifying any of the people she met directly, Wollstonecraft could keep the reader's focus continually on her narrative voice. These absences in the text allow the narrative to minimize and cloak the distraction that the purpose for the voyage and the relationship between the writer and her correspondent would have caused. In the process, Wollstonecraft's emotional intensity, although restrained, keeps rising to dominate and in its restraint, gains more force than if that emotion were fully expressed.

As a result of such complex motives and multiple audience anticipation, the writing in *Short Residence* presents a peculiar mix of rhetorical elements that, however, are not unusual in women's natural history travel narratives. It is as if there are levels of writing motives which the reader must peel away; there are apparent overt audiences and purposes, yet also hints of submerged, sometimes subversive, personal impressions.

While perhaps every travel account presents a complex rhetorical situation, in *Short Residence* Wollstonecraft's emotional intensity predominates. From the opening of the first letter the reader is continually teased with the unnamed "you" to whom she addresses the letters:

> Eleven days of weariness on board a vessel not intended for the accommodation of passengers have so exhausted my spirits, to say nothing of the other causes, with which you are already sufficiently acquainted, that it is with some difficulty I adhere to my determination of giving you my observations, as I travel through new scenes, whilst warmed with the impression they have made on me. (63)

In the process of reading this account, all other reasons and stated motives for publishing tend to retreat before this voyeuristic sense that somehow we gain a glimpse of the intimate details of someone else's life. It is as if Wollstonecraft, in her despondency, is reaching out to appeal not only to her unnamed correspondent, but also to her reader for understanding. The reader is placed in the position of looking over the shoulder of some mysterious silent correspondent and, moved by that correspondent's silence, of filling in the emotional void with a responding empathy. There is then a sense of cloaked intimacy, that somehow we have gained a glimpse into the intimate details of someone else's life without the author actually revealing her situation.[75]

"You Know I am Not Born to Trod in the Beaten Track"

However, as a travel account, *Short Residence* presents the narrator with an external world to comment on.[76] This not only gives relief to the introspection, but also provides another means to control her emotional response and the opportunity to establish intellectual authority and dignity. In a review written in 1789, Wollstonecraft particularly had found fault with one woman's travel account for its lack of dignified language which she felt weakened the author's knowledgable presence. She complained that

> [f]rom a lady who has had so many advantages, and whose knowledge of a dead language is so frequently displayed, we naturally expected more purity of style; yet we find in her journey all the childish feminine terms, which occur in common novels and thoughtless chat, *sweet, lovely,* dear dear, and many other pretty epithets and exclamations.[77]

In *Vindication*, Wollstonecraft showed that she was aware of a difference in men's and women's observations while traveling, which she characterized as follows:

> A man, when he undertakes a journey, has, in general, the end in view; a woman thinks more of the incidental occurrences, the strange things that may possibly occur on the road; the impression that she may make on her fellow-travellers; and, above all, she is anxiously intent on the care of the finery that she carries with her, which is more than ever a part of herself, when going to figure on a new scene; when, to use an apt French turn of expression, she is going to produce a sensation. Can dignity of mind exist with such trivial cares?[78]

These are the issues she sought to avoid in her own travel account in order to establish herself intellectually—those marking the text as feminine: discussion of clothing, others' responses to her, limited occurrences which cannot be developed into generalizations—

that is, big picture philosophical observations. In order to reaffirm her own "dignity of mind" both to herself and her audience, Wollstonecraft had to minimize such incidental distractions of the journey which would undercut her narrative presence, and which generally formed a major part of many women's travel accounts. Instead the focal point needed to be on issues worthy of contemplation: the impact of people on the environment and how the environment shapes culture, the effect of different types of government on individual life.

In order to reaffirm her own identity and authority in the text against a culture which defined authorship only in masculine terms, Wollstonecraft is very careful to show herself as directing and in charge of her voyage, as metaphorically she wishes to control and direct her own life. From occasional references, the reader becomes aware that, while her tone is introspective, Wollstonecraft is not physically solitary in her travels. She starts out accompanied by her one-year-old daughter, Fanny, and the nursemaid, Marguerite, but most of the time, when present, they blend into the background of the account. When Marguerite's presence is mentioned, it is skillfully used as a personification of female timidity and fears which (although they are not debilitating) serve as an indirect contrast to Wollstonecraft's own physical courage in traveling without a male companion. Thus, Wollstonecraft can call attention to her own daring while simultaneously treating her traveling as if it were normal behavior.

Although Wollstonecraft presents herself in control of her own voyage much as in the masculine explorer travel tradition, unlike the explorer travel narrative, Wollstonecraft's narration is not directed toward a particular geographic goal; her progress resists mapping since she makes side trips and give no particular reason for going to a specific town or staying in one place for a length of time. The general term, "business," is the only reason she offers for her movement. Perhaps because the purpose of the trip is Imlay's and Wollstonecraft has no desire to place him in control, Wollstonecraft has him exist narratively in a passive position, which requires marginalizing the purpose of her travel. In doing so, she can maintain control of the narrative, although as Imlay's agent she is actually in a position where her independence has been lost.

Despite the presentation of her travel as overtly conventional, Wollstonecraft was keenly aware of the anomaly of being an unescorted woman traveler and that Scandinavia was off the beaten track. It has been noted that women travelers manifest an underlying anxiety about their forbidden activities, both in the activities of

writing and traveling and in the narrative presentation of themselves
in the masculine stance of the explorer/discoverer. Mary Louise
Pratt has emphasized both in "Fieldwork in Common Places" and
her later *Imperial Eyes*, with the use of the arrival trope as an alle-
gory of the traveler's anxiety of travel.

In *Short Residence*, Pratt's general observation seems to be borne
out: the narration of travel begins with an emphasis on the difficulty
of landing on the coast at night. Winds blow Wollstonecraft's ship
past her destination in Norway in the darkness and then leave the
ship becalmed. Her eye fixed on a lighthouse, she awaits a boat to
answer the captain's signal and take her to shore, a "liberator" to
"emancipate me." The failure of rescue is blamed on the "despotism" of the government. Since the pilots are paid by the government, they lack the enterprise fueled by profit in Britain. (At this
point early in the account, Wollstonecraft's faith in capitalism is secure.) Since no rescuer appears, Wollstonecraft convinces the captain of her ship to row her ashore (63–64).

It is tempting to see in this opening an encoded reflection of Wollstonecraft's own life, her sense of being swept away both by the
ideals of the French Revolution and by Imlay, her hopes pinned to
a brighter future, only to be disappointed in her liberator /lover by
the commonness of economic forces and human frailty, finally
gaining her own release through her own power of persuasion. Too
much may, of course, be read into such passages. But certainly,
from the beginning, despite some evidence of encoded anxiety in
the process of reaching a strange land, Wollstonecraft resists that
self-doubt and emphasizes her own hand in controlling her fate. She
also suggests that she is responsible for her own progress and that
she must argue and impose herself on the men around her to move
toward independence.

This initial firm control of her passage is not, however, consistent
in *Short Residence*. As Wollstonecraft fails to repress hope of win-
ning back Imlay and as the narrative moves into a more distracted
darker mood, her expression of control over the journey changes.
Later in the text (Letter 16), she gives an account of the difficulties
she is having traveling. Trying to get back to her child (and an expected letter from Imlay), Wollstonecraft lays emphasis on the
problems caused by an overconfident captain who has turned out to
be unfamiliar with the route. The group is left lost among rocks
until Wollstonecraft orders the captain back to a settlement for
guidance. At this point, Wollstonecraft can still resist command
from a man, but there is a greater delay and the damage done to

her schedule snowballs as she misses one travel connection after another.

Finally, near the end of the journey (Letter 22), Wollstonecraft must decide whether to try to travel through the Little Belt (a strait between Denmark and Germany by the island of Fyn) where the wind is not reliable. The guide Wollstonecraft has hired advises them not to use that route, but a man traveling with them overrules the advice. This time Wollstonecraft does not challenge the male presence. The boat ends up becalmed for ten hours, leaving the ill-prepared occupants without food and Wollstonecraft must distract her daughter from her hunger. These accounts allegorically express Wollstonecraft's fear that the power that men in general, and Imlay specifically, have over her life has become first distracting and now finally immobilizing.

In response to this threatening loss of independence, Wollstone-craft's narration, like Rousseau's, exhibits a continual search for solitude. Despite descriptions of local households and evidences of conversations with residents she was staying with, Wollstonecraft's narrative stance is one of isolation. She seems to travel in a self-imposed vacuum. Although there is more individualization in her descriptions, as is common in women's travel narratives,[79] people are not identified by name. In general, Wollstonecraft seeks solitude while simultaneously observing; other people are oppressive to her, especially men. Social form seems devoid of meaning and those conversations and gatherings which would have been necessitated in the process of petitioning for Imlay are dismissed with little mention. This solitary presentation focuses attention on herself and her responses and also avoids mention of the painful fact that her intro-ductory letter identifies her as Imlay's wife and that, to a certain extent, she was probably forced (contrary to Tomalin's earlier gen-eralization of Wollstonecraft's personal and rhetorical weaknesses) to "wear a mask." Although she had to deal with business problems (this was the purpose of her travels), no details of those business meetings are given. Instead, Wollstonecraft focuses on the evenings and finds a refuge in the night away from the world of men.

It has been noted that there are influences from Edward Young's graveyard poetry in her description of night scenes, but she takes those images and transforms the lunar landscape into both a femi-nist landscape and a refuge. Such is her desire for solitude, that when she travels on a short side trip to Norway, she takes the daughter of a local family along so that she (Wollstonecraft) can view the scenery in peace "whilst the gentlemen were amusing themselves with her [companion]" (91). As evening passes, and her traveling companions fall asleep (not, she notes, snoring), she relaxes in the stillness of light with an almost pleasurable melancholy which follows the removal of stress and watches the dawn in peace, until the rising sun rouses the men and breaks her contemplation with the reminders of continued travel cares and stress.

In the book, this mostly male public world is generally associated with the day, while evening scenes represent a freedom in the natural world, a time when Wollstonecraft can be herself. In the evening, the winds die away,

> the aspen leaves tremble into stillness, and reposing nature seems to be warmed by the moon, which here assumes a genial aspect: and if a light shower has chanced to fall with the sun, the juniper the underwood of the forest, exhales a wild perfume, mixed with a thousand nameless sweets, that, soothing the heart, leave images in the memory which the imagination will ever hold dear. (99)

In such contemplations, Wollstonecraft finds a promise of something beyond Imlay, politics, and her social outcast status in the evening landscape. Here, the moon, a feminine symbol, paints a feminist utopian vision, a place where the moon/woman can "burst forth in all her glory to glide with solemn elegance through the azure expanse" (75).

Wollstonecraft asks, "Is not this the witching time of night?" and in a precursor to Coleridge and Wordsworth's belief in the affinities between nature and the mind, she escapes a personal sense of emptiness through a contemplation of nature which exists outside human time and, echoing *A Midsummer's Night's Dream,* connects to the world of the imagination.

> The waters murmur, and fall with more than mortal music, and spirits of peace walk abroad to calm the agitated breast. Eternity is in these moments: worldly cares melt into the airy stuff that dreams are made of; and reveries, mild and enchanting as the first hopes of love, or the recollection of lost enjoyment, carry the hapless wight into futurity, who, in bustling life, has vainly strove to throw off the grief which lies heavy at the heart. (75)

The night sky promises Wollstonecraft a hoped for future. Its crescent "hangs out in the vault before, which woos me to stray abroad . . ." (75), to stray and to live and to hope. This moon "is not a silvery reflection of the sun, but glows with all its golden splendour" (75), and in this image there is a suggested linkage between women and a contemplative side of nature that offers the hope of independence for women. The moon has its own light and, as ideally it should be for women, it is a source of power in its own right, not just a reflection of the sun's power, any more than a woman should be merely an adjacent figure to a man's life.

This relationship between the imagery of the moon and women is supported by the earlier use of moon symbolism in *Vindication*. Here the moon is also a symbol of modesty and chastity for Wollstonecraft. In *Vindication*, she writes,

> there is not a virtue that mixes so kindly with every other as modesty. It is the pale moonbeam that renders more interesting every virtue it softens, giving mild grandeur to the contracted horizon. Nothing can be more beautiful than the poetical fiction, which makes Diana with her silver crescent, the goddess of chastity.[80]

In *Vindication*, she imagines a "modest dame of antiquity" walking in the moonlight and inviting "with placid fervour" the moonbeams "to turn to her chaste bosom,"[81] as she criticizes the current double standard which makes it impossible for a woman to regain respectability by "a return to virtue."[82] Such a linkage of imagery suggests in Wollstonecraft's descriptions of moonlight feelings of regret over her position and perhaps a hope that somehow she can return to a chastity she connects with self-validation in the cleansing contemplation of nature.[83]

From her evening reveries in *Short Residence*, Wollstonecraft turns in contemplation to her own disappointments, asking, "Who fears the falling dew? It only makes the mown grass smell more fragrant" (75). The image is ambiguous but it suggests an acceptance of her own sorrow, which is inescapable, yet offers a contrast by which life can be measured, or at least as a strong emotion, serves as a substantiation of life. As she wrote prophetically in *Vindication*, "It is far better to be often deceived than never to trust; to be disappointed in love than never to love; to lose a husband's fondness than forfeit his esteem."[84]

THE PROBLEM WITH IMLAY

Throughout this critical discussion of Wollstonecraft's *Short Residence*, the figure of Imlay has kept reappearing. Considering that much of her reputation has been overshadowed by this figure, we need to examine how he is dealt with in Wollstonecraft's text, and what he represents. Holmes suggests that Wollstonecraft's struggle with Imlay provides the germ of inspiration for Coleridge's poetry as he is "slowly transformed into her demon-lover, and his shadow comes to brood over the Scandinavian countryside . . ." (36). Here, however, I would suggest that Imlay additionally embodies the imperialist activity surrounding the colonial context that we have seen as informing Wollstonecraft's travel account. In *Culture and Imperialism* Edward Said argues that "the facts of empire are associated with sustained possession, with far-flung and sometimes unknown spaces, with eccentric or unacceptable human beings, with fortune-enhancing or fantasized activities like emigration, money-making, and sexual adventure" (64), activities which describe much of Imlay's life. Such people as Imlay and such imperialistic activities formed the background of Wollstonecraft's journey and, although unacknowledged, the official purpose of her travel. She does not so much fight this purpose as ignore it in her account, making use of the situation to escape and seek isolation, separating herself from her own complicit involvement with the mechanics of nationalism and territorial expansion. As her account progresses, Wollstonecraft's response to Imlay's "business" becomes more outspoken as her personal relationship and power struggle with him becomes analogous to her involvement and struggle with the means of imperialism—the world of opportunism and plunder that constitutes Imlay's business.

Imlay's involvement in smuggling, which led to Wollstonecraft's travel, was not his first opportunistic activity. While Tomalin's biography suggests that Imlay was something of an intellectual lightweight, this is not quite accurate. It should be noted that Imlay's account of the back country of Kentucky encouraged emigration to the United States, along with land speculation. His *Topographical Description of the Western Territory of North America* was published in London in 1792 and republished in an enlarged edition in 1793 with articles by Benjamin Franklin, Daniel Boone, and Thomas Hutchins, among others. It is an impressively detailed work; the enlarged edition's text is just under six hundred pages. Like his novel, *The Emigrants* (also published in 1793, shortly after meeting Wollstonecraft), it is in the epistolary form, structured as a series of eleven letters, each beginning with the salutation, "My Dear Friend," describing the wilderness territory, especially with an eye to economic potential and development.

A shadowy figure, Imlay would most probably not be remembered today but for his involvement with Wollstonecraft and his early defense of the poet Phyllis Wheatley against Jefferson's disparagement (Imlay 229). His real estate ventures in Kentucky, his highly idealistic pastoral portrayal of the Ohio Valley, and his settlement schemes have largely been forgotten except as a sidenote to Coleridge's and Southey's Pantisocracy scheme.[85] His novel, *The Emigrants*, is interesting in that it is an early western novel and an example of what John Seelye calls the "Jacobin mode" set in an American locale.[86] One of a handful of critics to pay much attention to Imlay, Alexander Cowie sees *The Emigrants* as a transitional American novel that helped develop the intellectual content of the form.[87] Although little more than a footnote in most historical accounts, Imlay seems to have played several influential roles in American and European history.

Ralph Leslie Rusk's 1923 historical investigation, using court records and letters, and Oliver Farrar Emerson's independently researched 1924 literary scholarship together provide the most detailed record of Imlay's life, much of which was probably hidden from Wollstonecraft. Since Wollstonecraft's involvement with Imlay has been treated as evidence of a serious character flaw and even his abandonment of her has been considered somehow her fault, it will be helpful to examine Imlay's relationship to the circumstances behind Wollstonecraft's emotional turmoil in *Short Residence*.

In her brief biographical sketch, Virginia Woolf speaks of Wollstonecraft being torn between her revolutionary ideals and the horror of the French Revolution (a horror which probably shook many of her generation).[88] Similarly, Wollstonecraft is shown as giving Imlay contradictory messages about avoiding marriage, while simultaneously expecting loyalty. Woolf writes, "the plausible and treacherous Imlay cannot be altogether blamed for failing to follow the rapidity of her moods"[89] and Woolf continues along this vein:

> Imlay, the shrewd man of business, was exasperated by her intelligence. Whenever he saw her he yielded to her charm, but then her quickness, her penetration, her uncompromising idealism harassed him. . . . Tickling minnows he had hooked a dolphin, and the creature rushed him through the waters till he was dizzy and only wanted to escape. After all, though he had played at theory-making too, he was a business man, he depended upon soap and alum. . . .[90]

It is interesting but sad that a woman is so often held responsible for the inability of a man to control his own behavior, and Wollstonecraft has suffered from this double-standard. Here it should be pointed out that Wollstonecraft, rather than Imlay, was "rushed through the waters," and that many a scoundrel and confidence man has lurked under the euphemism of a "shrewd man of business."

In the advertisement that prefaces *Western Territory*, Imlay is presented as a frontiersman, a captain in the American revolutionary army and "Commissioner for laying out land in the Back Settlements." The unidentified writer of the introduction goes on to sketch Imlay as:

> A man who had lived until he was more than five-and twenty years old, in the back parts of America. . . , accustomed to that simplicity of manners natural to a people in a state of innocence, [who] suddenly arriving in Europe, must have been powerfully stricken with the very great difference between the simplicity of the one, and what is called *etiquette* and good breeding in the other.[91]

This description seems to agree with how Wollstonecraft perceived Imlay.[92] Records unearthed by Emerson and Rusk, however, give a different picture. Imlay was from a well-established family in New Jersey. He was briefly a first lieutenant in the American army during the Revolution. Later, he purchased land in Fayette county, Kentucky in 1783 and was appointed deputy surveyor of Jefferson county. By 1784, he was wanted in court to answer debt and trespassing charges. Among other speculative deals, he became a partner in an iron works project, which failed; after abandoning his associates, he arranged for sale of his land and Rusk speculates that he left the country by 1786. This chronology has generally been accepted.[93] Since Imlay's business dealings encouraged evasive behavior, it is not surprising to find evidence that, despite Imlay's claims to have written *Western Territory* in Kentucky from immediate observations, it was probably written in Europe.[94]

There are also strong indications from documents in French archives that Imlay was a spy in the French Girondist plot to regain Louisiana from Spain; French records include two reports by him on the advisability of involving Americans in a war with Spain.[95] Additionally, he may have been associated with General James Wilkinson's conspiracy to separate Kentucky from the U.S. in 1787.[96] All this was before he participated in European smuggling.

Despite the amount of time Wollstonecraft spent with Imlay in France, she seems to have been unaware of much of his past history. Even two months before Fanny's birth, Wollstonecraft still perceived Imlay through Rousseauian lens, investing him with some aspects of the noble savage ideal, uncorrupted by European social structure or political intrigue. As she wrote to her sister Everina on 10 March 1794, Imlay seemed

> [a] most worthy man, who joins to uncommon tenderness of heart and quickness of feeling, a soundness of understanding, and reasonableness

of temper, rarely to be met with—Having also been brought up in the
interiour [sic] part of America, he is a most natural, unaffected creature.[97]

In other words, Wollstonecraft believed Imlay was a person she
could trust and with whom she could form an egalitarian relationship. Blinded by Imlay's frontier facade, she seems to have forgotten her own observation in *Vindication* that even a reformed rake
cannot quickly get rid of old habits and "when he lacketh sense, as
well as principles" the consequence for the woman is "Verily misery, in its most hideous shape."[98] Eerily, although Wollstonecraft
knew what could happen and the risks she took, she convinced herself that, as a native of a republic and growing up with direct contact with nature, Imlay would be an entirely different creature.
Unknown to Wollstonecraft initially, Imlay, while presenting himself as a simple frontiersman, was a land speculator from New Jersey, a French spy, a smuggler, and a traitor seeking to involve the
U.S. in a war with Spain.

During her Scandinavian travel, Wollstonecraft came to understand more fully that Imlay was a con man who used his command
of revolutionary rhetoric to advance his opportunistic schemes. The
falseness of Imlay's self-representation and his use of the naiveté
and idealism of others bothered Wollstonecraft and shaped some of
her arguments in *Short Residence*. Thus her travel is illuminated by
reading it not only as a response to Rousseau, but also as a direct
response to Imlay's *Western Territory*. Although the intellectual
context of her discussion can most clearly be traced to Rousseau,
because of her personal situation, Wollstonecraft also used her
Short Residence to respond directly to Imlay's travel account by
making him her unnamed correspondent and by addressing assumptions he had made in *Western Territory*. Because Imlay's text
is not well known, it is necessary to discuss something of its nature
in terms of Wollstonecraft's issues.[99]

Imlay's discussion of the advantages of American life and its
legal code as compared to the European is particularly detailed in
the areas of development opportunities and religion, but shows little
interest in the type of issues which would have attracted Wollstonecraft's attention. *Western Territory* is a strange patchwork of Rousseauian sentiment and capital ventures, revolutionary ideals of
freedom and economic greed. Romantic musing is quickly followed
by a description of how fertile the land is and a pitch for the settlement of Kentucky (and purchase of land Imlay was speculating in).
The book has large sections composed of lists: types of grasses, the

cost of various wines, amount of grain produced, temperature ranges, rainfall, and Indian tribes. Imlay was less concerned with the status of women, who in this detailed account make only brief appearances as figures in the landscape, making maple sugar and tending to domestic chores. His one brief mention of the legal status of women is as follows:

> Respecting marriage and succession, more conformably to the laws of nature than the laws of Europe—women are permitted to enjoy all the privileges, and all that protection, to which reason and delicacy entitle them. (218)

This is a vague statement that suggests little real interest in the status of women. If, indeed, Wollstonecraft had been involved with the writing of this work (as Hare suggests), she would have been quite a bit more specific, and she would never have made a reference to "delicacy" as a limiting factor in women's legal rights. Indeed, the entire text of *Western Territory* gives the impression that a male audience is assumed and, as we have seen in *Vindication*, by this time Wollstonecraft was acutely aware of a readership that included women as well.

To his credit, Imlay does express abolitionist sentiments and is known for his repudiation of Thomas Jefferson's statement, "Religion has produced a Phyllis Wheatly; but it could not produce a poet" (quoted in Imlay 229). However, Imlay's interest in the African-American poet is focused on her enslavement, not her gender.[100] Similarly, a comment on French injustice includes a condemnation of "their unnecessary execution of females for mere political sentiments, . . . their whole system of proceeding against female delinquents, without allowing the political rights of females" (199). But this comment occurs only among other complaints related to the French Revolution.

More typical are the carefully timed hymns to American liberty, such as:

> O Liberty! how many blessings hast thou brought us! Man in promulgating his opinions, now finds security under the wings of an established freedom; and the dismal dungeon, which eclipsed the luminous mind of the celebrated Italian, would now be erected into a school for him to lecture in, instead of a prison to bewail the miserable ignorance and depravity of his fellow-creatures. (70)

With Imlay, there is always an underlying economic motive to such Republican rhetoric. These motives are evident, for instance, in the

long discussion he includes by Benjamin Rush of maple sugar making, including a claim for sugar's medicinal properties, pointing out
that unlike West Indian cane sugar, the extraction of maple sugar
does not involve the use of slaves, and thus can be used by those
boycotting sugar for this reason (156).[101] These economic claims
are supported with imaginative pastoral pictures (bear in mind that
what follows purports to be a firsthand description of Kentucky):

> The season of sugar-making occupies the women, whose mornings are
> cheered by the modulated buffoonery of the mocking bird, the tuneful
> song of the thrush, and the plumage of the parroquet. . . .—The business
> of the day being over, the men join the women in the sugar groves,
> where enchantment seems to dwell.—The lofty trees wave their spread-
> ing branches over a green turf, on whose soft down the mildness of the
> evening invites the neighboring youth to sportive play. (169)

This Eden-like setting suggests nothing of work, only amusement.
Somehow the northern trees, the March-April harvest of maple
sugar (which requires freezing night temperatures), summer-like
weather and southern birds all coalesce in this composite picture of
an American paradise. In such a scene, women are supposed to be
engaged in agricultural work without being actually involved in
physical labor. As Imlay continues with his description of the domestic life of American settlers, it becomes clear that his expectations for women's lives are fairly restrictive (although they do
involve the study of botany):

> Garden and fishing constitute some part of the amusements of both
> sexes. Flowers and their genera form one of the studies of our ladies;
> and embellishment of their houses with those which are known to be
> salutary, constitutes a part of their employment.—Domestic cares and
> music fill up the remainder of the day; and social visits, without cere-
> mony or form, leave them without ennui or disgust. Our young are too
> gallant to permit the women to have separate amusements; and thus it is
> that we find that suavity and politeness of manners universal, which can
> only be effected by feminine polish. (169–70)

Such idyllic pictures as Imlay's of life on the frontier, especially
women's lives, are in stark contrast to Wollstonecraft's sharp socio-
logically informed observations in *Short Residence*. Describing the
homes near the sea in Sweden, a sparsely settled land, whose people
are dependent on herring fishing, she notes that

> . . . there scarcely appears a vestige of cultivation. The scattered huts
> that stand shivering on the naked rocks, braving the pitiless elements,

are formed of logs of wood, rudely hewn; and so little pains are taken with the craggy foundation, that nothing like a pathway points out the door. (76)

Noting the lack of civil rights among Swedish servants, Wollstonecraft is also aware that the division of labor among Swedish servants portions out the more menial tasks to the women.

> Still the men stand up for the dignity of man, by oppressing the women. The most menial, and even laborious offices, are therefore left to these poor drudges. Much of this I have seen. In the winter, I am told, they take the linen down to the river, to wash it in the cold water; and though their hands, cut by the ice, are cracked and bleeding, the men, their fellow servants, will not disgrace their manhood by carrying a tub to lighten their burden. (76–77)

Such observations and, indeed, even the thought of asking specific questions about such daily labor, were outside Imlay's ken, and probably outside the awareness of most male travelers who did not have to concern themselves with household duties.

It would become apparent to later Victorians that such travel narratives as Wollstonecraft's could present one of the few historical records of women's work, especially the work of lower class, illiterate women, and later women travel writers who were engaged in natural history observations would make an effort to document the lives of women in other cultures. Women writers, in general, are more aware of the situation of other women, are more aware of the requirements of daily household work in a country's culture and economy and, most importantly, other women are more likely to speak freely and openly to an audience of women, whereas male travelers can easily ignore or minimize women and their work, and social constraints prevent easy familiarity among women and male travelers. This would become a major thesis of Martineau's work and one of the reasons she would give to justify the involvement of women in early sociological studies, and one which Kingsley would also use to support women's role in anthrolopology.

Along these lines, Wollstonecraft, with Imlay's work in mind, also challenges the kind of American utopian visions which *Western Territory* presents by pointing to the presence of servants with poor working conditions. The necessity of servants behind the scenes of the idyllic pictures painted by Imlay was often assumed and the contradictions posed by their presence in an egalitarian society were often ignored. When Coleridge and Southey debated the nature of their American utopia, they could not settle the problem of servants.[102] They had ignored the question completely until Southey wanted to bring servants along, defeating for Coleridge the whole idea of an egalitarian society.[103] The distastefulness of the idea of servants was in conflict with the equally distasteful idea of hard work. While Imlay does not place servants in his scene, he matter-of-factly answers the anticipated question: "how servants are to be procured," noting that American servants' wages are about twenty-five percent higher than European (192–93). The question of whether or not to have servants is never raised; the answer is assumed to be affirmative. After all, Imlay's intended audience was composed of those with enough money to invest.

Having been a governess, Wollstonecraft is far more observant of the living conditions of servants, especially female servants, and she uses their treatment as a measure of civilization in the countries in which she is traveling. She notes, for instance, that the serving class eat different foods than their employers, and that an employer may legally strike an employee (76). Wollstonecraft's passionate anger continues as she lists wages and working conditions. Addressing the general reader, she argues for understanding the conditions of servitude and is particularly upset that laws issued in order to finance the Swedish war against Russia have removed coffee and brandy from the hands of the peasants who have few creature comforts as it is (77). She similarly lashes out at the new restrictions on Sabbath activities in England in the anti-Jacobin atmosphere, which severely curtailed the leisure activities of workers who could only enjoy a Sunday rest (120–21).

Traveling on her own and feeling the weight of responsibility for her daughter, Wollstonecraft is particularly sensitive to the vulnerable position of women and to how marginal their existence can be. She describes a wet nurse, for example, who is paid $12 a year, yet must pay $10 for the nursing of her own child, who was abandoned by the father (115). And she approves of a provision that allows a widow of a clergyman to receive income for a year after her husband's death as a movement toward improving women's economic security (139).

As she continues her travels, Wollstonecraft becomes more and more critical of, yet also confused by the business activities centering around Imlay, as well as of the effect of politics, war, trade and shipping on the environment and on the social structure. Initially, she had come to Scandinavia optimistic about its progressive movements both in scientific exploration and democratic government. Reforms in the 1790s led to more humane conditions in Copenhagen's prisons, and social attitudes toward divorce became more tolerant.[104] In 1792, Denmark led the world in a movement toward the abolition of the slave trade by prohibiting the importation of slaves into its colonies.[105] Scandinavia then seemed to promise the enactment of the ideals of revolution, as there was a heightened interest in citizen participation in the 1790s,[106] while the region was distant from the horrors of the French Revolution. However, individual freedom did not seem to be related to the form of the government in the way Wollstonecraft had expected. Norway was a colony of Denmark (an absolute monarchy), yet Wollstonecraft found more personal freedom there than in republican France.[107] H. Arnold Barton's history of Scandinavia concludes that during this time period "[s]ubjects of the absolutistic Danish monarchy enjoyed far greater civic liberty—above all, freedom of expression—than those of the Swedish constitutional monarchy, which had evolved into a kind of ad hoc dictatorship."[108] Wollstonecraft believed "the inhabitants of Denmark and Norway [to be] . . . the least oppressed people of Europe" (105) and found the king of Denmark, although "the most absolute monarch in Europe," was so lenient that the government's laws could barely be felt (139). Yet, Norway was still a colony and, in Christiania, the Danish bailiffs represented the "cloven foot of despotism." Wollstonecraft observed that "though the Norwegians are not in the abject state of the Irish, yet this second-hand government is still felt by their being deprived of several natural advantages to benefit the domineering state" (144). So great was the support for the French revolution in Norway that she could not convince the Norwegians "that Robespierre was a monster" (141).

As the government structures she encountered seemed to bear no relationship to individual freedom, Wollstonecraft also found that issues of shipping often had more to do with war than with idealistic beliefs in progress. Imlay's "business" interests had placed Wollstonecraft in the midst of Scandinavian-European turmoil. As Imlay's agent, Wollstonecraft had to sort out the complexity of Scandinavian shipping laws and she found that Scandinavian social reform was supported by war profiteering. The economic survival of this area was dependent on its shipping neutrality. This trade was endangered when the British blockaded Scandinavian ports to prevent France from obtaining supplies and, in fact, the British war with France had begun when Britain seized almost two hundred Norwegian and Danish ships bound for France.[109] Earlier, similar British blockades during the American War of Independence caused Scandinavian trade to suffer.[110] In 1794, just before Wollstonecraft's visit, the Scandinavian monarchies were able to acquire some acknowledgment for their shipping rights as a neutrality, but this was just a step in a continuing battle which would lead to Sweden and Denmark joining Russia and Prussia in a challenge to the British control of sea, a challenge which culminated in Horatio Nelson's defeat of the Danish fleet in 1801.

There were no simple answers. Scandinavian prosperity was based on higher prices for their raw material and agricultural products, prices that had risen because of war. Scandinavia (along with the United States) were the principal neutral shippers, assuming much of the shipping trade both in Europe and beyond. With war, they gained control of the Mediterranean trade and increased business with North America.[111] Thus, war profiteering was at the heart of Wollstonecraft's business dealings. Indeed, the Scandinavian courts were more sympathetic toward Imlay's smuggling activities than might be expected because such smuggling was a large part of the rebirth of the shipping industry in Denmark and Norway. Gothenburg (which Wollstonecraft found to be vulgar) was headquarters of the Swedish East India Company, founded by English and Dutch merchants.[112] Additionally, Scandinavia supplied the raw materials to build ships. By 1750, Sweden supplied one-third of the European production of bar iron.[113] Norway supplied timber to Western Europe, stripping the coastal forests. Denmark also lost most of its forest due to unrestricted timber harvest, requiring legislation in 1805 to control logging.[114]

From this background, it can be seen that Wollstonecraft's increasing disenchantment with business activities in *Short Residence* is more than a personal reaction to Imlay; her realization of what Imlay's business meant comes to represent a realization of the entanglement of revolution, progress and imperialism, a pursuit "that wears out the most sacred principles of humanity and rectitude" (*Short* 143). Her movement toward nature and her meditation on the erosion caused by slash-and-burn farming techniques which leave the countryside "to mourn for ages" (152), displays a disenchantment with the progress she once had hopes for and which she now sees associated with destruction. She learned during her meetings with prominent traders "some tricks practiced by merchants, mis-called reputable . . . during the present war, in which common honesty was violated" (143). Coming into Christiania, she sees "the depredations committed on the rocks to make alum," a product Imlay exported. The mining operations burned the rocks, leaving them red, suggestive of a bleeding land, and she "regretted that the operation should leave a quantity of rubbish, to introduce an image of human industry in the shape of destruction" (142).

Such reflections lead to a better understanding of the abrupt conclusion of Wollstonecraft's narrative. Edward Said, among others, has noted that in the novel genre, closure is conservative; it tends to reestablish or reaffirm the status quo.[115] However, because it is ostensibly factual, travel narratives can resist closure in ways the novel cannot. Fussell points out that closure in travel narratives is obtained in most cases by a return to home or a return to one's starting location.[116] In some ways Wollstonecraft obtains closure by ending her narrative back in England at Dover, but she also resists it by ending her account suddenly and brusquely: the Cliffs of Dover are "insignificant," the place is dirty, her powers of observation have left her, her thoughts oppress her, and she leaves the letter unfinished (197). Although she has returned home, she does not feel at home; her return results neither in a resolution of her problems or an acceptance of her state.

Moreover, while a travel account, *Short Residence* also represents a nexus, interweaving Romantic subjectivity and scientific observation, so that it defies expectations of later readers. Yet the meditative leaps of association that often link these diverging modes sent ripples of influence through the next century, into the work of other women writers, who, for socially unacceptable purposes, set out to travel and support themselves from those travels. While their travels often were presented as serving a larger purpose, like Wollstonecraft's, their writings also served to establish authority, to shape public perception of the author, and, at times, to challenge established norms of scientific masculine discourse.

3

Harriet Martineau: An Investigative Observer

AMONG NINETEENTH-CENTURY WOMEN TRAVEL WRITERS, NO ONE obtained as high an intellectual status and respect as Harriet Martineau. Her successes were impressive, and her failures reveal how the travel genre was used in an attempt to gain a place for Victorian women in scientific endeavors as she attempted to apply techniques of observation developed for natural history to theories of social observation. Like Wollstonecraft in the eighteenth century, Martineau did establish for herself a position in the intellectual life of Victorian culture. Yet that success was limited to her lifetime; she was quickly forgotten, so that the reason for her success seemed ungraspable even by Edwardian commentators. While scholars have explained this latter collective amnesia in terms of the high concern with topical issues in her work, it is also linked to a change in how science came to be performed. Martineau's career, particularly her attempts to practice science, reflects this change in scientific culture, a change so major as to make it difficult to see today how early sociology could be related to natural history. As professional societies, often closely linked with colonial endeavors, became the voice of science, access to science became more limited and the term "scientific" was applied in a more restrictive sense, one which made it more difficult for women to engage in. Gradually, the sort of natural history with which Wollstonecraft was acquainted, one in which the individual natural historian could work outside any church or university hierarchy, was supplanted by the university- or government-employed scientist. Since women's intellectual success in Victorian society required a mode of writing which could not gain approval from a male-dominated social hierarchy, this removal of the freelance home-based access to scientific inquiry eventually closed science-related occupations to women.

In Martineau's career, we can see an initial movement into early sociology in her 1834–36 American travels, resulting in two well-received studies which shaped a call for science-based observation into a potential career field for women: the popular *Retrospect of Western Travel* and more scholarly oriented *Society in America*. Her theories of social observation were closely tied to the type of observation, indeed, a "science" of observation which was developed specifically for the study of natural history and was voiced in the public rhetoric of science. In contrast, her 1846–47 Mideast travel, *Eastern Life: Present and Past*, was far less successful. This travel narrative attempted to apply a pre-Darwinian evolutionary paradigm to describe the formation and development of religious doctrine at a time when Robert Chambers's publication of *Vestiges of the Natural History of Creation* (1844) challenged scientific authority. The controversy which accompanied the anonymously published *Vestiges* brought together "the tensions associated with the discussion of science in the public sphere."[1]

This chapter will examine Martineau's ability to shape travel writing into an investigative tool for scientific observation while substantiating her influence on others and her intellectual stature, and, at the same time, identify the limitations of her rhetorical strategy. Her intellectual goals required that she distance herself, on one hand, from more radical predecessors such as Wollstonecraft, whose readers too often focused on her life rather than her work, and on the other, from conservative ones, such as Frances Trollope, whose intellectual goals were in opposition to her own. Martineau had to create a narrative voice that was dignified and professional, yet non-threatening to conventional beliefs about women's proper social position and behavior. Comparisons with other contemporary travel writers will indicate both her position in a tradition of women travelers and her role in a continuing dialogue on the use of direct observation to aid the sociological/anthropological understanding of a foreign culture.

With her three travel works, *Society in America*, *Retrospect of Western Travel*, *Eastern Life: Present and Past*, and related writings, Martineau transformed the nature of travel writing, making it a more focused investigative tool of what would become the social sciences, a changing area of natural history where the provinces of sociology, anthropology, and political science overlap. In doing so, she also incorporated women's issues and concern for the domestic sphere into studies intended for a serious, academic, and thus assumed male, audience. In her travel books the domestic was presented as an essential part of society, so that careful attention to the conduct of household matters was a necessary part of sociological study. By highlighting the domestic role, Martineau drew attention to the importance of women in a culture, a role that male theorists generally overlooked or dismissed, and the need for women to engage in the study of sociology. In doing so, Martineau joined later women in natural history who similarly attempted to redirect/revise Darwinian narratives of the women's place (see Gates 154–57, 250–52), and establish women's role in science. Martineau was, however, postulating her ideas about the need to study women's work as part of any sociological study before the publication of Darwin's *Origin* in 1859. She was applying evolutionary ideas from pre-Darwinian sources: Spencer, Chambers and Lyell.

Martineau traveled not as a dilettante tourist nor as a colonizer, but as a professional working woman, and she presented herself not as an auxiliary member of a travel party headed by someone else, but as the sole director and organizer of her own journeys. Her travels established a model for the ideal traveler as one sympathetic and sensitive to the culture being observed, a role she saw as being particularly suited to women. At the same time, her work shows a nervousness about making the kind of sweeping, imaginative theoretical generalizations present in both the earlier Wollstonecraft writings and the travel writing of her contemporary Alexis de Tocqueville. In its careful substantiation of her conclusions especially, Martineau's writing shows an anxiety over potential challenges, reflecting the increasing antagonism of the emerging sciences to women's participation. This shying away from any discourse which would hint at speculative conclusions has been often noted, indeed it is reflected in the title of Valerie Sanders's study of Martineau's fiction, *Reason Over Passion.*

An examination of Martineau's travel writing in relation to her literary career is particularly important to this study since she was a prominent independent writer who was in a good position to expand women's vocational opportunities into scientific areas. Moreover, she was unusually conscious of the failings of perception and the effect of her own presence on what she saw and was, in effect, the sort of methodical observer which promoters of scientific method had called for. Her writing career also spanned a period of enormous change both in natural history, as it became influenced by evolutionary ideas, and in the development of travel writing, as Britain expanded its imperialist involvement with other areas of the world. These intellectual and social changes are particularly marked in the differences between her 1834–36 American travels and her 1846–47 Mideast travel, which also reflect the transformation of travel writing as travel became accessible to more Europeans. James Buzard points out that during the nineteenth century, travel came "to be characterized as an enterprise thoroughly mediated by literary texts and sponsoring a form of experience as second-hand or *vicarious* as that undergone by the readers of novels and tales" (216). This awareness is especially apparent in Martineau's Mideast travels where, in addition to dealing with gender-related writing anxiety, she also struggles to distinguish and distance herself from an increasingly codified tourism in order to understand and interpret a foreign culture within an evolutionary framework and in accordance to scientific objectivity.

Whereas in Wollstonecraft's day, terms such as "science" and "natural history" were used as if they were interchangeable, in the 1830s there was a growing awareness that the scientific enterprise lacked both stability and the sort of precise definition we now associate with science. This led to a need to promote scientific activities as accessible to a larger public, which included both women and the working class, in order to more firmly establish it and sharply define its professional borders. Eventually this would raise the so-called "hard sciences," those studies of physical phenomena which are easily quantifiable, to the top of a hierarchy of science while separating the term "science" from more subjectively based "natural history" and "moral sciences" such as political economy, sociology, and a cluster of fields now grouped around field biology and anthropology. However, at the beginning of Martineau's career, "science" was used less restrictively than it would be later on and several scholarly endeavors sought "scientific" status. With such loosely defined terminology, greater emphasis was placed on the method of study than on the object of investigation and individuals tended to drift across what we would perceive to be different disciplines, but which Victorians understood as a more unified discourse (Yeo, "Scientific" 272–82). Thus, a disciplined manner of observation was more important than the subject of study as science gave promise of clarifying everything.

Martineau's travel was central to her reputation in the Victorian era, and her travel writing helped shape much of her other work, establishing her independence and individualism. While her writings have now been critically rediscovered, modern study (with the exception of Richard L. Stein, who does discuss Martineau's epistemology) has been concerned primarily with her fiction, particularly with placing her novel *Deerbrook* within the context of the later work of such novelists as Charlotte Brontë, George Eliot, and Elizabeth Gaskell. Fiction writing, however, was not Martineau's central concern nor did it reflect her general writing purpose. As such, her travel writings should be examined more closely as the primary basis upon which her Victorian reputation was established.

For the purpose of this study, Martineau is an excellent example of a writer who successfully used travel as a way of establishing a vocation within a scientific discourse. As Maria H. Frawley notes in regard to her American travel, Martineau emphasized an orientation based on scientific method as a means of valid observation.[2] In order to do this, however, it was not enough to measure and evaluate; as a woman she also had to use an array of rhetorical strategies to keep her narrative within acceptable guidelines for feminine public discourse while simultaneously placing herself in a position of authority.

DEFENSIVE STRATEGIES AND THE DEVELOPMENT OF SCIENCE

Londa Schiebinger's history of the debate over the question of whether the mind is gender-neutral, *The Mind has No Sex?*, nicely defines the various arguments women have responded to and used to justify their own writings in cultures which would prefer them silenced. The increasing use of what has been termed sexual complementary ideology—"a theory which taught that man and woman are not physical and moral equals but complementary opposites . . ."[3]—to defend the inferior legal and social position of women particularly complicated how women could respond rhetorically in the early modern period. This ideology was usually substantiated with the newly authorized scientific terminology that claimed that innate physiological differences in women prevented them from high levels of intellectual achievement.[4] Many women writers countered with varying types of defensive strategies that resulted in multiple conflicting discourses. The earlier classical version of this ideology, which Schiebinger terms "essentialism," took as its basic premise that some unchangeable innate factor, psychological or physiological, limits women's intellectual achievement. The closely related doctrine of sexual complementarity was "developed in the eighteenth century as part of the ideological apparatus associated with the professionalization of science and the rise of motherhood."[5] Working on the assumption that scientific studies should be masculine, feminine ideals were designed to supply those social needs that were not valued professionally: religion, morality, and family relationships.[6] Since scientific societies believed there was evidence to support this stand, women in intellectually-oriented fields had to maneuver around these assumptions, a challenge which proved to be more and more difficult in the later half of the nineteenth century.

The two major strategies used in response to these restrictive ideologies are categorized by Schiebinger as "liberal or scientific feminism" and "cultural or romantic feminism." Beginning in the
seventeenth century, exponents of liberal feminism claimed that environment, not nature, was responsible for women's lack of success
in the sciences; for support they pointed out that no significant difference between male and female brains had been found.[7] In the
eighteenth century gender roles became more narrowly defined as
there were attempts to define male and female nature.[8] Since liberal
feminism based its arguments for equality on a supposition that
men and women were the same, it created the assumption that
women had to become men to achieve social equality. This often
led to frustration on the part of women who were trying to expand
their roles in society and better their condition. Such women often
felt that women who behaved frivolously or emotionally were holding the rest of the population back and that education would somehow result in better self-discipline among women in general. This
is exemplified by Wollstonecraft's at times confused pleas for
women to behave in a more rational (i.e., masculine) manner in *Vindication,* and in her sharp criticism of women's social behavior.
Similarly, later feminists distanced themselves from Wollstonecraft
when her life became publicly scandalous and her name became
associated with passionate, emotional behavior. It is also apparent
that Martineau's careful accounting of her own behavior, her anxiety to avoid the potential complexities caused by family life, and
her resistance to speculation in her sociological studies were linked
to such anxieties.

MARTINEAU'S RESPONSE TO WOLLSTONECRAFT

Wollstonecraft was a problematic figure for Martineau, as she
was for most nineteenth-century feminists. Martineau's second
published work, "On Female Education," written in 1823 when she
was twenty-one, showed Wollstonecraft's influence; in it, Martineau argued that differences between the sexes were the result of
different educational opportunities:

[W]e find that as long as the studies of children of both sexes continue
the same, the progress they make is equal. After the rudiments of
knowledge have been obtained . . . the boy goes on continually increasing his stock of information . . . while the girl is probably confined to
low pursuits, her aspirings after knowledge are subdued, she is taught

to believe that solid information is unbecoming her sex, almost her whole time is expended on light accomplishments, and thus before she is sensible of her powers, they are checked in their growth, chained down to mean objects, to rise no more; and when the natural consequences of this mode of treatment arise, all mankind agree that the abilities of women are far inferior to those of men.[9]

Similarly, in 1840, Martineau could write to Maria Weston Chapman and speak of the hard work she must take on to make it "easier for some few to follow as than [sic] it was for poor Mary Wollstonecraft to begin."[10] In her 1855 autobiography, however, she was careful to distance herself from Wollstonecraft, noting that women who wish to improve their condition must be "rational and dispassionate," make no complaints (especially of men) and never allow themselves to become victims of passion. From her description of her meeting with William Godwin, it is apparent that she was nervous about showing too much sympathy for Wollstonecraft. She was careful to state that her interest in Godwin was not related to his first wife (Wollstonecraft) and she emphasized her praise of his second wife (who was not intellectually oriented). While Martineau admitted to a predisposition "to honour all promoters of the welfare and improvement of Woman,"[11] Wollstonecraft still represented for her a lack of self-discipline or at least a yielding to the temptation to display to her readers too much emotion, a weakness which she believed posed an obstacle to women's causes.

This stance reveals Martineau's anxious anticipation of what could happen to her tenuously held power to affect public opinion if she should display spontaneity or emotional responses which would undercut her credibility. Not only did Wollstonecraft show her own personal unhappiness, Martineau thought, but she violated "all good taste" in her "obtrusiveness" and presentation of herself as "the victim of her husband's carelessness and cruelty, while he never spoke in his defence."[12] Martineau does not clarify if she is speaking of Imlay or Godwin here. The most likely reference is to Wollstonecraft's one-sided complaints of Imlay in *Short Residence*. But either way, what concerned Martineau was not the truthfulness of such an assertion, but that Wollstonecraft spoke of her distress in the relationship. For Martineau, true advocates of women's causes must not display their personal pain, must be objective, and must be careful at all times to give no grounds for scandal. In her most direct statement on women's struggles, written immediately following her criticism of Wollstonecraft, she stated, "The best friends of the cause are the happy wives and the busy, cheerful, satisfied single women, who have no injuries of their own to avenge, and no painful vacuity or mortification to relieve."[13] The tenor of the times, the turning away from any program which threatened the structure of government, meant that any reformer (such as Martineau during the Reform bills' progress through Parliament) must have a personal life as free from entanglements as possible and, in order for a woman to express her own views publicly, she must be either serving in what Deirdre David terms an "auxiliary," or supporting role to a husband (or other male relative), else remain a spinster.[14] Wollstonecraft was not, in other words, "a safe example" as a role model.[15]

Indeed, this public silence on the influence of Wollstonecraft was not unique to Martineau. Victorian feminists generally avoided any mention of her from the 1850s to the 1890s, not out of ignorance (for there are mentions in personal correspondence) but out of fear of being identified with loose morals.[16] The situation was such that Barbara Caine has characterized the position of Wollstonecraft as being "one of the dark secrets of Victorian feminism, haunting it as a shadowy and disreputable presence, constantly undermining the most earnest feminist attempts to insist on their respectability and propriety."[17] Several women writers who were clearly influenced by Wollstonecraft avoided speaking of her directly. As examples, Adele M. Ernstrom points to Anna Jameson's travel account *Winter Studies and Summer Rambles in Canada* (1839), Lady Morgan's *Woman and her Master* (1840), Marion Reid's *A Plea for Woman* (1843), and Mary Lemon Grimstone's 1835 *Monthly Repository* article, "Female Education."[18] As mentioned earlier, Jameson additionally shows some Wollstonecraft influence in her 1826 novel (initially taken as autobiographical), *The Diary of an Ennuyée*, where the emotional situation of the traveling narrator trying to forget a lover evokes the narrative stance of Wollstonecraft's *Short Residence* (while it also established Jameson's reputation in art history).

While Martineau made her sacrifices, taking refuge in her heavily structured workday and carefully limited social life, she looked forward to the future when women's advocates would be women with their own personal social power based on professional accomplishments: "the female physicians and other professors in America; the women of business and the female artists of France; and the hospital administrators, the nurses, the educators and substantially successful authors of our own country."[19] She placed her faith in the education of women, and in this faith the focus was especially on science. She was particularly hopeful that science as a vocational field would be gender-blind and that there a woman would only be judged on her achievements: "Whatever a woman proves herself able to do, society will be thankful to see her do,—just as if she were a man. If she is scientific, science will welcome her, as it has welcomed every woman so qualified. I believe no scientific woman complains of wrongs."[20] As with many women in the first half of the nineteenth century, science with its claims to rationality and objectivity appeared to be a future profession for women, one which was gender neutral.

Her optimism about the future position of women in science was echoed by scientific rhetoric in the 1830s. When Martineau was making her studies of American society (1832–34), a widespread rhetoric of the scientific method emphasized the role of careful observation in the development of science. It was not until the 1850s that Baconian methodology was seen as an obstacle and there was increasing emphasis placed on the importance of genius in scientific discovery.[21] This "genius" was perceived as being in opposition to the more routine and egalitarian methodology of Bacon; thus David Brewster described the role of genius in terms of its "impatience," which "spurns the restraints of mechanical rules" and does not "submit to the plodding drudgery of inductive discipline."[22] Prior to this new emphasis on those few (exclusively male) who were gifted enough to interpret the labor of observers, success in the dispassionate study of natural phenomena was seen by Martineau and other women as offering evidence of women's capacity for intellectual endeavor. At the same time, science could serve as a non-gender-specific sphere of study, a safe neutral ground where a woman, so long as she avoided speculation and worked within a carefully logical progression of ideas, could gain both a vocation and a voice in reform. Like Wollstonecraft, Martineau retained a faith in scientific observation as a particularly well-suited opportunity for women to advance professionally.

Much as Martineau wished to distance herself from Wollstonecraft publicly, she did share with Wollstonecraft a similar philosophical background. She was part of a second generation of women influenced by the progressive Wedgwood-Darwin family and other descendants of the old Lunar Society. Additionally, Martineau, like Wollstonecraft, had to find a way to support herself in a society that still offered few options for female employment.

Martineau's position in Victorian intellectual life was quickly established with her *Illustrations of Political Economy* project (1832–1834), which also gave her a direction for self-education in economics and political science (areas which were claiming a scientific methodology and thus a "scientific status"), and intensified her training as a writer. *Illustrations* required that Martineau devote immense concentration on studying an issue, then reinterpret it dramatically in her tales, fleshing out and illustrating abstract concepts in the process. The popular success of *Illustrations* gave her an unusual amount of political influence and she became aware that her writings could help effect political reform in addition to merely informing the public. Martineau's approval of a motion before Parliament could be transformed into public support. Her influence over current political issues was, as she pointed out, ironic, since, as a woman, she could not even vote. But this success allowed her to view herself as a sage capable of independent and original investigations.

Although she gained political power, Martineau avoided social censure in doing so by arguing that *Illustrations* served the needs of popular education, an endeavor that, with its ties to child care and uplifting charitable activities among the working class, was thus socially acceptable for women. As such scholars as Gates has noted, pedagogical work allowed women access to the margins of scientific scholarship. The initiating idea for the series came from another woman writer who was using educational texts as a means of moving into scientific studies. Her inspiration, Jane Marcet's *Conversations on Political Economy* (1816), however, was a classroom text oriented to a young adult audience.[23] Martineau saw that with the debate over the Reform bills, there would be general public interest in how daily life would be affected by economic change. She wrote that it had struck her "that the principles of the whole science [of political economy] might be advantageously conveyed . . . not by being smothered up in a story, but by being exhibited in their natural workings in selected passages of social life."[24] She took an approach used in a classroom and made it the vehicle for an adult audience, stating that she had a "thorough, well-considered, steady conviction that the work was wanted,—was even craved by the popular mind."[25] The series was sold by subscription but was also published by the Society for the Diffusion of Useful Knowledge as an approved self-improvement publication.[26] It gained an audience, however, far more wide-ranging than originally planned. By 1834, the series had sold an average of ten thousand copies per month and had showed up on nearly everyone's reading lists. Charles Darwin's notebooks reveal that he became quite a fan of Martineau's, quickly purchasing her books as soon as they were published.[27]

Notably, in explaining her reason for writing *Illustrations*, Martineau emphasizes that political economy was a "science." She viewed her approach to her studies as an extension of scientific methodology into the area of economics and human interactions and this claim to scientific status, while contestable in the 1830s and 1840s, was later supported by Huxley, Spencer, and Galton.[28]

Although Martineau had become successful in a theoretical area of study, this had come about via the rhetoric of popular education, an acceptable area of writing for women so long as she, like Marcet and Mary Somerville, was retelling or explaining a concept. While Martineau was influential, she was still to all appearances, as David explains, working in an auxiliary position. To bridge the gap between pedagogical and professional scientific status, she had to originate an idea and be recognized as an originator. This was a major barrier to women's involvement in science, as it required speculation, a difficult stance for a woman to take. Women were censored for not displaying much abstract thinking, for a failure to speculate. Speculation, however, with its close association with intuition, is a trait often associated with emotion, a feminine behavior, and is the sort of behavior which must be avoided by women seeking acceptance into male professional societies.[29] As a result, women's writing was only taken seriously if it conformed to a non-emotional rhetoric; but having learned to communicate in this manner, women's research was often judged to be plodding or unimaginative because speculation was nervously avoided or obscured amidst reams of supporting data.

Having achieved success in an auxiliary position, that is, one which is based on the reinterpretation of others' ideas, Martineau had reached the limits of success in popular educational writing. In order to advance professionally, to achieve a position of independent authority, Martineau had to find ways around the limitations of conventional feminine discourse through various justifications for her study and by finding an approach which avoided direct conflict with masculine authorities. She also needed a means of gaining direct experience which her readership would be interested in. One argument, or what might be called a liberating stance, available to her was cultural feminism.[30] Generally associated with the nineteenth century (although we have seen this stance used as early as Wollstonecraft), this response made use of the same duality employed in essentialist sexual definitions, but instead of viewing feminine attributes as a liability, they were advanced as assets which could overcome social ills. In contrast to claims that genius was inherently masculine, for example, cultural feminism celebrated a feminine genius which was divorced from the pursuit of power.[31]

Cultural feminism had general revolutionary potential in that it could provide a corrective to a belief that only by conforming to the dominant culture could success be obtained.[32] It was, however, limited in the spheres of knowledge where it could be used and in the degree of power that it could help women obtain, since cultural feminism's dualist epistemology ultimately restricted women's spheres of discourse, just as essentialism did. The trick would be to extend women's spheres of knowledge, something of what eco-feminists are achieving in modern times.

Another way of dealing with dominant cultural discourse was to circumvent the situation by essentially avoiding traditional paths of success and forming one's own discipline or approach to a subject. This is the approach Barbara McClintock used in the 1950s in her independent work on corn genetics, an object of study which was not being pursued in other labs and one which allowed her to work independently (and maintain ownership of the results).[33] McClintock was successful because she had a "feeling for the organism"—the maize plant in this case—the result of the sort of observation natural history taught and which women traditionally excel at. As Evelyn Fox Keller points out, McClintock would have been considered a naturalist in the nineteenth century because of her focus on a particular species and the telling differences between individuals.[34] Closely related to the stance of cultural feminism, such independent tactics answered the challenge of J. S. Mill who told women to write "with their sentiments and their feminine experience" and to ground abstractions in the concrete, and their practical daily experiences rather than attempting to duplicate male-dominated methodologies.[35] While this strategy posed some difficulty, since the new approach might not be taken seriously without professional accreditation, it at least allowed women to write in ways that were not in direct conflict with the established hierarchy. In McClintock's case, she was able to secure herself in established scientific theory before becoming an something of an outsider until her work in genetics was proven to be correct with the development of molecular biology. Until then, she viewed as something of an eccentric for years. Even in the 1940s, it was rare for a woman to achieve McClintock's initial success; for Martineau, such academic recognition would have been unthinkable.

However, Martineau's effort to establish a new field of study based on a methodology of observation that included the domestic was nicely tailored for her society and time. The approach could be justified with appeals to complementarist rhetoric: that women are more capable of sympathetic observation, that they are intimate

with family life and detail-oriented. In other words, women are mis-
tresses of what Martineau in "On Female Education" called "all
the little arts," "the important trifles . . . which render a home a
scene of comfort."[36] As such, they are well-suited to areas of study
in which their feminine attributes, particularly their training in detailed observation, could be presented as assets.

MARTINEAU AND THE BAAS: PROBLEMS WITH PROFESSIONAL SOCIETIES

   Since Martineau sought to establish herself professionally as an
authority in her sociological studies, involvement in a professional
society would be advantageous, although it was not a necessity. In
the 1830s, it was still possible for an independent scientific researcher to make a reputation based solely on publication, as would
any other writer. Writing, in general, offered an unusual access to
economic independence for such women as George Eliot, George
Sand, and the Brontës in part because they could use publication
to establish a masculine authority; no one had to know the author
personally; no professional membership was necessary to establish
an author's expertise. A similar situation existed in natural history
in Britain since the field, insecure in its social position and possibly
wishing to divorce itself from past radical associations, had sought
a broad foundation of public support with the argument that it was
a morally uplifting and non-controversial leisure activity which
anyone could pursue. At the same time, there was tension within
this public discourse as those in scientific research positions attempted to justify and strengthen its identity as a profession by clarifying the discipline's boundaries and standardizing its practice. By
the time Chambers anonymously published *Vestiges* (1844), it became apparent that the needs of the general public for an open,
flexible scientific discourse was in conflict with the specialists'
need to regulate how science was practiced and what would be considered "scientific." To the specialists, it became apparent that reg-
ulation of some sort had to be established to present a unified
cohesive scientific presence for the general public.[37]
   By the mid-nineteenth century, membership in scientific societies
became increasingly necessary for anyone working in the sciences.
Darwin's 1859 *Origin* was based on years of both extensive gathering of information and of correspondence with other established re-
searchers. When he published, therefore, he was a known name and
his work was anticipated by people such as Thomas Henry Huxley,

who were prepared to support him. Martineau's efforts to establish her American study as a ground breaking work would have been helped if she had gained acceptance and a voice through the backing of a professional society. As Keller explains in regard to the operation of modern science:

> A new idea, a new conception, is born in the privacy of one man's or one woman's dreams. But for that conception to become part of the body of scientific theory, it must be acknowledged by the society of which the individual is a member. In turn, the collective effort provides the ground out of which new ideas grow. Scientific knowledge as a whole grows out of the interaction—sometimes complex, always subtle—between individual and community.[38]

This process was just becoming formalized when Martineau was writing. In contrast to traditional explanations (or general disregard) of the absence of women in science, recent studies of the history of science indicate that as professional scientific societies became more prominent, it became more difficult for women to be accepted in scientific professions. The failure of women to make a greater impact in Victorian science was not the result of their lack of interest, research, or training. Rather, it was a failure to obtain sufficient support from established professional societies or to found their own societies.[39]

After Martineau's publication of *Society* in 1837, it would seem that she was in a position to make the sort of contacts necessary for professional recognition and advancement. Martineau had published under her own name, she was a public figure, and she represented her work as conforming to scientific principles. Moreover, the British Association for the Advancement of Science (BAAS) had just opened the geology and natural history section to women that year and the BAAS depended on women's attendance for a major part of their funding. What then happened to prevent Martineau from becoming more involved?

Martineau was sufficiently interested in this opportunity to attend the 1838 meeting of BAAS in Newcastle. Yet she found the experience to be discouraging and was surprisingly critical of the presence of other women at the lectures. This may be explained in terms of how the women's attendance and the meeting in general was being used by the BAAS. The 1838 meeting in Newcastle was an enormous affair. Besides the 1,100 women attendees, there were 2,430 members, and 4,500 people showed up at one evening promenade.[40] Some were delighted at the success of the meeting, others, such as John Phillips, called it "a vanity fair" and Charles Dickens observed that "the quackery is of an extra strength this year."[41] The carnival atmosphere, while publicly attractive, diminished the scholarly reputation of the meeting and this probably had much to do with Martineau's response to the organization. She was not impressed by many of the BAAS members; she spoke of "the conceit of third-rate men with their specialties, the tiresome talk of one-idead [sic] men, who scruple no means of swelling out what they call the evidence of their doctrines, and the disagreeable footing of the ladies."[42] Some of the speakers acknowledged the presence of the women in a condescending manner. Adam Sedgwick's, Charles Babbage's, and John Hershel's engagement in humorous flippancy at the expense of the women particularly caused annoyance.[43] Martineau expressed disgust at the behavior of both the men and the women and decided not to attend again:

I heard two or three valuable addresses; but, on the whole, the humbugs and small men carried all before them: and, I am sorry to say, Sir John Hershel himself so far succumbed to the spirit of the occasion as to congratulate his scientific brethren on the "crowning honour" among many, of the presence of the fair sex at their sections![44]

She continued to describe the undignified behavior of the women in some detail:

That same fair sex, meantime, was there to sketch the *savans*, under cover of mantle, shawl or little parasol, or to pass the time by watching and quizzing the members. Scarcely any of the ladies sat still for half an hour. They wandered in and out, with their half-hidden sketch-books, seeking amusement as their grandmothers did at auctions. I was in truth much ashamed of the ladies.[45]

This view of women as amateurs and unprofessional is a perception Martineau herself was trying to counter. While it is clear that the issue of women's presence at the BAAS meetings had been growing over the past seven years and that women had most probably been organizing in order to keep professional societies open by making their presence impossible to ignore, Martineau did not feel confident enough to become associated with the "carnival" atmosphere of these annual meetings. It is ironic that women's efforts to be admitted to the BAAS meetings backfired when the financial advantages became clear and the meetings became overwhelmed by entertainment designed to attract as many people as possible. The BAAS became a target for satire as *The Comic Almanack* held the

1835 meeting up for ridicule and Charles Dickens began "The Mudfog Association for the Advancement of Everything" sketches in 1837.[46]

To be taken seriously herself required that Martineau frown on less-than-serious behavior of other women, particularly when it had become associated with such satirical attacks. The necessity to maintain a dignified position, however, isolated her from those professional groups whose support she needed if she were to gain the recognition she sought. Martineau did not lose faith in her abilities. After all, she had no hesitation in criticizing the men for sloppy science. However, she made the decision to proceed independently of scientific societies, allowing her work to speak for her in a time when scientific recognition would become more heavily dependent on professional contacts. While this decision is understandable, since her independent stance had served her well as a political commentator, it is quite possible that the avoidance of such organizations as the BAAS made it more likely that *How to Observe Morals and Manners,* possibly the earliest sociology textbook written, would be ignored and that her later Mideast travel observations would be perceived as outside the realm of serious investigation.

A Search for a Vocation and Illustrations

To understand Martineau's particularly strong drive toward a vocation, it is necessary to look at her family's background and position in nineteenth-century Britain. As a Unitarian and a descendant of French Huguenot refugees who had emigrated to England after the Revocation of the Edict of Nantes in 1688, Martineau believed strongly in the importance of tolerance and free speech. She and her family, as descendants of emigrants, also maintained cultural links outside England, which would make the idea of travel fairly natural.[47] Although her family included many doctors and medicine was a family tradition, her father had gone into business and was a successful wine importer and bombazine manufacturer in Norwich, a city known for its connections to the Continent. Critics have thus pointed to Martineau's background as being typically middle-class bourgeois. But it was bourgeois with a difference.[48] Bombazine is a black cloth traditionally used in funeral mourning and in academic robes, an interesting reflection of the two areas of activity in which her family was involved outside that of business: religion and scholarship. The city of Norwich is also unusual in offering historical models of both women's travel and scholarship since it is the loca-

Harriet Martineau. From *Harriet Martineau's Autobiography,* **edited by Maria Weston Chapman (Boston, 1877).**

tion of Dame Julian of Norwich's (1343–1416) church, the same "Dame Jelyan" visited by the medieval travel writer Margery Kempe in 1415.

By the time of Martineau's birth in 1802, her father was concerned with the effect of war and decline in exports on the long-term success of his business, and this concern promoted Martineau's orientation toward self-support. Although the family was initially well-to-do, all the children were raised with the expectation that they would eventually provide for their own livelihood and they were taught to care for themselves and to see their education as their only dependable inheritance. Martineau early internalized this realistic need for economy and learned to sew her own clothes to spare expenses and prepare for a lowering of her living standards. She also knew very early that she would have to support herself.

Martineau's childhood education bespoke her family's belief in the intellect and this training prepared her well for her later writing. Although she was the sixth of eight children and the third daughter, her early education was not stinted. She received an unusually good education at home in language, classics, rhetoric, and philosophy, a curriculum usually reserved for boys; it was assumed that she would eventually work as a highly qualified governess.

Such expectations for her future employment were dashed when she started losing her hearing at the age of twelve. Her disability was, ironically, a liberation because it meant she could not work as a governess, or at least not in the highly qualified position for which she was being trained. Such a position required musical training and, up until this time, Martineau had shown musical ability and was receiving tutoring. But the onset of deafness quickly limited what few vocational opportunities were available to her. Only needlework remained and Martineau was strongly encouraged to pursue this occupation. (She enjoyed this activity and later donated "fancy-work" to abolitionist groups for fundraising.) Writing was not seen as an acceptable option, at least for the daughter of a business owner. But when the family business failed, the situation changed. Later, in 1829, Martineau would happily remember when "we had lost our gentility," and, thus, could write openly rather than secretly in the early morning hours.[49] This fall in social status allowed her family, in Martineau's estimation, to truly live instead of vegetating.

It was not uncommon during the early Victorian period for women writers to have difficulty finding editors who would consider publishing their works; however, politically radical and religious publications were more accepting of women's writing. Martineau found both types of publications in William Johnson Fox's *Monthly Repository*, a radical Unitarian publication, and she became its only paid contributor (submitting fifty-two articles in 1830). Despite this output, she still could not earn a livelihood from her writing and was sewing during the day and writing at night.

It was only after she had achieved phenomenal success with her *Illustrations of Political Economy* (1832–34) that she could give up the sewing. This writing project required an immense effort: she committed herself to essentially writing a novella-length story on a monthly basis from 1832–34. At first, she planned on publishing quarterly, but her publisher and her brother James pressed her to publish monthly. The workload she established with this project was necessary to maintain her income and the rest of her writing life was dedicated to producing an immense oeuvre, an output which she could only achieve by restricting herself to first drafts, at times written so quickly that she admitted later to having no memory of the contents of some of the essays she had written. Despite her attempts to justify this practice on the grounds that rewriting weakened the quality of the prose, it did create unevenness in her writing.

Even when time for editing and rewriting became available to her, Martineau still resisted revision, an attitude she shared with other women writers. Her insistence on validating those initial thoughts present in the first draft and her avoidance of rewrites recalls Wollstonecraft's declaration that her first spontaneous impressions should not be altered because they were closer to the source of artistic genius. But Martineau was distancing herself from that Romantic ideology, especially with its dangerous emotional associations. Rather, although she insisted on the necessity of this writing process to fulfill a utilitarian purpose, her reliance on first drafts also may be read as a symptom of the gender anxiety which resulted from working in a masculine discourse, especially since, unlike George Sand and George Eliot, she wrote under her own name.[50] Rewriting her drafts would create the temptation to alter, perhaps weaken, the opinions she presented to make them less controversial. Since Martineau exhibited enormous intellectual bravery in continually writing unpopular and certainly unladylike editorials, her publishing such forceful opinions might well have been made even more difficult if she allowed herself second thoughts.

THE "NEED OF TRAVEL"

While Martineau had achieved a certain level of authoritative discourse in her *Illustrations,* her authority (like that of many women involved with natural history) was still based in the feminine realm of popular education. In order to establish herself professionally, she had to market her information by way of the discourse of direct experience, since she did not have access to the assumed authority which a male writer could gain through education and work credentials. Travel outside England was one of the few ways for a woman to gain such authority. In her travel writing, Martineau made use of the cultural feminism stance by justifying her analysis of American society with the argument that the feminine experience was needed to truly understand the workings of any social group. This did not mean, however, that she attempted to claim any moral superiority for women outside this limited vocational arena.[51] Rather, she emphasized the domestic details in her observations, such as the maintenance of a household and the daily needlework of the women. These observations were not unique to Martineau; Wollstonecraft had used similar observations in her travel. But Martineau placed herself within the dominant culture, and supported the domestic role for women. This made her analysis less overtly revolutionary, and thus, more likely to be accepted by the intellectual establishment because it was less threatening.

Martineau's domestic discourse was the approach necessary to counterbalance her potentially subversive act of creating a new scientific discipline. Travel was the means by which she could obtain material to both substantiate her methodology and her authority. Her travel writings, particularly the methodological *How to Observe Morals and Manners* and the investigative *Society in America*, were attempts to form the groundwork of a new discipline, the scientific study of modern societies based on family structure, in essence, what Susan Hoecker-Drysdale and Michael Hill have identified as early sociology.

Her purpose in these travel writings was not obvious since she did not emphasize those arguments that would generally be expected in a work designed to persuade others to take up a text as a guide to future study. That is, Martineau did not explicitly state in her studies or in her autobiography that her goal was the establishment of a new field of study, nor did she indicate her preparation for field work, be it in terms of past publications, personal questions or mandates from others. In his 1856 Mideast travel, for example, Richard Burton introduced his institutional affiliation, the Royal Geographical Society, and explained the specific reason for his travel in order to substantiate and legitimize his narrative authority.[52] The curious absence of any such explicit declaration of Martineau's work as pioneering in nature may be understood in terms of the restriction of feminine discourse. A woman lost respect if she was seen as too aggressive or pushy in her behavior. Correspondingly, it seems that a woman's writing would be perceived as more acceptable if her argument proceeded implicitly. This would allow the reader to make important connections or conclusions from the evidence she gradually accumulated. By avoiding direct statements, which could be interpreted as too aggressive, the woman writer could allow the reader to feel in control and unthreatened, since the authorial voice would not be a dominating presence. Yet, by choosing to present her travels as essentially solitary, Martineau was able to implicitly maintain ownership of her ideas.

While the lack of an explicit statement as to why her work was ground breaking may be understood in terms of Martineau's nervousness over directly challenging guidelines for feminine discourse, the absence of any discussion of her own intellectual preparation for her travel is more problematic. Such discussions are fairly common in men's travel writing, especially if the travel was being presented as a scholarly endeavor promising geographical, anthropological, and/or sociological discoveries. This preparation research helps establish the scientific traveler's credentials and separates him from more touristy accounts. For example, David Livingstone's *Missionary Travels* (1858) begins with a personal sketch showing how his studies and experiences led to his departure to Africa. This is similar to Edward Granville Browne's autobiographical first chapter of his *A Year Amongst the Persians* (1893) which also details his studies. Even the well-known explorer Richard Burton provides in his travels in North America, *The City of the Saints* (1862), a brief indication of his readings before his trip. In contrast, Martineau's details of her preparation are more difficult to establish. Some of her preparation for travel is presented implicitly in her choice of subjects for her *Illustrations* series and these at least indicate the range of her reading. While most of these illustrations were concerned with issues involving England, Martineau also wrote some foreign-based illustrations based on travel accounts and studies since, up until this time, she had done no traveling outside Britain.[53]

Even though Martineau gave no description of her studies in preparation for her voyage, it is apparent that she did prepare herself. Even while she was working on *Illustrations*, travel was on her mind. In her autobiography, she confessed, "My pleasure in Voyages and Travels is almost an insanity."[54] She listed as sources for her writing: "Lichtenstein's South Africa for 'Life in the Wilds'; Edwards's (and others') 'West Indies' for 'Demerara'; and McCulloch's 'Highlands and Islands of Scotland' for the two Garveloch stories."[55] This reading indicates that she was studying how other travelers presented their experiences. She also produced several local color accounts in relation to her work on Ireland, France, Siberia, Holland, the United States, and Ceylon. Her work on Ceylon, a topic chosen as sort of a personal indulgence, also required that she locate and interview travelers who had just returned from that country because she could not find sufficient printed information.[56]

Additionally, although Martineau does not speak directly about her readings in the natural sciences, nineteenth-century theories of development clearly influenced her travel writing. She was familiar with Charles Lyell's *Principles of Geology* by the time of her American travel and Chambers's *Vestiges* by her Mideast voyage. Later, she received a copy of *Origin* directly from Darwin's brother, Erasmus, and she commented on it.[57]

As a genre, travel writing is heavily influenced by the work of previous travelers and from these indications in her autobiography, it can be seen that Martineau, as did many travel writers, prepared herself by acquiring a library of works by earlier travelers and studying their observations. Yet, while knowledge of past work in the field is generally perceived as an indication of expertise in a subject, Martineau does not want to stress this preparation, since it might leave her open to charges of traveling with publication in mind, a critical attack "often made against women on the basis of their proverbial garrulousness and exhibitionism."[58] Martineau's need for travel also contained an element of personal desperation. She timed her travel so that she finished her final tale for *Illustrations* just one day before her departure date. Her workload had been overwhelming and she lived with her aging mother, who was going blind, and a frail elderly aunt. She may have been escaping social expectations. An unmarried woman in her position would normally be expected to remain at home, isolate herself and nurse elderly family members.

In addition to avoiding an emphasis on herself as an authority in her field of study, Martineau was also careful to downplay her personal bravery in traveling, either by emphasizing the positive aspects of a potentially dangerous activity or by simply avoiding mention of it all together. The strenuous and dangerous endeavor was presented in terms of self-discipline, "rest and recreation."

> My first desire was for rest. My next was to break through any selfish "particularity" that might be growing on me with years, and any love of ease and indulgence that might have arisen out of success, flattery, or the devoted kindness of my friends. I believed that it would be good for me to "rough it" for a while, before I grew too old and fixed in my habits for such an experiment.[59]

In her autobiography, she acknowledged that the anti-abolitionist climate of 1830 America placed her at greater risk than she indicated in *Society* or in *Retrospect*. But she never mentioned the more immediate danger of the New York cholera epidemic of 1834, the

year of her American visit, which she must have exposed herself
to during her visits to New York schools, hospitals, and prisons.[60]
Similarly, her 1847 Mideast travels gave no hint of the threats made
against European women, documented in Florence Nightingale's
unpublished Egyptian letters of 1849–50.

As a woman traveling without a man, Martineau was what would
later be referred to as "unprotected." It was assumed that women
required continual shielding and watching while traveling. James
Buzard points out that "the very involvement of women . . . represented a threat to the ideals associated with independent, 'masculine' travel."[61] Aware that she was treading in a masculine area of
discourse, Martineau showed a nervousness about publicly admitting the dangers of travel. In an effort to normalize traveling, she
may have been hesitant about directly taking an explorer stance
which could lead to an outcry against women traveling.

THE "RESULTS OF TRAVEL": EXAMINATION OF AMERICAN TRAVELS

Martineau's travels to America gave her the personal experience
necessary to validate a more authoritative voice in her writing. Having made her literary reputation in her *Illustrations,* her ambitions
expanded from the popularization of topical economic issues to independent political and sociological studies. She eventually published three books from her experiences. In *Society in America*
(1837), she presented a sociological study of American institutions;
Retrospect of Western Travel (1838) is a more personal and popular
account of her travels; and *How to Observe Morals and Manners*
(1838) outlines her methodology for sociological study. Additional
details of her travel experience that she considered too sensitive for
publication during her lifetime were included in her *Autobiography.*

Society in America was necessary to establish Martineau's authority and, underlying her rigor, there is a self-conscious anticipation of the criticism which would seize upon any evidence of
female elements—those which could be termed unscientific or unprofessional—to dismiss her work. At the same time, her reputation
and sales depended upon her ability to treat difficult subjects in an
entertaining manner, thus the anecdotal, narrative elements were
treated in a separate volume, *Retrospect.* Maria H. Frawley discusses the implications of Martineau's division of her study into
separate books. Pointing to Martineau's prefatory remark, "There
seems no reason why such a picture should not be appended to an

inquiry into the theory and practice of their [American] society" (9), Frawley explains that,

> By describing the second study as a "picture" that has been "appended to" the more rigorous "inquiry," she unambiguously places her allegiance with the first. She sought to safeguard her public identity as rational, masculine social investigator by overtly separating the spheres of her travel writing and suggesting that the "lighter" and hence more feminine book, *Retrospect of Western Travel,* was written only to satisfy the less serious-minded reading public.[62]

Thus, the division of material according to her anticipated audience indicates Martineau's desire that her studies be accorded scientific status. However, at this point in her literary career, it may be more accurate to say that rather than "safeguard," she hoped to *establish* her public identity, since her previous success was due to her short stories, not her social investigation.[63]

While at sea, before she had reached America, Martineau prepared for possible critical attacks by starting work on *How to Observe Morals and Manners*, which explained how she went about observing American society. She started this project by first writing a chapter for a book (proposed by an unnamed friend) to be called "How to Observe." This writing allowed her to consider systematically and abstractly how to perceive and form general conclusions about another society prior to her actual American observations. The chapter eventually formed the basis for her own volume in an aborted series of books on "How to Observe," of which Martineau's was the second and final volume. This project was originally intended to be a multiple-author series on the topic of observation from the perspective of several scientific fields. The first volume was *How to Observe Geology* (1835) by Henry Thomas de la Beche. Disciplined observations were considered to be an important, if not defining, aspect of natural history. Emily Shore, who wrote on bird behavior in the 1830s, noted that natural history is a study in which "it is particularly important not to come too hastily to conclusions, but to study facts from observation frequently and most carefully before any inference is drawn from them."[64] This type of observation was what Martineau was trying to transfer from natural history to the study of society.

The placement of her book in this series indicates that Martineau's travel was intended to be viewed within the discourse of science. H. Bellenden Kerr's preface to the series in de la Beche's volume begins by quoting from John Herschel's *Discourse on the*

Study of Natural Philosophy that "there is no branch of science" in which "an immense mass of valuable information might not be collected from those who in their various lines of life at home or abroad, stationary or in travel, would gladly avail themselves of opportunities of being useful" (Martineau, *How to* 248–49). Martineau's own volume was not published until 1838, after the publication of her two other books on the United States. Although her book went out of print almost as soon as it was published and her subsequent reputation was obscured by later writers of the history of sociology,[65] *How to Observe* shows a rare glimpse into the formation of a professional discipline as it makes a call for travelers to exercise a more disciplined regimen in their travel writings to serve the needs of developing sociology and anthropology. Rejecting the argument that the purpose of travel writing is merely to entertain because the writers' reports are subjective, Martineau proclaimed that travel writing was an important tool, producing the data needed for a universal understanding of important moral issues, especially "the domestic [which] are the primary interests among all human beings" (*How to* 224–29). This stance justified her travel and raised its status from entertainment to that of providing data and valid scientific generalizations. However, she was still careful to indicate that others, men presumably, would provide the speculation and shape the final conclusions after the travel observations are somehow absorbed.

Martineau, of course, was not the first to write a travel account on the United States. Books on travels to the United States developed into an important literary market for many authors as the British public desired personal accounts of the results of American democracy. Such attention by British writers created an atmosphere of suspicion among Americans toward British travelers. This is reflected in Charles Dickens's original 1841 opening chapter to his *American Notes* in which he speaks of a dissatisfaction among Americans "with all accounts of the Republic whose citizens they are, which are not couched in terms of exalted and extravagant praise."[66]

In her work, Martineau's attempts to differentiate her account from previous writings showed that she was intensely aware of the atmosphere which motivated Dickens's irritation. In particular, she wished to avoid such fault-finding perceptions as that of Basil Hall's *Travels in North America in 1827 and 1828* (1829) and Frances Trollope's *Domestic Manners of the Americans* (1832). Trollope's book had been published just before Martineau's travel and it became for her a cautionary model of what to avoid in her own accounts.

MARTINEAU AND THE "LYNX-LIKE OPTICS OF THE FEMALE"

Trollope's and Hall's travels were written for clear political purposes and Americans saw close similarities between the two, enough to move an "American Editor" of a one-volume 1832 New York edition of *Domestic Manners* to write a preface claiming that the real author was not Trollope but Hall himself.[67] In *Domestic Manners,* Trollope makes clear the effect she hopes her book will have on a British reform-minded reader (her intended audience):

> How often have I wished, during my abode in the United States, that one of these conscientious, but mistaken reasoners, fully possessed of his country's confidence, could pass a few years in the United States, sufficiently among the mass of the citizens to know them, and sufficiently at leisure to trace effects to their causes. Then might we look for a statement which would teach these mistaken philanthropists to tremble at every symptom of democratic power among us. (359)

Her travels are primarily designed to teach a lesson on the dangers of reform to a British audience. Yet, within a fairly consistently negative view of American society (she did like the blackberries), is a concern with the treatment of women and an implicit cultural feminist assertion that the health of a society is dependent on an active female presence to maintain a strong social order, a presence Trollope found to be lacking in American society.

Trollope describes American women as being "guarded by a seven-fold shield of habitual insignificance" (69). She points out that all male social enjoyments take place in the absence of women and discusses the effects of the social segregation of the sexes at such occasions as a supper at a ball (154–57). An illustration in *Domestic Manners* shows the women at a ball lined up in single file against the wall on chairs, balancing plates in their laps, outcasts from the celebration which can be seen beyond in a next room where the men, seated at a table, are engaged in toasting one another (Plate IX, 161). Such concerns are, however, not uniformly expressed. When sexual segregation is consistent with British practice, as with the exclusion of women from the House of Commons, at a time when the U.S. House of Representatives had a ladies' gallery, Trollope manages to justify the British practice by claiming it is necessary so that members will keep their minds on the business of government and not be distracted (225).

Unlike Trollope, Martineau was prepared to applaud evidences of social equality that she observed in the United States; however, like Trollope, Martineau supported the position that a woman traveler's access to the domestic sphere gave her important insights into the social fabric of a society and that the position of women in society was important. In contrast to Trollope's approach, Martineau stressed social science rather than politics as the purpose for her travel. And whereas Trollope had no hesitation in making value judgments about American society based on personal values, Martineau attempted to keep her observations bound to a scientific methodology.

In keeping with conventional expectations for feminine discourse, Trollope was careful to offer her observations (at least initially) in a self-deprecating manner. She wrote in *Domestic Manners*:

> I am in no way competent to judge of the political institutions of America; and if I should occasionally make an observation on their effects, as they meet my superficial glance, they will be made in the spirit, and with the feeling of a woman, who is apt to tell what her first impressions may be, but unapt to reason back from effects to their causes. Such observations, if they be unworthy of much attention, are also obnoxious to little reproof: but there are points of national peculiarity of which women may judge as ably as men,—all that constitutes the external of society may be fairly trusted to us. (46)

Here Trollope characterizes her observations as "superficial" and "unworthy," acknowledging a sexual complementary ideology that defined how much abstraction women could use. But she also argues that so long as women restrict themselves to a limited sphere of ambition, even though they avoid the "big" issues of causation and widely encompassing theory, their observations may equal a man's. In her notebook, which she kept while writing *Domestic Manners*, Trollope explicitly states what her work implies.

> The study of manners, though greatly important, is not too profound for their [women's] capacity, and the minutiae of which it is composed, suits better the minute and lynx-like optics of the female, than with the enlarged and elevated views of things taken by the male traveler. (46–47 n. 3)

While Martineau discarded the traditional feminine self-denigration of Trollope's discourse, she uses a similar cultural feminist argument to justify her own travels. The "lynx-like optics of the female" identified in Trollope's private notebook was the position Martineau took publicly in her own account, arguing in *Society in America* that being a woman traveler was far from being a disadvantage; rather, it was an advantage since she had "seen much more of domestic life than could possibly have been exhibited to any gentleman travelling through the country" (xvi).

With this argument, Martineau was able to make use of a cultural feminist position to justify her travel while avoiding the associated sexual complementary corollary that women were inherently incapable of rigorous judgment or the sort of generalizations which lead to risk-taking predications. Essentially, Martineau managed to make use of the same argument as Trollope but without Trollope's need for ingratiating apologies for writing. This position, however, did have its drawbacks. For while maintaining a dignified narrative voice, Martineau also stayed close to the safe Baconian methodology developed for natural history that limited the number of risks she took in her writing. As a result of this care in providing support for her conclusions, Martineau's writing, when compared to her more famous male contemporary, Alexis de Tocqueville, seems rather dry.[68] This careful use of the argument that women are in a better position to observe, along with a need to prove that women could work within a rigorous methodology, helps explain why, as Frawley has observed, Martineau's investigative approach appears to be "excessive in its asceticism" and reflective of a "fear of the impressionistic, the immediate, the spontaneous."[69]

The attempt to maintain a scientific investigative methodology can be seen functioning in the multiple perspectives Martineau provided for in her American itinerary. As with natural history observation, Martineau attempted to make direct contact with her social observation and see American on its own terms, without preconception. Upon arrival in New York on 19 September 1834, Martineau planned her travel so as to make observations from as many social perspectives as possible. By comparing her observations, she hoped to be able to verify the accuracy of her conclusions. Similarly, she attempted to vary the type of locales she reported on. She traveled as far north as the Great Lakes region and as far south as New Orleans, then went up the Mississippi by riverboat. She ventured through Tennessee, Kentucky, and into Ohio, ending with a series of trips to New England. Although never in very good health, she cheerfully endured the discomfort of long-term travel, often by coach, on rough, rugged roads. Like many Victorian visitors, she visited prisons, hospitals, schools, factories, and farms. Aware of the difficulty involved in trying to make large generalizations about a country, Martineau attempted to anticipate charges that her knowledge was too shallow by staying with families and attending whatever social opportunities were made available to her as part of her fieldwork. She prided herself on being able to fit into the daily domestic routine. Martineau explained that she visited with different households, gossiped and sewed with the women, and attended local churches and weddings, noting that "[a]bove all, I was received into the bosom of many families, not as a stranger, but as a daughter or sister" (*Society* 1:53). This emphasis on the intimacy of her position with Americans supports the argument that women travelers can obtain experiences denied to male travelers. Women's eyes are not just sharper. They are allowed access to a private realm of life hidden from male visitors and this expanded access made their observations more scientifically valid.

Martineau uses a similar argument of increased intimacy when she acknowledges the limitations of her own deafness.[70] Anticipating that her conclusions would be attacked on the basis of her handicap, Martineau raised the issue herself in her writing. In her travel accounts she made her hearing problems quite obvious: she carried a large hearing-trumpet with her, which apparently drew quite a bit of attention. She admitted that her deafness (which apparently was complete in one ear but only partial in the other) did not allow her to hear comments made by people on the streets, and there were cases, as in the House of Representatives, where the acoustics prevented her from hearing discussions. However, she argued that the presence of her hearing trumpet inspired intimacy in conversation and made up for her hearing limitations.[71]

While Martineau implied that both her sex and her handicap gave her unusual access to the personal sphere (presenting perceived weaknesses as actual strengths), it is apparent from her autobiography that in actuality her deafness was of greater value in allowing her to control and distance herself from unwanted intimacy. She could "cut" a person by refusing to extend her hearing trumpet to those she considered rude, unmannerly, or boring. It also permitted her to ignore what she did not want to deal with, allowing her to distance criticism from herself and, thus, take on controversial issues to an extent which was very unusual for women of her class. When she was attacked for raising Malthusian issues (and suggesting birth control) in "Weal and Woe in Garveloch" (the sixth in the *Illustrations* series), her response was: "If any other should come whispering to me what I need not listen to, I shall shift my trumpet, and take up my knitting."[72] Thus a tendency to exaggerate her hearing loss was, in part, an adaptive behavior that allowed her to function publicly, yet distance herself from personal criticism.

Since Trollope was her immediate female predecessor in American travel writing, it was important that Martineau distance herself as well from the views of the United States presented in *Domestic Manners*. From the beginning of her travels, Martineau was aware that she could be viewed by Americans as another Trollope and she worried that Americans, as a result, would not be receptive to her and she would lose the American market. (Martineau was careful to obtain American copyrights for her publications.) Although Martineau's argument was similar to Trollope's in that she was using the importance of the domestic as a cultural feminist justification for her writing, she neither agreed with Trollope's political purpose nor with her sexual essentialist argument that serious issues were not suitable subjects for women's writing.

With her American travel writings, Martineau, unlike Trollope, always showed an awareness that her audience included both the American and British reading publics, and she shaped her narration accordingly. While she spoke out against the mistreatment of disenfranchised groups in her discussions on the issues of slavery, the displacement of Native Americans, and women's rights, Martineau was encouraged by evidence she found of a less rigidly class-defined society. By presenting a generally positive response, she was writing against fears expressed by de Tocqueville and Trollope that such an egalitarian culture would result in a rejection of traditional intellectual authority, that popular belief rather than truth would rule in the absence of a class structure with an intellectual elite. Instead, Martineau noted with great approval the wide availability of a basic education and how talented individuals could be found from varying backgrounds, evidence for her own progressive reform agenda in Britain. With a keen eye for detail, she pointed out that there was a better distribution of wealth than in Britain, as shown by the fact that, "Every factory child carries its umbrella and pigdrivers wear spectacles" (*Society* 1:16). While she was annoyed by the heavy use of chewing tobacco, especially the accompanying spitting, she tried not to dwell on it since Trollope had already gained notoriety in the United States for her complaints about the habit.[73] In general, though, Martineau, with a sensitivity toward her trans-Atlantic audience, made an obvious effort to speak highly of American hospitality wherever she could to counteract the previous impressions made by Trollope and to emphasize her own pursuit of objective truth.

Martineau additionally separated herself from Trollope by criticizing a bazaar Trollope had constructed in Cincinnati. The bazaar was originally founded by Trollope to sell luxury goods and raise the aesthetic sense of Americans, but it quickly lost money. Trollope attempted to recoup some of her losses by staging musical entertainments there from 21 November to 19 December 1829, but was not able to attract a large enough audience (Trollope xl–xlix). She returned to England on 5 August 1831 before Martineau's arrival. When Martineau visited Cincinnati, the building with its large ballroom was apparently being put to use. She first describes the building as an architectural monstrosity:

> . . . the Cincinnati public was pouring into Mrs. Trollope's bazar [sic], to the first concert ever offered to them. This bazar is the great deformity of the city. Happily, it is not very conspicuous, being squatted down among houses nearly as lofty as the summit of its dome. From my window at the boarding-house, however, it was only too distinctly visible. It is built of brick, and has Gothic windows, Grecian pillars, and a Turkish dome, and it was originally ornamented with Egyptian devices, which have, however, all disappeared under the brush of whitewasher. (*Retrospect* 2:54)[74]

Martineau is attacking Trollope's lack of culture (as Trollope herself had attacked American culture for its collective lack of culture and manners) and is essentially accusing her of vulgar taste in her combination of so many different types of architecture for an exotic effect, rather than for cultural instruction. Trollope's introduction of musical performance in the city, however, meets with warm approval, so long as the Americans can also be shown in a good light:

> The concert was held in a large plain room, where a quiet, well-mannered audience was collected. There was something extremely interesting in the spectacle of the first public introduction of music into this rising city. . . . The thought came across me how far we were from the musical regions of the Old World, and how lately this place had been a canebrake, echoing with the bellow and growl of wild beast; and here was the spirit of Mozart swaying and inspiring a silent crowd as if they were assembled in the chapel at Salzburg! (*Retrospect* 2:54)

The American crowd may be new to this experience, but they know how to behave and are quiet and absorbed. This report challenges Trollope's representation of an American audience as a noisy, spitting crowd that bore little resemblance to a church scene.[75]

These contrasting impressions of American life are carried over in Martineau's descriptions of the natural world, which, in contrast

to the emotionally-laden personal descriptions of Trollope, similarly reflect her emphasis on objectivity, calmness, and dignity,
both in her persona and in the scenes she describes. Trollope entered the United States via the mouth of the Mississippi, which she
called "utterly desolate," remarking that "[h]ad Dante seen it, he
might have drawn images of another Bolgia [trench where the
damned are placed] from its horrors" (4). The mounds of driftwood
particularly drew her attention:

> Trees of enormous length, sometimes still bearing their branches, and
> still oftener their uptorn roots entire, the victims of the frequent hurri-
> cane, come floating down the stream. Sometimes several of these, en-
> tangled together, collect among their boughs a quantity of floating
> rubbish, that gives the mass the appearance of a moving island, bearing
> a forest, with its roots mocking the heavens; while the dishonoured
> branches lash the tide in idle vengeance: this, as it approaches the ves-
> sel, and glides swiftly past, looks like the fragment of a world in ruins.
> (4)

In this "murky stream," Trollope's first encounter with American
land, the image of Dante's hell is continued in the disengaged roots
which mock the heavens and dishonored vengeful branches, a world
outside heaven, or at least England, populated with fragments of
ruins. This tangle is suggestive of Trollope's view of the settlers of
America as composed of misfits and castoffs from other countries,
ill-suited to form a stable government.

In contrast, Martineau's response to a similar scene outside
Memphis invests the land with a tranquil solitude, moving the perspective imaginatively outside herself and focusing first on the people skillfully navigating amongst natural dangers which are devoid
of any divine retribution.

> No object was more striking than the canoes which we frequently saw,
> looking fearfully light and frail amid the strong current. . . . sometimes
> crossing before our bows, sometimes darting along under the bank,
> sometimes shooting across a track of moonlight. Very often there was
> only one person in the canoe, as in the instance . . . of a woman who
> was supposed to be going on a visit twenty or thirty miles up the stream.
> (*Retrospect* 2:23)

The picture is of frailty and strength embedded in the form of a lone
woman on the river in the moonlight, suggestive of Wollstonecraft's
own solitary rowing. In a sublime moment common in women's
natural history, Martineau imaginatively moves her perspective out

to the lone woman in the canoe and then looks back to observe her-self from an outsider's perspective:

> I could hardly have conceived of a solitude so intense as this appeared
> to me, the being alone on that rushing sea of waters, shut in by untrod-
> den forests; the slow fishhawk wheeling overhead, and perilous masses
> of driftwood whirling down the current; trunks obviously uprooted by
> the forces of nature, and not laid low by the hand of man. What a specta-
> cle must our boat, with its gay crowds, have appeared to such a solitary!
> what a revelation that there was a busy world still stirring somewhere;
> a fact which, I think, I should soon discredit if I lived in the depths of
> this wilderness, for life would become tolerable there only by the spirit
> growing into harmony with the scene, wild and solemn as the objects
> around it. (*Retrospect* 2:23)

The trunks are clearly part of nature, a natural part of the forest, not a Dantesque vision. Rather than being outcast from the heavens, Martineau imagines a dweller in these woods casting out the rest of the world in preference to a harmonious dignified existence in the wilderness. And this is a position with which she feels personally sympathetic, imagining herself as "liv[ing] in the depths of this wil-derness." By looking back at herself from the imagined position of the woman in the canoe, taking an insider/outsider position, Marti-neau attempts to understand how such isolation could shape one's perspective.

Martineau's participation with the woman in the canoe, however, must remain imaginative. Unlike Wollstonecraft, she is not able to represent herself as having immediate physical involvement with her surrounding. Such a representation at this time would involve assuming the explorer role, a narrative position too closely associ-ated with male discourse to be entered without a higher degree of self-confidence. So Martineau remains the observer—sensitive and perceptive, but still detached.

When Martineau did depart from her careful controlled observa-tions, it was under the guidance of science, which granted her a de-gree of authority that made such speculation possible. One of the few examples of risk-taking speculation in her American travels took place under the auspices of Charles Lyell's *Principles of Geol-ogy* (1830–33), the same text Darwin took with him on the *Beagle*. Lyell's perception of geologic time allowed her to envision a distant geologic future at Niagara Falls. Standing under Niagara Falls, Martineau was able to imaginatively see into the future when the place she was standing on would become covered by ocean:

I saw something of the process of world-making behind the fall of Niagara, in the thunder cavern, where the rocks that have stood for ever tremble to their fall amidst the roar of the unexhausted floods. Foot-hold
upon foot-hold is destined to be thrown down till, after more ages than
the world has yet known, the last rocky barrier shall be overpowered,
and an ocean shall overspread countries which are but just entering upon
civilised existence. Niagara itself is but one of the shifting scenes of
life, like all of the outward that we hold most permanent. Niagara itself,
like the systems of the sky, is one of the hands of Nature's clock, moving, though too slowly to be perceived by the unheeding,—still moving,
to mark the lapse of time. Niagara itself is destined to be as the tradition-
ary [sic] monsters of the ancient earth—a giant existence, to be spoken
of to wondering ears in studious hours and believed in from the sole
evidence of its surviving grandeur and beauty. While I stood in the wet
whirlwind, with the crystal roof above me, the thundering floor beneath,
and the foaming flood before me, I saw those quiet, studious hours of
the future world when this cataract shall have become a tradition, and
the spot on which I stood shall be the centre of a wide sea, a new region
of life. This was seeing world-making. (*Society* 210–11)[76]

David terms this a "sibylline" perception[77]; however, it is still a
vision without people and, thus, a more limited and safer image
than the type of predictions concerning the course of American development contained in de Tocqueville's book or even the pre-Mal-
thusian vision of a crowded world in Wollstonecraft's travels. It is
only later in the Mideast travels, after Chambers helped enlarge the
scope of science speculation and created an intellectual climate
which asserted "the right of the lay public to speculate on general
questions about the natural world,"[78] that Martineau would try to
make predictions about such sensitive issues as culture and religious development.

While *Retrospect* was an accessible, entertaining account intended for the general public, the three-volume *Society in America*
was intended to provide for Martineau's entrance into a rigorous
area of intellectual study; it was the sort of project, which, in its
theoretical ambition, was considered to be beyond a woman's intellectual capacity. In this work, she helped change the nature of travel
writing by making use of a comparative methodology to analyze
American society and to criticize the social structure of Britain indirectly.[79] Her original title, *Theory and Practice of Society in
America* (which was rejected by her publishers) was a more accurate indication of this work's purpose. Martineau does not explain
why her publishers wished a shorter title, but there may have been
a desire to avoid attaching such a word as "theory" to a work by a

woman, suggestive as it is of a masculine intellectual realm. The study's three volumes attempt to compare the state of American society with the principles expressed in the Declaration of Independence and the Constitution. This discussion of American society also gave Martineau a vehicle to support increased political representation of women in Britain at the time of her travels. In her examination of the nonrepresentation of women in the political process in the United States, she compared the woman's position with that of American slaves. In this context, she was able to generalize her argument so it was applicable to all women, not just Americans.[80]

Speaking out, writing directly, in *Society* did not come easily. In a letter to William Tait, of the *Edinburgh Magazine*, Martineau indicated that she had been steeling herself for a hostile reaction upon publication. She wrote,

> the reception of my book has taken me wholly by surprise. I fully expected it would ruin me, and the writing of it was, I think, the most solemn act of my life. I hope I shall never again want faith in the sympathies of my readers, for never can I put their generosity to a severer test than I have now done, and I have met with nothing but the most entire trust and generous sympathy . . . from all kinds of readers.[81]

These comments, of course, refer to the more reform-minded critics. She gave no public recognition to the heated attacks from her Tory critics, who called her a "female Quixote" and a "maiden malcontent."[82]

Interestingly, those more hostile critical attacks help illuminate and chart the areas where she was intruding into masculine discourse: her position of non-dependency and independence, political activity and theoretical innovation. By remaining single, she was able to anticipate and defuse potential personal attacks that might claim she was abandoning her proper domestic sphere. All that was left then were accusations of being unnatural in her behavior, as was charged by John Wilson Croker in the *Quarterly Review.* Here her unmarried state was grounds for a hysterical cry that Martineau was "A *female Malthusian. A woman* who thinks child-bearing a *crime against society! An unmarried woman* who declares against *marriage*!!"[83] The suggestion here is that since she was unmarried, she could not know the true satisfaction of dependency. This attack was later taken up by American critics when they added such adjectives as "masculine" and "Amazonian" to their name calling.[84] Her claim that she had the capacity to be able to form abstract, "big picture" analyses of contemporary society was attacked first on the grounds of accuracy and then of originality. This is evident in Benjamin Disraeli's 1837 review in *The Times* which charged her with describing America according to her own image of what should be there, based on the "cockney authorities" to whom, he declared, she was indebted. Comparing Martineau's account of America to Volney's travel to Egypt and Syria, Disraeli declared:

> She doubts nothing, she desides upon everything. She explains how everything occurred, and announces how everything must happen. With no learning, and, as we suspect, with very limited reading—with no experience of human nature derived either from books or men, armed only with the absurd axioms of an arbitrary scheme of verbiage which she styles philosophy, and which appears to be a crude mixture of Benthamism, political economy, and sans-cullotte morality, she hurries over the vast regions of the United States in half the time that Volney spent in Damascus and Aleppo, analyzing resolving, defining, dividing, subdividing, and mapping out "the morals" of America, to adopt her own favourite jargon, not as they appear to her or to any other chance speculator, but as they ought to figure according to the principles which she imbibed before her visit, and the crude meditation of which probably amused her outward voyage.[85]

Because women were kept out of the professional sphere via an argument that emphasized their supposed innate inability to reason abstractly, any acknowledgment of Martineau's originality would threaten this supposed biological determinism of women's intellectual potential. Also underlying Disraeli's distrust was an uneasiness over using a natural history-based observation approach on a contemporary British-settled country, whereas such observation would be acceptable in an "exotic" or ancient civilization.

Although Martineau wished to speak with authority on political theory, her attempts were not entirely successful and, since she received little public encouragement, this led to her having second thoughts about her movement into abstraction. Rather than abstract generalizations, what appealed most to her readers were her sketches of contemporary figures of Jacksonian America. Thomas Carlyle seems to have represented the response of her readers when he wrote to her "that he had rather read of Webster's cavernous eyes and arm under his coat-tail, than all the political speculation that a cut and dried system could suggest."[86] Noting this response and torn between a desire to prove herself in an intellectual arena and a strong desire to be marketable, Martineau later expressed regrets that she had chosen an abstract framework for this book rather than focusing more on concrete topics. But it is clear that the original purpose for this framework was to show she could "do" theory, that she was capable of masculine discourse. Ultimately, however, her attempts seemed to have been ignored.

While *Retrospect*, which gave a more personal account of her travel, was the most popular of her American travel books, in it Martineau was still careful to maintain a dignified narrative voice and presentation which supported her argument that women are well-suited as observers because of the insights made possible by their gender. Her narrative voice was structured to communicate a sense of control and authority in her travel. Her narrative portrayal of herself was that of a levelheaded intelligent individual, very sensitive to the feelings of others but accustomed to making her own decisions, quite in contrast to the traditional declarations of inferiority made by many women travel writers at this time. (In this regard, Trollope's self-denigration was a more typical narrative stance.)

In the beginning of *Retrospect* before the trip even gets underway, Martineau's sensitivity and ability to project herself into others' positions is established in order to emphasize the differences and advantages of a woman's empathic awareness in her observations. As Martineau and her friends travel on their way to the dock, they are told that the wind is against them and they cannot sail that day. Martineau's response is that "[t]his was uncomfortable news enough. We had bidden farewell to many friends, half the pain of parting was over, and there was little pleasure in having it all to go through again" (13). She describes the commonly encountered point of awkwardness in social interaction when, after carefully bringing a meeting to a point of closure, the process has to be interrupted, breaking the set pattern of interpersonal expectations which form an understanding of manners. The captain does not help the situation. He

> was fidgeting about, giving his orders in a voice rather less placid than ordinary; a great number of inquiring persons, who had come down to see us off, had to be told that we were not going to-day, and why; and several of the American passengers were on the spot, looking very melancholy. (13–14)

Here Martineau establishes the weakness of the male captain's character. This parallels the situation in the opening of Wollstonecraft's travels when the captain is unable to make a decision and Wollstonecraft takes over. But in Martineau's sketch, the problem with the captain is not related to taking action. Rather, the captain's weakness lies in the area of interpersonal relations; he cannot project a calm presence and gives way to impatience. These character weaknesses provide a contrast to Martineau's own strengths as well as support for her cultural feminist thesis that because women are more empathetic and aware of details of behavior and manners, they are more sensitive and, thus, better observers.

Implicit in Martineau's criticism is the suggestion that she could do a better job. However, unlike Wollstonecraft, Martineau does not take command or directly challenge the male authority figure. Rather, having established the inability of the male captain to improve the comfort of the passengers, she moves the perspective of the narration to a sensitive portrayal of the American passengers:

> They had entered the 8th in their journals as the day of sailing, brought down their portmanteaus, paid their bills at the hotel, and taken leave of Boots and chambermaid. Here they were left with four-and-twenty dreary and expensive hours upon their hands, and who knew how many more than four-and-twenty? (14)

Considered in relation to the journey as a whole, the delay is a minor happening. But when considered in relation to the domestic problems it causes, its ramifications increase: Martineau's host will be distracted from his Sunday sermon writing; the women's "sea-dresses" (designed to be disposable because they will be made irreparable by the effect of salt and mildew in route) are not usable for attending Sunday service in Liverpool; and all the passengers' books and work are stored away on board. In this way and from the beginning, the importance of the often overlooked domestic details and manners are established along with Martineau's ability to observe them.

In these American travel accounts, Martineau writes against the stereotypical presentation of women as timid travelers, resistant to change or hardship.[87] Rather, she emphasizes a fascination with the sights of travel, a capacity for discomfort, and an open mind to new experiences. Wind conditions delay departure one day, and occasional weather problems follow them on the voyage. At times during the trip, the winds left them becalmed, and once they experienced hurricane-force winds. Even in such danger, Martineau is careful to project an enthusiastic upbeat narrative voice. With high winds roaring on the deck, she is so in awe of the sight that she goes back down to the cabins "to implore the other ladies to come and be refreshed" (*Retro.* 1:28). After being ignored, she goes to the captain to persuade him to lash her to a post, a vantage point from where she could safely experience the force of the storm. Here Martineau transforms a dangerous situation, defusing it, so it appears as if no danger was really involved, and in separating herself from the other women, identifies herself as both adventurous and authoritative in her perceptions.

This need to establish herself as different and, therefore, more authoritative and scientific in her narration also extends to a need to distance herself from non-serious travelers. Although Martineau usually projects a highly emphatic sensitivity of others' feelings, she is also capable of satiric commentary, which she uses to distance her travel from "tourist" traveling, particularly at well-known attractions such as Niagara Falls. Similar to the above mentioned shipboard sketch, on these occasions the ability to withstand discomfort is used as the distinguishing mark of the serious traveler. At a hotel near Niagara Falls, she describes one Englishman who "was so anxious about where he should settle, so incessantly pettish, so resolutely miserable, as to bespeak the compassion of all the guests for the ladies of his family, one of whom told me that she had forgotten all about the [Niagara] falls in her domestic anxieties" (*Retrospect* 1:99). Interestingly, this is a reversal of the usual gender roles used in stereotypical comic accounts of tourists. Buzard's study of continental tourism notes that "[i]n the record of cultural self-promotion . . . , women and members of the commercial or lower classes of British society often functioned as the *bêtes noires* of an anti-touristic rhetoric . . ." (217). Usually, the male head of the traveling family must endure the inflexibility of his female family members. Here it is the man, not the woman, who is presented as being the ill-prepared traveler and the female family members who must suffer through the complaints.

In addition to showing her commitment to a higher, more scientific level of understanding by rising above immediate discomfort in her accounts, Martineau also makes use of aesthetic awareness of scenery as a means of establishing her voice as more authoritative than other travelers. While at a mountain lookout over the Hudson River, she observes "the gradual lengthening of the shadows and purpling of the landscape," noting that this sunset "was more beautiful than the sunrise of this morning, and less so than that of the morrow." Yet she does not attempt to give a description because "I would not weary others with what is most sacred to me" (1:62). This privileged sense of sacredness in her response to the natural world is an inheritance from early Wordsworthian romanticism and the Romantic tradition of the Grand Tour, one which Ruskin and other later European travel writers would use to distinguish their own perception as particularly authentic.[88] It is also a carryover from the natural theology tradition in natural history as Martineau looks to the landscape to experience a spiritual relationship.

To illustrate why she feels such descriptions would "weary others," Martineau mentions the response of some fellow travelers, who, having been persuaded to stay a little longer in order to see the sunrise, quizzed her on what she had expected to see. When she explains that "it was the effect of the sun on the landscape that I had been looking for," she is astonished to hear the response, "Upon the landscape! Oh! but we saw that yesterday" (*Retrospect* 1:62–63). By the time of her travel on the Mississippi, such lack of interest is expected. Looking at the other women on board, Martineau remarks,

> Nothing surprised me more than to see that very few of the ladies looked out of the boat unless their attention was particularly called. All the morning the greater number sat in their own cabin, working collars, netting purses, or doing nothing; all the evening they amused themselves in the other cabin dancing or talking. And such scenery as we were passing! I was in perpetual amazement that, with all that has been said of the grandeur of this mighty river, so little testimony has been borne to its beauty. (*Retrospect* 2:11)

On the other hand, Martineau also targets the pretentious hyperbole associated with others' romanticized posturing. A woman questioning her on her response to Niagara Falls, asks, "Did you not . . . long to throw yourself down, and mingle with your mother earth?" To which Martineau dryly answers, "No" (*Society* 3:81). Such contrasts serve to reinforce Martineau's pragmatic common sense persona, part of her authoritative stance.[89]

As Martineau presents a narrative persona balanced between a position of higher aestheticism and practicality, she also attempts to maneuver between a cultural feminist rationale for writing and the necessity to separate herself from traditional feminine discourse. This balancing act was needed to maintain an authoritative position. When we consider that she also had to exhibit care in not undercutting her liberal feminist political agenda nor in upsetting American readers' sensitivities, the enormous difficulties for Martineau and other women who attempted to extend the sphere of women's professions at this time become evident.[90] The stress involved in her task is seen in Martineau's strong need for repose and reflection in the process of sorting through and analyzing her travel observations. A small waterfall near Niagara Falls which catches her eye seems a reflection of herself: "solitary in the midst of the crowd of waters, coming out of its privacy in the wood to take its leap by itself" (*Retrospect* 1:98). The solitary position was necessitated by these conflicting rhetorical demands.

This requirement for contemplation is also linked to her acute capacity for sympathy and identification with others, an awareness that called for more responsibility on the part of the observer. Martineau knew that travel meant she would inadvertently hurt someone's feelings through ignorance of another's culture.

> Worse than our own little troubles, probably, has been the fear and sorrow of hurting others. One of the greatest of a traveller's hardships is the being aware that he must be perpetually treading on somebody's toes. Passing from city to city, from one group of families to another, where the divisions of party and of sect, the contrariety of interests, and the world of domestic circumstance are all unknown to him, he can hardly open his lips without wounding somebody; and it makes him all the more anxious if, through the generosity of his entertainers, he never hears of it. No care of his own can save him from his function of torturer. He cannot speak of religion, morals, and politics; he cannot speak of insanity, intemperance, or gaming, or even of health, riches, fair fame, and good children, without danger of rousing feelings of personal remorse or family shame in some, or the bitter sense of bereavement in others. (*Retrospect* 2:235)

Despite the masculine pronoun, such sensitivity to the feelings of others is a behavioral trait valued particularly in women. However, this unavoidable "fear and sorrow of hurting others" made it difficult to evaluate a society and Martineau felt she could make an honest sociological report and show her masculine objective rigor of mind only when she had placed some physical distance between herself and the subject of her study. Indeed, she chose the word "Retrospect" for her title because of her belief that it "is only after sitting down alone at home that the traveller can separate the universal truth from the partial error with which he has sympathized, and can make some approximation towards assurance as to what he has learned and what he believes" (*Retrospect* 2:234). The situation bears some resemblance to the social anxiety Virginia Woolf personified as the "Angel in the House," the mental hurdle each woman writer/intellectual must overcome in order to publicly express herself. But whereas a woman writing at home could feel the angel of woman's socialization breathing down her neck, the woman traveler at least had the advantage of a buffer of physical distance at her disposal to separate her from the subject of her writing. Practicing sociology or anthropology at home is far more difficult than practicing it abroad.

MIDEAST TRAVEL

In 1846, after a long-term illness, Martineau felt she had regained enough of her health to take what would be a last long trip, this time to the Mideast, a journey which both in purpose and circumstance marked a very different approach to travel from her earlier excursions and reflected changes in Victorian culture as well. This trip was additionally different from her American travel in terms of her social relationships with both her fellow travelers, who paid the traveling expenses, and the inhabitants of the land which formed the subject of her study. While Martineau always had to struggle with gender-related writing anxiety, here the situation was worse. Traveling as part of a male-headed group of other Europeans in countries where she did not know the languages, Martineau was also more isolated from the native culture by her fellow tourists and the cocooning apparatus of tourism.[91] While still prepared to respond emphatically to those she met, her isolation from the native culture, her self-conscious awareness of fellow travelers, and her own lack of personal control and independence during travel caused *Eastern Life: Present and Past* (1848) to reflect more typical Eurocentric colonial attitudes, as it also tested her observation methodology.

In addition to differences in travel procedure, Martineau's purpose in writing about the Mideast was very different from that of her American writings. Here she wished to show Christianity to be part of a continually evolving religious movement that started in Africa rather than a unique development in religious thought. Influenced by developments in higher criticism and pre-Darwinian evolutionary theory, Martineau attempted to show that religious thought could be viewed as an adaptation to a particular environment and that Christianity was merely a variation of a philosophy that was rooted in the sands of Egypt.[92] In 1846, the year Martineau left for Egypt, George Eliot translated David Friedrich Strauss's *The Life of Jesus* (1835–36), that explained the development of the Gospel as a mythological process. Martineau was familiar both with Strauss's book and with pre-*Origin* evolutionary theory.[93] Working from higher criticism assumptions and guided by an evolutionary paradigm, Martineau interwove the account of her travel with Biblical history; adapting geologic observation methods and trying to read ancient monuments like layers of strata, she offered speculation on how the historical evolution of religious tradition could occur.[94]

In her autobiography, she explained that her search for "the true character of the faiths which ruled the world" was based on "a view of their genealogy" obtained from direct observation in the field. Her observations led her to the conclusion that

> a passage through these latter faiths is natural to men, and was as necessary in those former periods of human progress, as fetishism is to the infant nations and individuals. . . . More advanced nations and individuals suppose a whole pantheon of gods first, and then a trinity,—and then a single deity . . . in proportion as this stage is passed through, the perceptions of deity and divine government become abstract and indefinite.[95]

The emphasis of movement from lower to higher stages of development is all too apparent here as the early evolutionary ideas of the development of a species provide a metaphor for a continuous development of religion. Martineau regarded as original this application of what would have been at this time a legitimate scientific hypothesis for the historical development of religion. Yet, Martineau's efforts to see Mideast culture as a sort of vestige of cultural development based on Chambers's work conflicted with her own desire to focus on continual progress in modern society. This conflict is related to the emphasis of Victorian Orientalist study on pre-Islamic history and antiquarian methodology, rather than modern Islamic culture. While Martineau was able to resist the traditional pilgrimage discourse, she could not sufficiently distance herself from the enormously authoritative Orientalist scholarship to resolve the incompatibility between seeing the evolution of the history of ideas as a methodical process through a series of stages and seeing modern history as being shaped by adaptation to economic pressure.[96] In a rather muddled form, this ideological conflict suggests later conflicts in Darwinian theory as the Victorian belief in a progressive development in evolution was found to be incompatible with adaptation through natural selection.

Related to this belief in progress and to her sense of gradual development, Martineau always traveled with a particularly Victorian sense of historical time, an awareness that the present she was recording would one day become history, that her mode of transportation would be superseded by other means. She had seen the sail, used in her voyage to America, replaced by steam and had seen the railroad bring new groups of tourists to her home in the Lake District (for which she wrote a travel guide). This sense of her own place in history is reflected in the preface to her second edition of *Eastern Life*, written thirty years later. In it, she explains that she decided not to make changes to her travel book to reflect changes in the Mideast, feeling that the account is in itself a historical document, reflecting the era of the travel, not just a guide to a locale (iv–v).

At the same time, her travel to the Middle East reflects a more typical Eurocentric and imperialistic view of other lands as being historically static, offering a view of the past as if it were trapped in amber, an interpretation which circumscribed any native visions or perception. In a 31 January 1847 letter to Richard Milnes, a previous traveler to Egypt, she wrote, "I rode, day by day, through the glorious sterile valley which leads one among the population of the dead, feeling the same ideas and emotions *must* have been in the minds of those before whose eyes, as before mine, lay the same contrasting scenery of life and death."[97] For Martineau, traveling through the Mideast was imaginatively similar to traveling through geologic strata while examining the embedded fossils of past cultures.

This limitation was noted even within the nineteenth century; one contemporary, Lucie Duff Gordon, remarked of Martineau's description of modern Egyptians, "The people are not real people, only part of the scenery to her, as to most Europeans. She evidently had the feeling of most people here [Egypt] that the difference of manners are a sort of impassable gulf, the truth being that their feelings and passions are just like our own." [98] While still displaying an unusual sensitivity to other cultures, Martineau's *Eastern Life* was not written with that same awareness of a dual audience that made her American travel accounts so progressive. It is obvious that she did not consider the people of the Middle East to be part of her reading public, and this, along with her isolation from daily Egyptian life, affected her observations.

Rather than trying to perceive the Egyptian culture from as many viewpoints as possible, as she did in her American travel, the itinerary of this trip was designed to follow the historical development of Christianity, since Martineau wished to see the landscape in the same order as it is presented in the Old and New Testaments to emphasize the connection between Egyptian mythologies and Christian beliefs. Thus from Cairo, Martineau and her companions retraced the Hebrews' path across the Sinai, Jerusalem, Damascus, and finally Lebanon.

During the initial part of her travel, Martineau is preoccupied with two closely related issues: the need to define the Other and to identify the moment when awareness of difference, the exotic, has been obtained. In *Retrospect,* the travel started with the difficulty of leaving Britain; here Martineau's confidence is better established; she is surer of herself and has organized this travel narrative for a more narrowly defined purpose. She begins not with the ill ease of departure, but with her arrival to the destination. There are questions here, however, as she ponders what is Africa? when does one really arrive there? when is Africa recognized? and how is Africa to be perceived? These are questions that were not raised in the American travels, where the quest for the Other, the exotic, was not a component of the American traveler's perception.

The complexity of the possible multiplicity of answers to these questions of definition and classification is suggested in Martineau's different interpretations of the first sight of Africa. The first view of the continent is dark and distant with an ominous red-tinted sea between her and her destination, suggestive of a view through the battles of history. The second early morning sight of white level sand and a single Arab tower appearing and reappearing with a "milky blue" sea, is lighter, idyllic, representing another side of the imaginative construction of the foreign. This is followed by a third sighting of recognizable ruins and the passengers' consensus that they have arrived. This moment of recognition serves as a reminder that when Martineau went to America, she was describing a land that was still being defined for the European gaze; Trollope and de Tocqueville were contemporaries of Martineau. By the time of her Mideast voyage, however, there was prior knowledge and preconceptions of what Egypt looked like; the land had become, in Buzard's words, "scripted."[99] Martineau, therefore, is speaking to an audience whose expectations have become set.[100] She does not bother to describe Cleopatra's Needle or Pompey's Pillar because "everyone has seen them in engravings" (7). This sense of "belatedness" in travel, of following what has already been recorded, produces a self-conscious need to transcend previous work, "to stake out new territories with one's own text."[101]

These questions also indicate a change in European perception of the Other contained in the Orient. Martineau's text shows those "moments of discursive uncertainty" identified by Edward Said and Ali Behdad as indicating a questioning of previous authorities, uncertainty about European authority and the possibility of complete mastery of oriental knowledge and representation of that knowledge. This self-doubt on a basic epistemological level reveals itself in *Eastern Life* as a compulsion to search for authenticity.[102]

One of the most dramatic ways that *Eastern Life* betrays its hesitation is through the trope of the landing, which with its delays is suggestive of a more general uncertainty about how the Orient can be recognized. Unlike Wollstonecraft's account of her landing, there is no physical barrier to push through or authorities to argue with. Like Martineau's earlier *Retrospect,* however, the virtue of patience is exhibited as the landing is delayed. Everyone stands around waiting for the pilot and it is nightfall before they anchor. While Martineau points out ineptitude, as Wollstonecraft did, she states it objectively, draws no conclusions, and takes no active involvement in directing events, a reflection of her new position as a woman who is part of a travel group.

Because of the evening light, the scenery looks dramatic: the ships are imposing, the pilot turbaned and robed. At this point, authenticity has been momentarily achieved, difference has been found, the scene is "a perfect feast to western eyes" (4). But Martineau is not satisfied with this image and continually looks for indications of something undefinably different, some source of Orientalism.

The next morning in her rooms, the questions raised at the landing are reconsidered as Martineau looks again for a reaffirmation of arrival. Her search for Africa is disappointing as she looks out her window to see an ordinary square with large but shabby houses, "nothing peculiarly African" (5). The view is saved by the bright sunlight backlighting the minaret, "as little like England in November as could well be." Then a string of camels pass through the square, welcome to her for their exotic touch and the indication that, yes, she is faced with the Oriental. But then the camels become disappointing. They reveal a malignant expression which is disrupting to fantasies formed from pictures and Martineau takes an immediate dislike to them, finding the animals almost as ugly as ostriches, and, in a description more typical of Trollope, sees them fitting creatures for a portrayal of hell—"a *damned* animal" (5).

Martineau's desire to extend human understanding also conflicts with her sense of European superiority. She yields to common complaints of the "multitude of screaming Arabs," as loud as "a frog concert in a Carolina swamp" (4) (reminding the reader of her own previous travel experience and expertise). Yet, while she sees no problems with comparison of people with animals, she is bitter about the racist responses of some other travelers, sarcastically termed "amiable gentlemen," who, with stout sticks, clear a way through the crowd by force with the "philosophical conviction that this is the only way to deal with Arabs" (4).

Despite her surface Eurocentric assurance of her own capacity for understanding which is apparent, there is an underlying concern that perhaps she will not and cannot understand this culture. When sailing on the Nile in the beginning of her travel, she listens to the crew make "wild music" and give forth "mournful song" (18). Noticing that the music is in a minor key and searching for some evidence of an instinctive, bird-like sense of music, she mentions that she has "been struck by its prevalence among all the savage, or half-civilized, or uneducated people whom I have known," even though in the same sentence she admits a lack of knowledge about whether all "primitive" music is indeed in a minor key. Additionally, the string of terms used to identify those who sing in a minor key—"savage," "half-civilized," "uneducated"—suggest a redefining, a reconsideration even as she writes of just what she is trying to identify.[103] From this generalization, she moves to assert that

> the music of Nature is all in the minor key—the melodies of the winds, the sea, the waterfall, birds, and the echoes of bleating flocks among the hills: and human song seems to follow this lead, till men are introduced at once into the new world of harmony and the knowledge of music in the major key. (18)

Having equated the crews' music with nature and concluded that knowledge of musical harmony and major keys are ways of distinguishing the civilized from the primitive, Martineau returns her observation to the boat's crew and seems to entertain a notion of bringing improvement to them by singing to them, as if the sound of a major chord would be instantly recognized as superior and produce a catalytic effect leading to an improved sense of harmony. This idea, however, she gives up because she realizes that the crew is singing too loud to even hear her. The situation frustrates her urge to push self-improvement: "They kept time so admirably, and were so prone to singing, that we longed to teach them to substitute harmony for noise, and meaning for mere sensation," for "the nonsense that they sing is provoking" (18).

Because Martineau does not understand their language, she asks Alee, their interpreter (dragoman), to translate the repetitive words of the song, only to be told that they mean "put the saddle on the horse" or "pull harder." Initially, she accepts this report, but then follows it with a comment that indicates second thoughts. She advises her readers that, "if the dragoman appears unwilling to translate any song, it is well not to press for it; for it is understood that many of their words are such as it would give European ears no pleasure to hear" (18). Notably, this caution is not addressed to women only, but to all Europeans. Her advice suggests a realization that she was not being told the full meaning of the songs and that she would not learn them. The barriers to her understanding, the restrictions of the tourist world, would not yield here as they did in America.

Although not explicitly stated, Martineau seems to understand that she cannot be intimate with the people here or be invited into households as a guest in the same way she was in America. Later on, she remarks that the village women often ran from her company and that she resorted to checking out domestic arrangements in the villages by walking into the empty houses while their owners were out working (62), giving the impression that there was little difference between walking in an ancient Egyptian tomb and a modern village hut, and, at other times, that she was some sort of poor-law inspector.

Aware of the effect her fellow European travelers had on her perceptions, Martineau tried to counteract this influence by riding away from the group or taking long walks alone, increasing the sense of isolation her deafness generally imposed. In this way, she felt she could best recapture the past she believed was contained within the landscape and could see it divested of traditional pilgrimage associations. Aware of and wrestling with her European biases, she focused on the domestic details of an encampment in an attempt to gain an insight into native perception (64). In addition to the religious intolerance, she observed the aspect of Mideastern life, the Egyptian harem, which most vividly illustrates her struggles with European bias. In the harem, Martineau found the women "the most injured human beings I have ever seen—the most studiously depressed and corrupted women whose condition I have witnessed" (245).

In describing the harems she visits, Martineau is struggling not only with her own biases but also with her anticipated readers' expectations. She knows her readers expect such a description since only women could enter harems and the image of the harem, invested by Europeans with an imagined illicit sexuality, had become the predominating image of Orientalism.[104] While women visitors were expected to be shocked, they were also expected to report their reactions, although it meant dwelling on subjects Victorian women were not supposed to have knowledge of, and would, in effect, require that the woman writer expose herself in the process. The restrictions and expectations were thus contradictory, posing a difficult writing situation.

Martineau handles this problem by acknowledging her own distress that she cannot shed a favorable light on this tradition. She describes her struggles with her preconceptions but reluctantly concludes, echoing the imagery used in her first description of the camels, "if we are to look for a hell upon earth, it is where polygamy exists: and that, as polygamy runs riot in Egypt, Egypt is the lowest depth of this hell" (236). Despite the absolute judgments made on the institution of the harem, however, she is still haunted by her need to understand, yet frustrated by the barriers to her understanding. While her earlier travels projected confidence in the validity of her observations, here we see struggles with doubts underlying her descriptions. Martineau considers the possibilities of misreadings as she wonders if she is expressing cultural prejudice or if the harem could fit into a paradigm of gradually evolving progress. Finally, she has to conclude that the limitations placed on women and the disruption of family life that slavery causes is worse than what she had seen at home, that "a visit to the worst room in the rookery in St. Giles's would have affected me less painfully" (239). But all Martineau can do is resolve to speak to a European doctor about introducing jumping ropes into the harem so the women could get more exercise. She concludes that this institution is a negative aspect of the culture, but one no worse than those found in other cultures: it is as well entrenched "as our representative monarchy, or German heraldry, or Hindoo caste" (240).

At the same time, in its focus on the idleness of its residents rather than on sexuality, Martineau's response to the harem differs from that of her contemporaries.[105] By focusing on the effect of idleness on the women in the harem, Martineau made use of a liberal feminist argument for the importance of environment in shaping women's character and, by doing so, was able to desexualize what was for Europeans a highly erotic subject. This rhetorical solution would provide a model for later women travelers.

Finally, in *Eastern Life*, an earlier determination to be scientific survives in Martieanu's efforts to devise a unifying theory describing religious development and her desire to make her observations objective. Once again, Martineau attempted to break away from that "auxiliary intellectual" position by which Deirdre David identifies her (93) and to test the limits of feminine discourse. Although dependent on J. G. Wilkinson's *Manners and Customs of the Ancient Egyptians* for the argument that Christian tenets originated in ancient Egyptian religious beliefs,[106] *Eastern Life* is quite clear on her view of religion as an evolutionary process, a stance which reflects her own personal religious movement toward agnosticism as a series of gradual modifications of her original liberal Unitarian position. While Pichanick's assessment of the book is that it shows that Martineau's "scholarship was inadequate and her method of hasty composition too incautious to comprehensively trace the evolution of Christianity. . . ,"[107] the book is particularly her own in the sense that it is not a retelling or a compilation of observations, data for a masculine theorist. Rather, it is an argument justifying through historical evidence the development of her own philosophical stance. Additionally, the work is of interest because, according to Hoecker-Drysdale, religion, a feminine subject, is presented here by a woman as an area of investigation and intellectual understanding, a rhetoric associated with masculine discourse, not in the more traditional form of personal revelation.[108] As Martineau's American travels made domestic and family relationships a key to understanding the operations of a society, her Eastern travels examine the feminine sphere of religion in a rational, scientific manner.

Eastern Life essentially ended Martineau's attempt to use travel writing as a means to secure an authoritative voice within a discourse of science. She briefly attempted to move back into an auxiliary position with her translation and condensation of Auguste Comte's six-volume *Positive Philosophy* (1830–42) in 1853. While, in this work, Martineau is not developing her own ideas, in a sense, her translation of Comte can still be seen as part of her involvement with the debate over the purpose of science. Comte succeeded in establishing a school of study by applying scientific method and observation to the social sciences, what Martineau was trying to do in her American travels. By making Comte, the founder of positivism, more available to an English reading audience, her translation and abridgment serves as a continuation of Chambers's message that natural science could serve as a starting point for a broader social philosophy.[109] And Martineau's work still serves as the standard English edition of Comte's work. But finally, Martineau directed her energies to the political journalism where she had gained the most recognition.

While Martineau's travels provided her with a means of retreating from a social atmosphere which limited and discouraged women's intellectual achievement beyond particularly prescribed feminine areas of influence, the authority which could be transferred to her back in Britain was limited. At first, she found that a scientific discourse would allow her to speak more authoritatively to a general audience. But with the increasing dominance of a professional elite, she could not gain the support needed to found a new area of scientific research. Similarly, her Mideast travels were even less successful in enabling her to participate in contemporary philosophical discussion. Her Mideast journey did, however, allow her to realize the limitations of her ability to understand when faced with the complexities of a strikingly different culture, underscoring her early sense that the presence of travelers changes the very nature of the native culture, a realization which informed her later editorials against British colonial practices.

4

Isabella Bird Bishop: An RGS Fellow

AMONG THE GROWING NUMBER OF WOMEN TRAVEL WRITERS IN THE
later half of the nineteenth century, Isabella Lucy Bird Bishop stood
out in the scientific community. She was the one woman traveler
whose geographical credentials were well secured and not questioned by Victorian readers.[1] Even Lord Curzon, a vocal opponent
of women's membership in scientific societies, could not fault Bird
Bishop's abilities. Unable to ignore his fellow traveler when making his argument against women's memberships in the increasingly
government-involved geographic societies, Curzon emphasized instead the rarity of women such as Bird Bishop, an argumentative
position that avoided making a personal attack on her qualifications.
Bird Bishop achieved this unusual position, one which allowed her
to lead the initial movement of women into the Royal Geographical
Society (although she avoided taking a public stand), through a
combination of impeccable respectability, both domestic and religious, and the sheer number of miles and corresponding pages she
racked up in her travels.

In all, she wrote eleven travel books, most of them four to five
hundred pages long. These books were among the most popular
travel books of the late nineteenth century, especially the personally
revealing *A Lady's Life in the Rocky Mountains,* which went
through seven editions in its first three years of publication.[2] Her
readers followed her journeys through mountainous, difficult
stretches as she proved that a woman could handle long journeys in
rugged terrain, thus opening fieldwork in distant realms to later
women naturalists. Although interested in the marketability of her
books, Bird Bishop was also conscious of the increasing involvement
of colonial government interests with activities of the ethnographic,
anthropologic, and geographic societies, and she shaped her later
narratives in response to both governmental and scientific interests.
In the process she also changed the theme of her travel writing from
personal liberation in her early writings to the success of British

imperial expansion as she moved from pedagogical writings typical of women naturalists to writings aimed at the new government-funded scientific professional societies.

Bird Bishop wrote on Hawaii and the Rocky Mountains, but eventually decided to become an authority on Asian physical and cultural geography. She traveled in Iran, Turkey, Japan, Korea, Siberia, and central China. In her later books, she gave an overview of the physical geography, summarizing previous descriptions of the region and official government reports and she evaluated how the lay of the land, its rivers, mountains, and natural resources relate to the development of the inhabited areas and the culture of its people. Her works presented her readers with a useful summary of what was known about an area, along with her on-the-spot evaluation of the relations between Europeans and the native population. Generally, she traveled in areas where Europeans had seldom ventured, so her writings provided first glimpses of unfamiliar cultures, bridging the gap between foreign ministers' reports and popular studies of foreign lands. Her descriptions of the landscape were sure and detailed as to the particulars of geology and botany, but she was also able to take a broader map-based view, showing how mountain ranges and riverways shaped the countryside. The following description from *Journeys in Persia and Kurdistan* is fairly typical:

> From Dehnau the path I took leads over gravelly treeless hills, through many treeless gulches, to the top of a great gourge, through which the Sabzu passes as an impetuous torrent. The descent to a very primitive bridge is long and difficult, a succession of rocky zigzags. Picturesqueness is not a usual attribute of mud villages, but the view from every point of Chiraz, the village on the lofty cliffs on the other side of the stream, is strikingly so. They are irregularly covered with houses, partly built on them and partly excavated out of them, and behind is a cool mass of greenery, apricot orchards, magnificent walnut and mulberry trees, great standard hawthorns loaded with masses of blossom, wheat coming into ear, and clumps and banks of canary-yellow roses measuring three inches across their petals. Groups of women, in whose attire Turkey red predominated, were on the house roofs. Wild flowers abounded, and the sides of the craggy path by which I descended were crowded with leguminous and umbelliferous plants, with the white and pink dianthus, and with the thorny *tussocks* of the gum tragacanth, largely used for kindling, now in full floom. (1:358)

At this time, geographic exploration was an activity which gripped the Victorian imagination as it combined military prowess and hunting with the pursuit of scientific knowledge. The scientific aspects of the exploration were not well defined as separate from the imperial colonizing activities. Rather, the explorer might emphasize any of a range of scientific interests—biology, geology, geography, anthropology, ethnology—while exploring and the field was open to anyone who could claim to have described accurately a new region, especially if that region was of interest to the British government and/or involved physical endeavors. The role of the explorer was, however, a particularly masculine one. And Bird Bishop (and Kingsley) had to cope with the gender specific nature of this activity.

Here with Bird Bishop, the general sense of what a naturalist did has changed. Whereas Wollstonecraft and Martineau traveled essentially on their own with letters of introduction but no driving need for institutional recognition in their attempts to use their travel narratives to establish scientific authority, by the 1870s these scientific organizations which Martineau viewed with some distrust now became better established as they had access to government funding, especially if they promised information useful to the expanding British empire. Connection with such organizations, and a reputation of being a good speaker who could draw in crowds, became an important part of establishing a name in serious scientific work. In Bird Bishop's writing career, we see a movement from journalism intended for women's periodicals, which still featured natural history essays, to a more pedagogical emphasis that was still open to women writers, to finally, a narrative that elicited at least token acceptance from the major British geographical society, The Royal Geographical Society (RGS). Bird Bishop accomplished something fairly remarkable in obtaining a place in this increasingly masculine world, one which was attempting to move out both women and those who still practiced natural theology. In doing so, Bird Bishop, as did Martineau, felt a need to maintain conventional behavior, although she quickly found that the restrictions involved were at odds with the fieldwork she was attempting to do.

As Bird Bishop became a more experienced traveler, she realized the professional advantages of traveling far from European settlements and routes as her travels could gain more respect as she moved into areas where Europeans had not established a firm foothold. Her travels differ from the journeys of Wollstonecraft and Martineau in that she journeyed farther from the sight of most Europeans. By traveling on the edges of the British empire, she was able both to gain respect for her writings as politically valuable sources of information and to engage in behavior which otherwise would have ruined any social reputation she had.

In presenting these experiences to her readers, however, Bird Bishop needed to take into account the limitations of feminine discourse. In many ways, these restrictions were similar to the ones Wollstonecraft and Martineau had to circumvent. However, Bird Bishop's accounts also reflect an increasing concern with the justification of her travel, dress, and the maintenance of respectability while traveling alone with groups of men, indicating a more narrowly restrictive code of behavior for women in the latter half of the nineteenth century.

These new areas of concern were shared by many British women travel writers of the 1880s and 1890s, resulting in markedly contradictory modes of narrative presentation as the women attempted to be both adventurous and domestic. As Frawley has noted, although women writers during this period may have written about very different regions, there are still similarities in the sort of narrative identities they constructed. In addition to Bird Bishop, other writers such as Florence Dixie, Amelia Edwards, Constance Gordon-Cummings, and Mary Kingsley would travel in remote areas and then exaggerate or otherwise capitalize on their distance from England. In this way they were able both to justify their unconventional behavior, and at the same time, present a conventional image so as to justify the act of traveling.[3]

While recognized as important, Bird Bishop's work has received little critical attention. Although many of her travels are available as modern reprints, the sheer volume of her writings presents a daunting task for the researcher. In this study, I will focus on the rhetorical strategies Bird Bishop used to establish a position of scientific authority in her texts and, once this authority was achieved, how her texts changed in response to new audiences as she moved from popular to more technical accounts. Bird Bishop is unusual in that she did manage to make the movement from the traditional education-oriented natural history narrative common to women writers to the new professional, and increasingly more masculine, professional audience. This change was, however, made gradually over several publications. Rather than try to present an overview of all her travel books, I will treat in detail particular texts which reflect important changes in Bird Bishop's writing as she responded to her acceptance by geographical societies. Along with the frequently cited and popular early work, *A Lady's Life in the Rocky Mountains*, I will also examine the generally disregarded *Journeys in Persia and Kurdistan*, a less engaging work, but one written for a professional geographic audience.

Bird Bishop was very successful in gaining recognition among professional geographic societies for her travel and this recognition allowed her to redefine for the Victorian public women's capacity for physical stamina and independence. As with the other writers in this study, her success was based on a combination of unquestionable personal respectability at home, and careful control of the persona she revealed in her narratives. In her travel narratives, she presented herself and her observations as authoritative, based on immediate experiences available to only a few. Additionally, when planning her travels, she made a conscious effort to make herself useful to those in power, particularly in regard to colonial affairs, and learned that, by avoiding the company of other Europeans, she could escape many conventional social restrictions. However, it was not easy to maintain a narrative position that was both conventional and authoritative, and the anxiety resulting from trying to present herself in appropriate ways to British readers is apparent in her early writing.

As with the others in this study, Bird Bishop was a working author, dependent on her writing for her living. At the beginning of her career she anonymously published *The Englishwoman in America* (1856) and *Aspects of Religion in the United States* (1859), and then worked as a journalist after her father's death. When she started traveling she was a "redundant" woman, the daughter of a struggling minister, in poor health and a spinster at the age of forty. Generally, she spent her first forty years conforming to those duties expected of women of her age and position, performing charitable activities and suffering increasingly more debilitating ill health. Travel presented opportunities that were unobtainable at home, leading to a dramatic rebirth both physically and mentally. This rebirth as it was evidenced in her vigorous travel narratives suggested to the Victorian public that limited social roles for women caused individual ill-health and, in general, represented the loss of potentially useful individuals to society.[4]

Her writings showed a distinct interest in and orientation toward science. Like many young Victorian women, she was trained as a botanist and eventually studied early microscopic botany with her husband. Bird Bishop received critical attention for the precise identification of native flora in her early writing. Later, when traveling with Major Herbert Sawyer in Persia, she learned survey methodology and the expectations for observation in geographic work. As a result, in her later travel accounts, she expanded the range of her scientific observations to meet geographic requirements by including descriptions of geologic formations, natural resources and local commerce.

In contrast with the other writers in this study, Bird Bishop seems to have occupied a more secure socio-economic position, or at least anxiety about her financial position has not been highlighted by her biographers. As a young woman, her class identification appears to have been solidly middle-class. I say "appears" because, while her grandparents were well-to-do, Bird Bishop's early journalism, the limited travel equipment, lack of a personal maid, and use of rental lodging in Britain, all point to a decrease in her standard of living (which was possibly disguised) during the years between the death of her father in 1858 and her marriage to John Bishop in 1882. The social awkwardness apparent when Bird Bishop described meeting the aristocratic traveler Marianne North in 1880 and her emphasis on being a "lady" when titling her second travel account, *A Lady's Life in the Rocky Mountains*, provide some additional clues about her insecurity over her class position.

While Bird Bishop often found herself by necessity part of a traveling group, like Kingsley, she had a preference for solitary travel with native attendants who had not accepted European cultural conventions and who would perceive all foreigners as equally strange, making little distinction between the behavior of foreign men and women. Travel with other Europeans produced the same sort of anxiety and need for isolation we have seen in Martineau's 1846 Egyptian travel. For example, in her Persian travel account, Bird Bishop did travel with Major Sawyer. Her correspondence reveals that he was not an amiable companion and she was often at odds with him, especially in regard to his treatment of the native workers they hired. In order to continue traveling with him, she requested that they keep separate camps and had him agree to allow her to "keep my rough ways in dress, etc.," that is, to maintain a more tolerant attitude toward her unconventionality during the trip.[5] These details, however, were not included in the travel account.

By keeping other European members of her traveling party out of her text as much as possible, Bird Bishop could emphasize her voice as the controlling one of the narrative. This authoritative and solitary voice continues in all her books and is one consistent trait she shares with the other writers in this study. While not unusual in men's travel accounts, this narrative stance is quite different from that of other women travel writers who more often took the position of the trip's scribe, rather than its director.[6] The solitary stance is indicative of Bird Bishop's efforts to achieve a professional scientific reputation in her own name. In Bird Bishop's Persian travels, for instance, instead of acknowledging Sawyer's views, Bird Bishop presents only her own impressions and, although scrupulous about referencing earlier geographic studies, she implicitly refuses to identify herself as an auxiliary member of a group. Even non-Europeans in the party are generally ignored during travel unless they become part of her immediate experience.

With Bird Bishop, we return to the issue of the epistolary form discussed in relation to Wollstonecraft. Bird Bishop's initial writings were in the form of letters, based on her journals, notes, and actual correspondence sent to her younger sister Henrietta. The first two books bearing her name, *Six Months in the Sandwich Islands* (1875) and *A Lady's Life in the Rocky Mountains* (1879), were dedicated to her sister; and she wrote her subsequent books with her sister in mind as her immediate audience, a writing strategy which

Title page of *A Lady's Life in the Rocky Mountains* **by Isabella Bird Bishop (London, 1879).**

helped many women writers in the eighteenth and nineteenth century overcome anxiety over the public disclosure of authorship. After the death of her sister in June 1881, Bird Bishop struggled over how to restructure her travel writing now that her immediate audience was gone. But she continued to use the letter format as the one she was most comfortable with, seeing it, as did Wollstonecraft, as the one most likely to encourage a sympathetic identification of the reader with the traveler, "enabling him to share, not only first impressions in their original vividness, and the interests, but the hardships, difficulties, and tedium which are their frequent accompaniments!" (*Journeys* 1:ix). With *Journeys in Persia and Kurdistan* (1891), she attempted to replace her sister with the general reading public, dedicating the book to "The Untravelled Many."

Although the specific economic pressures she worked under have not been identified, her earlier prose was market-shaped for women's magazines. As with many women Victorian and Edwardian natural history writers, her early writings were written journalistically with the goal of popular education. She directed her writing to her very proper and religious sister, who represented the conventional, pious readers she wished to reach. However, by her last two books, the letter format was dropped completely and her writing shifted toward a more scientific discourse as her purpose for writing and her audience changed, and as she became more successful in her inroads into the masculine realm of professional science.

During the second phase of her travel, which began in 1889 with her arrival in Karachi, Pakistan, Bird Bishop reoriented her writing toward the expectations of a scientific readership. At this time, two life-changing events occurred. Besides the loss of her sister, the archetypal reader of her travel, she became a widow in 1886 after five years of marriage. Additionally, she was older and past the childbearing age when Victorian society would have been most concerned with her behavior. As a matron and a widow, she was less bound by social restrictions than she had been as a spinster traveler in her forties. Widowship brought her automatic respect along with full control of her income, both inherited and earned.

With this increased freedom, Bird Bishop looked now toward establishing herself within scientific and political archival projects and shaped her writing to answer the British empire's call for information. This is not to say that she abandoned her earlier audience. But they no longer set the standards for her writing and she was less self-conscious about their anticipated response. Now, she was informing her readership directly with new material from unexplored territory, rather than simply presenting known scripted colonial areas through a woman's view and merely repackaging previously published information in a more entertaining form. Her voice is sure as she corrects overly simplistic assumptions about a place, as in this paragraph describing the outskirts of Baghdad:

> The "Desert" sweeps up to the walls of Baghdad, but it is a misnomer to call the vast level of rich, stoneless alluvial soil a desert. It is a dead flat of uninhabited earth; orange colocynth balls, a little wormwood, and some alkaline plants which camels eat, being its chief products. After the inundations reedy grass grows in the hollows. It is a waste rather than a desert, and was once a populous plain, and the rich soil only needs irrigation to make it "blossom as the rose." Traces of the splendid irrigation system under which it was once a garden abound along the route. (*Journeys* 1:48)

Bird Bishop's description of the landscape is informed, not only in what is present, but what has been there in the past (and perhaps will be in a colonized future).

Although much could still not be mentioned by a woman narrator, Bird Bishop could relieve her own travel-related tension by voicing irritation and did not have to apologize for her dress or horseback riding as she did in her early travels. (It may also be possible that being postmenopausal made traveling in the outlands easier.)

In particular, her journey first to Tibet, then Persia marked a movement into a new type of travel writing for Bird Bishop. In this journey, she first ventured into the outskirts of what was for the British the most mysterious area of the world, and then, in Persia, was introduced to new expectations for her writing as she traveled with Major Sawyer, a military surveyor and spy. From these experiences, she learned that her travel could be of service to both science and government.

GAINING ACCEPTANCE FROM THE RGS

Having established a reputation for popular travel accounts with her early writings, Bird Bishop eventually turned her attention to the higher status and prestige associated with acceptance from professional geographic societies. Such acceptance would indicate that she was a scientific explorer, not just a traveler. In the late-nineteenth century geographic societies had gained much power and attention as the British Empire extended its range. Of course, travelers' accounts have always been a source of information about

foreign lands that help inform traders and settlers. After 1870, however, the British government developed a more systematic process
of gathering and collecting geographic information both for trade
and for military tactical purposes. Thomas Richards's *The Imperial
Archive* examines the implications of this interest in the establishment of a centralized surveillance agency "in which the production
of knowledge could act as the vanguard of the state" in areas not
fully under British control.[7] While the British Museum organized
the collection of information, scientific societies such as the Royal
Society, The Royal Asiatic Society, and the RGS developed the
geographical, demographical, and ethnographical practices which
would alert military and colonial government agencies of possible
invasion or unrest.[8] This was especially true for the RGS, which at
its founding in the 1830s explicitly stated that geography's "advantages are of the first importance to mankind in general, and para-
mount to the welfare of a maritime nation like Great Britain, with
its numerous and extensive foreign possessions."[9]

Eventually Bird Bishop chose her destinations not only for isolation but also with an eye to what sort of information would be valued by an audience concerned with geographic and foreign policy
issues. After her third book on Japan, which focused on areas that
had earlier been off-limits to Western travelers (she needed an inter-
nal passport to travel), her observations attracted government attention and she obtained government help in her travels to sensitive
areas where the need for covertly gathered data was important. This
movement into areas in which the British government was particularly interested helped Bird Bishop secure an authoritative reputation far greater than was generally available to women travel
writers. In particular, her two travels in the region of Tibet, a sealed
off and unmapped area, advertised by her publishers as "less explored than most parts of Central Africa," clearly marked her travels as serious, professional work. The Chinese government refused
foreigners access to interior Tibet for most of the nineteenth century, and as a result, the city of Lhasa acquired a mystical reputation, such as today's Nepal, as a place of hidden knowledge.[10] Bird
Bishop did not attempt to enter Lhasa, but at this time the area in
which she was traveling was viewed as frontier by the British.[11] Her
descriptions of Tibet lacked any sense of spiritual mystery common
in literary accounts of the time. Rather, although she liked the people, her account conformed to more "scientific" discourse as she
took the stance that the lamas were ignorant parasites who preyed
on Tibetan superstitions.

By the time of her journey to Persia, she was able to count among

her fellow passengers Major Sawyer, a military surveyor, and the
then M.P., George Curzon (later Viceroy of India), who was on a
fact-finding mission for his book, *Persia and the Persian Question*.
Curzon was convinced that Russia was moving toward the domination of Central Asia and this view influenced Bird Bishop's report
in *Journeys in Persia*.[12] The increasingly militaristic overtones of
what Kipling in *Kim* called "The Great Game" carried over into the
scientific societies as they became an arm of the imperial archive.
As a result, exploration became even more closely identified with
masculine military strategy.[13] This identification of scientific exploration with colonial government interests increased the marginal
nature of women's involvement with scientific societies. Yet the
economic motives which gave women access to the BAAS meetings in the 1830s continued to allow women erratic participation.

These economic motives allowed Bird Bishop and a few other
women to become members of the RGS, formerly a male bastion.
This softening on the stand against women was not the result of
progressive thinking or an effort to do the right thing, rather it was
the unforeseen consequence of a turf war. Concerned over competition from regional geographical societies (especially when the
Scottish Geographical Society opened a London branch just around
the corner from the London RGS office in 1892), the RGS decided
to admit members of other geographical societies, then found that
this decision meant admitting women.[14] As Bird Bishop had established herself as a speaker to a wide range of missionary societies
and was a fellow of the Royal Scottish Geographical Society, she
was one of the women who gained entrance.[15] When she returned
from Persia in 1891, she gave the anniversary address to the Scottish Geographical Society on "The Upper Karun Region and the
Bakhtiari Lurs," followed by another address at the new competing
London office on "A Journey to Lesser Tibet," which attracted a
large audience.[16] However, despite her recognition, she still had to
borrow books from the RGS library under the name of her publisher.[17] In response to the popularity of such lectures as Bird Bishop's from competing geographical societies, on 28 November 1892,
the RGS admitted the first group of fifteen women, including Bird
Bishop, Kate Marsden, and May French Sheldon, and then slowly
admitted a few others in 1893 for a total of twenty-two women.[18]
Shortly afterwards, Curzon led a revolt of members (including
many military men), who felt the prestige of the organization was
threatened. Bird Bishop felt ill-used by Curzon, with whom she had
traveled in Persia, but also sensed that a response from her on this
issue could become awkwardly personal, especially since she beat

Curzon to publication; her book on Persia was out before his. She did not contrive this situation. Curzon's publishing delay was the result of his own political ambition. After returning to Britain, he was appointed Under-Secretary for India; this appointment then necessitated some censorship after the British government concluded that Curzon's outspokenness in the book could cause diplomatic problems.[19]

However, it was generally noted that Curzon had a rather proprietary attitude to Persia, regarding it as his personal area of expertise, and Bird Bishop was probably wise not to make matters worse and to stay out of the conflict between Curzon and the women fellows. She confided privately in a letter that "The fellowship as it stands at present is not worth making any trouble about. At the same time, the proposed act [the exclusion of women] is a dastardly injustice to women."[20]

Her failure to challenge Curzon does not imply that Bird Bishop did not value her membership. The title page of her 1894 *Among the Tibetans*, reads: "by Isabella Bird Bishop, F.R.G.S.; Hon. Fellow of the Royal Scottish Geographical Society, etc.; Author of *Unbeaten Tracks in Japan,* etc. etc."—all the professional apparatus is present. Those initials indicating she was a fellow of the Royal Geographical Society are used to add prestige in the same way they would to a man's work and her name is stated plainly without the "Mrs.," which would signal a more conventional feminine authorial stance. The "etc., etc." suggests a long stretch of credentials, so many that enumeration would be tiresome. While admittedly such a title page is conventional enough for a man, it was certainly unusual for a woman to present herself in this manner.

Thus Bird Bishop's lack of involvement in a fight with Curzon may be read as a practical response rather than a lackluster commitment to feminist goals, as was suggested by Barr. Barr's biographical assessment was that Bird Bishop "did not have enough faith in or sympathy for the great majority of womankind to be any sort of suffragette" and that she "seems always to have assumed that she was an inexplicable and not very laudable exception to the general rule, and that most women were neither deserving of nor particularly fitted for the greater freedoms allowed to men."[21] However, Curzon was, after all, a powerful man who could make access to future travel more difficult, so too much should not be read into Bird Bishop's response. She had good reasons to stay out of the fray.

Rather, Bird Bishop's interest in establishing a professional reputation can be seen in her continued involvement with the RGS after the furor over her admission had died down. Although the problems with the admission of women has received attention from Birkett[22] and Blunt,[23] admission was just the start of the effort women had to make. In order to achieve true recognition on their own merits, the women who were admitted to professional scientific societies needed to be more than minor or token members and this required both continual professional activity and private self-advertising. While happy that some women had been admitted, Bird Bishop suspected that they were held to different standards than the men and their achievements were not being fully recognized. She was particularly irritated that RGS medals and grants went to men whose achievements, she felt, were no greater than her own. In 1897, she wrote to John Scott Keltie, Secretary of the RGS (after the society had presented a medal to Curzon), pointing to the success of her talk to the Scottish Geographical Society: "I hear myself so continually spoken of as 'the distinguished traveller' that I am arriving at the very natural conclusion that I am as well entitled to a medal as Mr. Curzon or some others!"[24] When Warrington Smyth (who made a comment on one of Bird Bishop's papers), received the Murchison grant from the RGS for travel expenses, Bird Bishop fumed to her publisher John Murray,

> Though my work has not been distinctly geographical yet I think that I have contributed so much to the sum of general knowledge of different countries that I had [sic] been a man I should undoubtedly have received some recognition from the Royal Geographical Society. I consider myself to deserve it at least as much as Mr. Warrington Smyth![25]

Other women felt similarly left out. Birkett's account of the situation indicates that although accepted as fellows, Lilly Grove and Ella Christie, speakers at regional societies, were not invited to speak at the RGS. The Anthropological Institute similarly ignored Marianne North and Lady Brassey, while the Royal Asiatic Society snubbed Lady Anne Blunt and Agnes Smith Lewis (a friend of Kingsley).[26] And although Bird Bishop and the other women remained RGS fellows, no other women were admitted.

A MINISTER'S DAUGHTER

Initially, Bird Bishop's life was fairly conventional and this made her contrasting travels after age forty even more striking. Some explanation of Bird Bishop's anxiety about conventional respectability and how she came to seek personal independence through travel can be found in her family background. She was from a family which, with its connections to William Wilberforce and its numerous missionary members, was strongly committed to religious philanthropy and causes.[27] The family drank sugarless tea as a protest against slavery in the West Indies, even after slavery had been abolished. Their religious beliefs were strict and rigid and the father was not a popular minister (largely because he insisted that local businesses close their shops on the Sabbath). Intellectual achievement was valued, however, and she was allowed to gain the background she needed for later scientific study. She learned Latin and botany from her father and pursued interests in chemistry, metaphysical poetry, and biology.[28]

Despite later biographers' representations of Bird Bishop as a woman who started her travel writing career fairly late (that is, in her forties), she actually began writing and traveling as a young woman. Bird Bishop made her first voyage at the age of twenty-two after recovering from an operation for a tumor at the base of her spine.[29] At first, she was able to travel with the justification that her doctor recommended it and she wrote an anonymous account, *The Englishwoman in America,* in 1856, based on letters written during the trip. In 1857, Bird Bishop made a second trip (this time citing the interest of her father to investigate American religious revival movements) and met Emerson and Thoreau. Acting in an auxiliary position, she edited her father's observations on the American religious scene, *The Revival in America by an English Eye-Witness,* then wrote her own account, *The Aspects of Religion in the United States of America,* in 1859.[30] As with *The Englishwoman,* this work was also written anonymously. Although she did not sign her name to her first books, they were apprenticeship works which prepared her for future writing.

Notwithstanding her continuing ill health, she continued writing as an invalid when she returned home for such magazines as *Good Words, The Leisure Hours,* and *The Family Treasury.* After her father's death, she, along with her mother and her sister, moved to Edinburgh where she wrote descriptive pieces on Scotland and supported causes for the poor. She organized emigration to North America and Canada for the poverty-stricken crofters she came across in the Outer Hebrides (1862–66), visiting them later in Canada to see how they were doing and did some muck-racking journalism by describing slum conditions in Edinburgh.

Although she had been active with her writing and social work in Scotland, Bird Bishop had not attracted much national attention.

Additionally, her back problems were still troubling and she had to use a neck brace in order to write. Barr's biography (which makes use of Anna M. Stoddart's 1906 *The Life of Isabella Bird*), paints the picture of a woman trapped in a very conventional and restrictive upbringing where the only justifiable escape was through charitable endeavors. While in Britain, Bird Bishop suffered from continuing spinal problems, insomnia, and the vague Victorian ills generally associated with depression and the intense intellectual frustration to which middle-class women were subjected. Remembering that she felt better when traveling fifteen years before, Bird Bishop decided to make a trip to Australia at the age of forty-one for her health. Although miserable in Australia, she saw little reason to return to Scotland, and so made the decision to travel to California.

This trip gave Bird Bishop the material with which she established herself as a popular writer and gave her the realization that she could escape the limitations of proper behavior through travel. Looking back on the account of this trip, we can see the beginnings of themes that she would develop in her next three books. She noted, for instance, that when she encountered a hurricane and became involved in shipboard emergencies, she felt more alive and was more able to dismiss the pain she had endured in Britain. Nursing a fellow passenger who needed to be placed off the ship, she found herself in the Hawaiian islands; and here, she discovered the liberation of riding astride instead of sidesaddle. As a result of these experiences, she apparently resolved to seek out areas away from heavy colonization where her unconventional riding behavior would not be censured. From the islands, she then went to Estes Park in the Colorado Rocky Mountains to put her ideas into practice.

After returning home, she wrote up the successful *Six Months in the Sandwich Islands*; reviewers singled out her book for its display of energy in the troublesome tropical climate suspected of encouraging indolence and sexual laxity (in the *Pall Mall Budget)* and for its accuracy in botanical description (in *Nature*).[31] The lush colorful botanical descriptions of her early work particularly caught the critics' attention. Observing the Hawaiian flora, she notes how

[t]he delicate tamarind and the feathery algaroba intermingled their fragile grace with the dark, shiny foliage of the South Sea exotics, and the deep red, solitary flowers of the hibiscus rioted among familiar fuchsias and geraniums, which here attain the height and size of large rhododendrons. (*Six Months* 17)

Such descriptions would work well in tandem with the popular botanical paintings of Marianne North as they evoke a sensual feeling
for color and form. Yet Bird Bishop's sure sense of botanical identification and knowledgeable comparison inspires trust in her observations, dismissing any question of imaginative exaggeration.

After some activity at home, she again complained of health
problems and left in 1878 for Japan, then the Malay Peninsula.
Only in 1879, after returning from Malay, did Bird Bishop publish
"Letters from the Rocky Mountains" serially in *Leisure Hour* along
with various other popular magazine articles on "Taxation and the
Working Classes," fossil footprints, natural history observations,
and "Female Education in China."[32] The letters were quickly published in book form by John Murray III as *A Lady's Life in the
Rocky Mountains.*[33] After completing the manuscript for *Unbeaten
Tracks in Japan,* her sister developed what would eventually become a fatal case of typhoid fever and she was attended by Dr. John
Bishop, whom Bird Bishop married after her sister's death. She
then wrote *The Golden Chersonese,* based on her Malaysian travels
and dedicated it to the memory of her sister. Later, her husband
became ill and they went to Europe to escape the severity of Scottish weather. He died in 1886 after five years of marriage.

It is after these deaths that Bird Bishop changed her writing style
and switched her audience focus, aiming for a more authoritative
and professional voice for a new audience consisting of geographers, explorers and colonial government officials rather than the
readers of ladies' magazines who had been her original audience.
She prepared to travel again by taking a three-month nursing course
at St. Mary Abbott's Hospital in London to learn how to perform
minor surgery (during her travels she stitched up both people and
horses). She also took photography courses and resumed the journalism she stopped practicing while married. In 1889, she escaped
the duties of Victorian widowhood for the outskirts of Tibet to
begin founding a series of medical missionaries, which she helped
support with the proceeds of her books.[34] From Tibet, Bird Bishop
continued to Persia and Kurdistan, publishing the two-volume *Journeys in Persia and Kurdistan* in 1891. Upon returning to Britain,
she began giving talks to regional geographic societies and was admitted to the RGS. Another two-volume travel account, *Korea and
Her Neighbours,* followed in 1898. As a result of these works, she
was viewed as an "authority on the political situation in the Far
East."[35] Her last book-producing trip was to China and further into
Tibet, after which she gave several lectures, was the first woman to
address the RGS, and wrote her final book, *The Yangtze Valley and*

Beyond, in 1899. This book gained additional attention after the 1900 Boxer Rebellion attracted Western interest to that part of the world. Although the reason for traveling, establishing medical missionaries, was not highlighted in her writings (she seems to have provided funding, but left the organization to others), she did succeed in establishing the John Bishop Memorial Hospital in Kashmir, the Henrietta Bird Hospital for Women in Punjab and three other hospitals in China and Korea.[36] At the age of seventy she was in Morocco writing articles on the local situation and riding five hundred miles at a stretch. After returning to Edinburgh, she died in 1904.

"To Do the Most Improper Things"

A continual theme of Bird Bishop's writing is the escape to solitude away from people, especially Europeans, into a fast disappearing wilderness. As we have seen, this desire to be alone is expressed by Wollstonecraft and Martineau, but it becomes more intense in the writings of Bird Bishop and Kingsley in the late nineteenth century. Just as European men made it difficult for women to achieve professional recognition, so men tended to enforce conventional and inhibiting expectations for women. Sometimes this was done directly through the belief that women needed "protection"; other times, the influence was subtler as the woman, intensely aware of the male authoritative presence, felt she needed to support and acquiesce to male wishes. It is because of such subtle pressures that traveling alone becomes increasingly important for women. This was very noticeable to D. Amaury Talbot, who, in her 1915 anthropological study of the Ibibios of Southern Nigeria, *Women's Mysteries of a Primitive People*, looked back to such solitary travelers as Bird Bishop and Kingsley with some envy because they managed to travel on their own. Talbot noted with some irritation that she and her sister, on the other hand, were surrounded by "never-failing watchful care," from which they needed to escape in order to write with "no intervening male influence."[37]

As Bird Bishop pursued behavior which challenged ideas of women's proper roles and capabilities, she placed her travels in increasingly more isolated places where she could be alone. Her early and best-selling account in the Rockies opens at Lake Tahoe early in September and quickly establishes the area as a place of solitude and thus an area where a woman could escape conventional expectations. The region is described as a "strictly North American

beauty," pure and distant, quiet except for the distant sound of a
lumberman's axe. This is contrasted with the best-forgotten "clang
of San Francisco," a place of overabundant food, fruit of "startling
size," and dry stifling dust which continues into Sacramento. This
contrast implies that Bird Bishop's senses were continually jarred
and disturbed when surrounded by people and that isolation provided a welcome relief to the psychic tension produced by crowds
(thus securing a pseudo-medical excuse for her isolation).

The later intrusion of settlers into the region is underscored by
notes inserted in later editions which updated changes in the area,
and thus, the solitude of the place becomes temporal in addition to
geographical. While these footnotes provided a connection with her
Sandwich Islands book, they also updated the reader on changes
that had taken place in the Rockies since the book was first published.[38] As a result, the reader can see in these notes that the conditions she had originally described were already gone and, thus, that
the Estes Park area she remembers is now accessible only through
her nostalgic recall. This presentation is consistent with her view in
later travels—the peace and solitude in the wilderness, the unsettled
or uncolonized outlands of the world, disappear under western development almost as soon as she leaves the area.

This regret, however, does not indicate that Bird Bishop necessarily celebrates non-European culture. She commonly emphasizes
the backwardness and dirt of indigenous peoples even as she notes
their passing. The Digger Indians in Colfax are described as "perfect savages, without any aptitude for even aboriginal civilization,
and are altogether the most degraded of the ill-fated tribes which
are dying out before the white races" (4). Comments such as,
"They were all hideous and filthy, and swarming with vermin" (4),
are added with descriptions of bows and arrows. Yet there is a certain sympathy in the remark that this vanishing tribe was "a most
impressive incongruity in the midst of the tokens of an omnipotent
civilization" (4), especially in the context of her reactions to the
horrors of such an "omnipotent civilization" as she found in San
Francisco or continual later expressions of disgust over urban areas
in Asia where the British presence was well established. These settled areas were always left as quickly as possible and with much-
expressed relief. And finally, as Barr points out, it is the indigenous
peoples, these incongruities, whom Bird Bishop sought out in her
travels, even as she lay such emphasis on dirt that her publisher,
Murray, asked her to tone down similar descriptions in her Japanese
travels.[39] These contradictory views of native populations continue
through her books as her belief in the superiority of European civi-

lization conflicts with her sympathy for the powerless, so that Persian peasants in *Journeys*, for instance, are characterized with a range of alternating positive and negative qualities: "grossly ignorant, hardy, dirty, bigoted, domestic, industrious, avaricious, sober, and tractable . . ." (2:250).

Bird Bishop assumed the superiority of European influence, but she viewed its physical presence during her travels with dread. In her later travel to Tibet, when she was in her sixties, the unexpected sight of a British liaison in an isolated area did not bring pleasure but elicited the moan, "I never felt so extinguished. Liberty seemed lost, and the romance of the desert to have died out in one moment!" (*Among* 145). In *Journeys in Persia* a major highway ("a road of dreary width") is dismissed as a "beaten track," the most tedious part of the journey (172). It is possible that Bird Bishop felt she needed to stress the poor conditions in which native peoples dwelled in order to justify in her own mind the necessity of those westernizing influences, even though it was western culture with all its restrictions on her activities which she was continually attempting to escape.

In examining the tension contained within such narrative positions as Bird Bishop's, the practicalities of women's travel are often overlooked. Understanding the difficulties women had to overcome while traveling on their own in the context of Victorian expectations for women's behavior, allows us to better appreciate how innovative Bird Bishop's traveling was as well as its importance for women of her time. Additionally, such a discussion reveals features of Bird Bishop's persona and helps us understand the rhetorical strains within her narration.

For one, a woman traveling alone was viewed as particularly unfeminine. Speaking in the plural, traveling with a companion, and with readily apparent tour guides, lent a degree of respectability to the female traveler. This more typical stance is the rhetorical position Amelia Edwards takes in *Untrodden Peaks and Unfrequented Valleys* (1873). At one point, she and her companion (another woman) encounter an unaccompanied solitary woman traveler, a German, while traveling in the Italian Dolomite Alps. In Edwards's description, this woman is objectified as being beyond the civilized pale, identified as being "a Phenomenon." She is depersonalized in Edwards's text and is identified as "it":

> [W]e encounter a Phenomenon. It stands in the little yard between the Albergo and the Dependance [inns], discoursing and gesticulating. . . . It wears highlows, a battered straw hat, and a brown garment which may

be described either as a long kilt or the briefest of petticoats. Its hair is sandy; its complexion crimson; its age anything between forty-five and sixty. It carries a knapsack on its back, and an alpenstock in its hand. The voice is the voice of a man; the face, tanned and travel-stained as it is, is the face of a woman."[40]

This woman rejects the male guides, declaring "Fatigue is nothing to me—distance is nothing to me—danger is nothing to me" and "I am afraid of nothing—neither of the Pope nor the devil!"[41] Edwards is relieved to find this traveler is a foreigner, a German, and not English. Traveling is one thing, but to go it alone moves the woman traveler beyond civilized acknowledgement and labels her as nearly mad. Edwards and her companion do not speak to the woman, although they note that she paints, botanises, and maybe even writes. Edwards must distinguish herself as separate from such unEnglish and unfeminine behavior. Written just a few years before Bird Bishop's Hawaiian account, Edwards's distancing of herself from the German traveler marks the social norm against which Bird Bishop was writing. Bird Bishop would also travel alone and reject physical fatigue in her writing, but she did not want to become "a Phenomenon" and had to take care to avoid being categorized as such.

It should also be noted that for women gaining solitude through travel was not easily done even if a woman headed off the beaten path. In order to travel on their own in isolated areas, women needed a form of transportation they could manage alone, a continuing difficulty for women, especially if they wished to maintain the appearance of gentility and respectability associated with the title "lady" of Bird Bishop's Rocky Mountain book. This helps explain the interest shown in rowing by Wollstonecraft, Kingsley, and imaginatively, by Martineau. At this time, respectable women had to ride horses sidesaddle. It was a difficult position to maintain and even five years after Ethel Brilliana Tweedie wrote *A Girl's Ride in Iceland* (1889), riding horses astride was still nearly unthinkable. But Bird Bishop's books helped establish a respectable precedence that other women could cite. This is what Tweedie did when, after an outcry arose over women riding astride (apparently stemming from her book), she needed to justify her own riding position in Iceland. Tweedie expanded on this issue in later editions of *A Girl's Ride* and pointed to Bird Bishop's experiences as proof of the unnecessary pain imposed by the sidesaddle.[42] She pointed out also that, even after knickerbockers and short skirts were acceptable for bicycle riding, the sidesaddle was still retained for horseback riding.[43]

As riding sidesaddle indicated class position, it is likely that changes came slower to this activity than to more novel pursuits such as bicycle riding.[44]

Riding sidesaddle caused problems for women travelers because assuming this riding position meant more than using a particular saddle. The horse had to be specially trained to the sidesaddle for the rider to have a smooth ride and such horses would usually be part of a large stable. Consequently, for women, riding, as opposed to traveling in a carriage, was a skill learned only if one grew up in well-to-do circumstances.[45] Bird Bishop most likely learned to ride during her childhood spent with her grandparents and she mentions accompanying her father on horseback as a girl while he visited his parishioners in the country. When women traveled away from Europe, they commonly carried their own sidesaddles with them. Edwards recommended that women bring their own sidesaddles to Italy, for there were "only two in the whole country, and but one of these for hire."[46] Even when women brought their own saddle, however, a rough ride could be expected since the horses were not accustomed to the uneven weight distribution caused by this riding position. The roughness of the ride explains Bird Bishop's preference for the Mexican saddle (now called the Western saddle) when riding sidesaddle. This saddle is heavier and has a horn, originally intended for securing lassoed cattle, but also useful to simply hang onto during a rough ride.

More than a fashionable convention, the insistence that women ride sidesaddle produced practical problems at a time when horseback riding was a major means of transportation, and certainly the only form of transportation in mountainous regions. The sidesaddle seemed almost to require that a woman be accompanied by men, since mounting the sidesaddle was not something a woman could do alone. She needed a platform and at least one man to lift her into the saddle, while another held the horse's head.[47] This posed a difficult problem for a woman who wished to be on her own.

Additionally, the sidesaddle was dangerous when used in rough terrain or over long distances, the sort of riding Bird Bishop needed to do in order to travel in such areas as Persia. This problem was recognized by an earlier woman traveler. In 1894, four years before Bird Bishop's trip to Persia, Ella Constance Sykes, an upper-class Englishwoman, joined her brother's enormous entourage through the passes of Persia as he went to found a British consulate. As part of a male-headed group, Sykes was compelled to keep up the sort of appearances associated with British civilization by riding sidesaddle. In her book, *Through Persia on a Side-Saddle* (1898), the saddle is an irritant as much as it is a symbol of her sex:

> The more I rode, the more I saw the disadvantages of the saddle to which I was condemned. The side-saddle is by no means an ideal invention in my eyes. It is difficult to mount into it from the ground; it is dangerous in riding among hills to be unable to spring off on either side in case of an accident; the habit is very apt to be caught on the pommels if the rider falls, and the position in which she sits cramps her much if persisted in for many hours at a slow walk, which is the usual thing in hilly and stony countries.[48]

The cramping caused by a position women were "condemned" to hold seems to have caused more than discomfort. The rider was, after all, facing forward while her torso was turned sideways. Tweedie mentions as a matter of common knowledge that many young women "become crooked when learning to ride,"[49] and this raises the possibility that Bird Bishop's lifelong back problems may have stemmed from sidesaddle riding when younger.

Then there was the more immediate problem of maintaining one's seat when jumping or making sudden turns, an additional difficulty alluded to by Sykes. Bird Bishop's contemporary, Florence Dixie, in *Across Patagonia* (1880), raised this issue when describing an ostrich hunt she participated in where she said she would have been killed if she had attempted to ride sidesaddle:

> The class of fall . . . is the most frequent and by no means the least perilous part of the hunt and generally knocks the breath nigh clean out of one's body! I know that several which I got in this manner did so, and I am quite certain that had I not been riding on the cross saddle [riding astride] I should have been killed. . . . The moral of this is that all ladies who go to Patagonia should abjure the use of the side saddle.[50]

Despite these practical considerations, the linkage between being a lady and riding sidesaddle remained so well established that Bird Bishop felt continual anxiety about riding astride and was careful to be seen riding sidesaddle if she was within sight of Europeans. When she remained in England for five years during her marriage, she rode sidesaddle with her husband and felt like a "crippled fool."[51]

Considering the problems posed by the sidesaddle, it is understandable that Bird Bishop was so struck during her Hawaiian visit with the sight of a woman riding "along the road at full gallop, sitting on her horse as square and easy as a hussar" (*Six Months* 16).

The sense of freedom and ease embodied by the Hawaiian women stirred her imagination and she quickly made the connection between riding astride and the freedom to travel on her own. She described the Hawaiian women riders as "free-and-easy," "flying along astride, bare-footed, with their orange and scarlet riding dresses streaming on each side beyond their horses' tails, a bright kaleidoscopic flash of bright eyes, white teeth, shining hair," in contrast to the British naval officers, "riding in the stiff, wooden style which Anglo-Saxons love" (22–23). With such free-flying women, Hawaii was a "fairy land [in which] anything might be expected" (23). While riding astride could be done on this distant "fairyland" where it was part of everyday life along with other such unbelievable sights as volcanoes and surfboard riding, transferring such behavior to places where it was not the norm and defending her actions to her British readers was more difficult.

In her next book, which was situated in the Rocky Mountains, Bird Bishop presents herself riding astride and thus challenges the linkage between gentility and the dependency related to riding side-saddle. She approaches the issue of riding astride cautiously, indicating her nervousness about her desires. As she introduces the issue of riding position, she first circumvents the controversy by raising the question of the type of saddle to be used. A stablekeeper is mentioned who tells her "some ladies preferred the Mexican saddle" (7). Having been thus encouraged, she goes to the stables where she is shown "three velvet-covered side-saddles almost without horns" and is then told some ladies used the horn on the Mexican saddle, but no one rode "cavalier fashion." Faced with the expectation that she should ride sidesaddle, Bird Bishop wrote she "felt abashed"; but then her spirits lifted as she is told that in the town of Truckee "people can do as they like" (8).

This careful building of suspense, along with the indication that permission has been given by a man described as "the very type of a Western pioneer" (7), serves to simultaneously show Bird Bishop's hesitation to do something unconventional (a hesitation which validates her claim to being a lady), and, through the representation of the stablekeeper, permission from the frontier culture to show herself riding astride. Permission granted and respectability intact, she is then able to proceed with her ride of liberation. She straps an extra skirt to the saddle, dumps her long cloak (which hid her divided skirt) in a corn bin and is on the horse with no need of help from the men in the stable, who are shown lounging about. The observers are reported as showing no astonishment (and remaining respectful), reinforcing her declaration that she would not be judged or found lacking in social credentials here. Leaving her socially imposed embarrassment behind, she then rides out of town. The dust of the town, symbolizing the restricting conventions, is now behind her and there is "an elasticity in the air which removed all lassitude, and gives one spirit enough for anything" (9). She thus presents herself not only as having made her escape but as having also maintained her respectability in doing so. Her nervousness, however, about towns continues and, when she rides into Colorado Springs, she rides sidesaddle with a skirt, "though the settlement scarcely looked like a place where any deference to prejudices was necessary" (141).

Associated with women's riding position was the issue of women's dress. How women travel writers negotiated the representation of their dress while engaging in exploratory travel became a complex part of their rhetorical strategies. This was in response to a growing public backlash to the increasingly visible position of women apparent in Britain during the 1880s and 1890s. Whereas Wollstonecraft and Martineau purposefully avoided bringing up the issue of dress while traveling because it was associated with feminine frivolity, later women travelers such as Bird Bishop (and later Kingsley) did raise this issue because they wished to separate themselves from the various developing women's movements (later to be lumped together under the term "New Woman" movement), including the rational dress movement, which were being mocked in the popular press.[52] A comic illustration in *Punch* in 1894, labeled "Donna Quixote," serves as an illustration of the women's issues which were regarded as impractical and unrealistic—appropriate targets for satire. This cartoon, with accompanying rhyme, expresses the popular view of women's struggles against restrictive conventions. In it, a woman is featured sitting with a raised key and book in hand surrounded by images of the "disorderly notions picked out of books": battles against marriage laws, chaperons, and "tyrant man." One figure raises a banner labeled "divided skirt" against a dragon titled "decorum."[53]

This illustration also underscores the association of women's progressive movements with literary treatments of such issues, so much so that, by the 1890s proposed changes in women's social status had gained a fictive quality. In "Donna Quixote," the New Woman reader is accused of mental confusion over the difference between reality and imagination: "Mere book-bred phantoms you for facts mistake. . . ."[54] This raises the possibility that if a woman traveler presented herself in a manner that would be considered Amazonian, she would lose credibility; her observations would be

"Donna Quixote." *Punch* 28 April 1894, 194.

dismissed. The more exotic or unusual the locale or means of travel, the more conventional and less imaginative the presentation needed to be if the traveler was to be believed. For the traveling woman naturalist, this potential loss of credibility required careful consideration of how she should appear in her accounts.

Because of the imagery of women as deluded in the popular press, women travelers during the later half of the nineteenth century experienced anxiety over how to present to the British public their appearance in the field. Bird Bishop wrote that "Travellers are privileged to do the most improper things with perfect propriety, that is one charm of travelling."[55] This belief, however, did not remove the anxiety over "improprieties" present in her writings. In *Six Months in the Sandwich Islands*, she was careful to include an engraving of a woman on a horse in full gallop. Labeled "The Pau or Hawaiian Ladies' Holiday Riding Dress," the full folds of the divided skirt are shown as almost covering the horse as well as the rider (22).[56] The costume was obviously impractical if the rider ever had to dismount or was thrown.

Bird Bishop modified her riding dress for the Rocky Mountains and this (along with being unchaperoned) caused her concern because she noted with relief that not only were the reviews favorable for *A Lady's Life in the Rocky Mountains* but the reviewers had not "scented out any imagined impropriety."[57] *The Times,* however, in a short review which played up the Wild West elements of her travel (calling her "the feminine counterpart" of "Ruxton's *Adventures in the Far West*"), claimed she "donned masculine habiliments for her greater convenience and backed such half-broken horses as she happened to hire." The reviewer also noted that she climbed a peak in a pair of borrowed man's jackboots and "spent weeks in the depth of winter in a mountain cabin with a couple of young sportsmen for company, a bare larder, and a temperature considerably below zero."[58] These were not the elements of her book that Bird Bishop would have preferred to be advertised, even though these experiences were present in her text. In response to this review, Bird Bishop wrote in protest to her publisher, Murray. Rather than complaining about the general misrepresentation of her behavior in the book, however, Bird Bishop chose to target the description of her dress, explaining that her costume was "a dress worn by *ladies* at Mountain Resorts in America and by English and American *ladies* on Hawaii. The full-frilled trousers being invaluable in mountaineering or riding." Very much enraged (possibly because of suppressed guilt over riding astride), and having emphasized the word "ladies," she continued, "My indignation and disgust have not cooled down yet. I can imagine a lady who 'dons masculine habiliments' quite capable of thrashing an editor on less provocation."[59] Murray suggested adding a note and a sketch emphasizing the femininity of her riding dress to derail such comments. This sketch appeared in the seven later editions of *A Lady's*

Life[60] and seems to be the one featured in Middleton's study.[61] It shows a woman with a mid-calf-length skirt over bloomers that are carefully secured at the ankles to maintain modesty. Bird Bishop's response to the drawing was that it was "rather Amazonian," but at least not masculine.[62]

Eventually, in her later travels, Bird Bishop partly resolved the problem of dress by adopting native costume when possible.[63] When she was in her sixties, she was a well-established figure and could publicly indulge in variations of Chinese dress in Asia, although still with some residual anxiety. However, rather than displaying herself in native dress in a frontispiece to her books, as was traditional for male explorers, she buried the photograph in the middle of the text.[64]

Combined with the anxiety over dress and riding manner, and perhaps underlying those two concerns, was Bird Bishop's difficulty in presenting herself in her narrative when indoors and unchaperoned with men, one experience picked out by the anonymous *Times* reviewer. The social code in regard to unchaperoned women was particularly strict and, at one point in *A Lady's Life*, Bird Bishop was snowed in high in the mountains at Estes Park with two young men, occasionally visited by a courting "desperado" with "not a woman within twenty-five miles" (187). Rather than state her authorial anxiety about such improprieties directly, she distracts attention from herself by saying she felt sorry for the men who had to put up with her presence. As supplies were very limited and the mountains were intensely cold in November, her anxiety, the overwhelming isolation, and sexual tension produced a state of claustrophobia evident in her description of her situation:

> . . . when storms sweep down from Long's Peak, and the air is full of stinging, tempest-driven snow, and there is barely a probability of anyone coming, or of my communication with the world at all, then the stupendous mountain ranges which lie between us and the Plains grow in height till they become impassable barriers, and the bridgeless rivers grow in depth, and I wonder if all my life is to be spent here in washing and sweeping and baking. (194)

Alone with the men and freezing temperatures, Bird Bishop keeps the text focused on "washing and sweeping and baking"—her "endless" mending and the limited flour. When Martineau mentions sewing and mending activities, they provide a reassuring domestic element to her travel. But here Bird Bishop's domestic concerns have an intensity that suggests that they substitute for is-

Isabella Bird Bishop. From *The Yangtze Valley and Beyond* (London, 1899).

sues which cannot be discussed.[65] She presents her day as one of continual busyness, in which she "never sat down till two." Nervously, she cleans:

> I cleaned the living room and the kitchen, swept a path through the rubbish in the passage room, washed up, made and baked a batch of rolls and four pounds of sweet biscuits, cleaned some tins and pans, washed some clothes, and gave things generally a "redding up." (194)

The guilt and anxiety over her highly improper and sexually charged position is transferred to concern over domestic matters. Additionally, she broods with a strange fixation over her lack of clothing. She says she came with a small carpetbag for luggage, a black silk dress and a flannel riding suit (194–95). Having little to wear does not make the close quarters any easier and she frantically mends. But what she does not touch on is the inherent immodesty in this situation, a situation which is too suspenseful to simply leave out of her narrative yet contains sexually charged elements which are too risky even to intimate.

To alleviate readers' possible concerns that she, in her unprotected state, would be in danger of rape, Bird Bishop makes reference to a popular Rousseauistic belief in the nobility of the frontiersman. She claims that because of some sort of code native to the wilderness, if a woman behaves with fortitude, she will not be touched. To reinforce this idea, she quotes a stablehand who tells her, "There's nothing Western folk admire so much as pluck in a woman" (*A Lady's* 16). The "pluck" in question was her calm response when thrown by her horse after it was startled by a bear on her first ride in the Rockies. Again, this reassurance is placed in the mouth of a native to indicate its authenticity and to emphasize the moral distance of the American West from England. At the same time, however, Bird Bishop does not want to suggest that there was absolutely no danger, since that would undercut her own courage. As a way of persuading her readers that the area she was traveling in was dangerous enough to make her account worth reading and that she was not in immediate danger because of her own mental stamina, she adds such stories as the account of cannibalism among the Donner party with her description of Donner Lake, suggesting an illustration of just how ruffian the local lowlife could be if it were not for her particular self-control. Generally, however, she highlights the lawlessness, and the lack of humanity in such places as Cheyenne, associating such behavior with towns, where she does not wish to dwell.

Traveler for the Empire

Having been successful with her personal reminiscences in Hawaii and the Rocky Mountains, Bird Bishop moved her travel accounts into the realm of popular education with *The Golden Chersonese and the Way Thither* (1883). In this Malaysian account, her tone is upbeat, laying emphasis on the grace and picturesque nature of the scenery. Here she takes on the role of the popular pedagogical writer, explaining to her sister and readers what she is seeing. (Although she does include descriptions of Chinese jails and torture which her publisher wanted her to remove.[66]) Indeed, so positive and popular was her general picture of Malay that Emily Innes, the annoyed wife of a government official in Malay, wrote an exposé, *The Chersonese with the Gilding Off* (1885), in response to Bird Bishop's account.[67]

The Golden Chersonese represents a movement toward the more professional narrative voice represented in her Persian and later journeys. Here she indicates her awareness of the use of travel writing to supply information valuable for colonial policy.[68] Thus now, in justification for writing, she emphasizes both its importance to the British empire and the need for this information. She describes the area as "practically under British rule, and . . . probably destined to afford increasing employment to British capital and enterprise" (viii). This new economic awareness is bolstered with supporting RGS maps and reports to make the letters "useful." Aware of her writing as part of a larger project leading to an increasing store of information, she now represents the goal of her endeavor as the creation of a "little volume" for "the ever-growing library of the literature of travel" (ix). In addition to providing reports useful for government purposes, what is different in this travel is the new emphasis on being not just off the beaten path but in fairly unmapped areas. Bird Bishop calls the area "a little-travelled region" often confused with the Malay Archipelago and more than half unexplored (vii).[69] With *The Golden Chersonese*, Bird Bishop is making a move into the area of the independent explorer, rather than the visiting traveler.

By *Journeys in Persia and Kurdistan* (1891), Bird Bishop is much more assured and self-confident in how she presents her travel. At this stage, her reputation had grown beyond the limited expectations usual for a woman writer. While Tweedie's and Dixie's books were marketed for both adults and children, Bird Bishop's writing was targeted for an adult audience and was attracting more scholarly notice. The Persian journey was made a year before she attained her fellowship in the RGS, and it shows what sort of discourse and type of information was expected for scientific acknowledgment of her work.

What is apparent in Bird Bishop's career is a pattern similar to Martineau's: a movement from popular or educational works to more independent study. However, whereas Martineau repeatedly attempted to gain recognition for theoretical work and worked outside scientific organizations, Bird Bishop established as her goal acceptance from a specific and well-established scientific community. In pursuit of this goal, her aim seems to have been to make her writing so strategically useful to the British empire that she could not be ignored.

While her early travels made very specific botanical identifications, by the trip through Persia she is also carefully noting the geologic details and trade information which a military strategist would consider vital. Her descriptions of the local geology are precise and show a knowledgeable understanding of terminology. At one point, she speaks of the brown alluvial soil as "a series of low crumbling mounds of red and gray sandstone, mixed up with soft conglomerate rocks of jasper and porphyry pebbles" which "mark the termination . . . of the vast alluvial plains of the Tigris and Euphrates, and are the first step to the uplifted Iranian plateau" (1:59). When she travels over routes which have been described before, she shows her awareness of scientific work by footnoting and giving credit to the previous explorer, often by citing an article in the Royal Geographical Society journal or Foreign Office reports. Such careful acquisition of the language and details of professional courtesy signal her desire to be acknowledged by the geographical societies. The awareness of trade issues is registered immediately with *Journeys in Persia*'s opening at landfall in Bushire, identified as an important seaport, and Bird Bishop notes the types of ships present, their country of ownership and the nationality of officers. A footnote adds information on tonnage and imports. As she traveled, she itemized information such as data on the date industry (1:7) and the production of gall for ink (1:44). This is not just entertainment for the armchair traveler at home but also information for the businessman interested in overseas investment, and for policymakers in the government and military who could foresee the possibility of British control of this region and who depended on geographic exploration to provide the needed maps and descriptions.

Even though Bird Bishop states, "I have no books of reference with me, and can seldom write except of such things as I see and hear" (1:60), her accounts are clearly documented and checked against other sources. She establishes her authority by warning about the unreliability of Turkish statistics and dismissing a male travel writer's account as being "charming," a telling word choice as this is the sort of language generally used in referring to (and diminishing the importance of) women's writing (1:28). If we approach Bird Bishop's accounts by taking the viewpoint of a military strategist, her identification of sources of water, natural resources, travel conditions, shipping lines and control of trade gain new meaning as we see that her attention is clearly directed toward the very aspects of the landscape important for military control of the region. While still retaining her contact with the general public, with *Journeys in Persia* Bird Bishop became part of the Imperial Archive and there is little wonder that the British government took notice of her travels.

Along with her sensitivity toward information of strategic importance, her continuing efforts to increase the geographic usefulness of her travels can also be seen in Bird Bishop's efforts to acquire expertise in photography, increasing the number of photographic plates with each travel book. Anticipating the need for film development in the field, she devised techniques for developing her film in the camp. While her Persian and Malaysian travels are illustrated with drawings based on her photos, for her later Korean and Chinese travels, she used photographs as illustrations. Her final book, *The Yangtze Valley,* was illustrated with one hundred and seventeen photographs, including Tibetan scenes, a subject of much interest for the British.

Much of this new awareness was probably stimulated by her contact with Major Sawyer, the military officer and surveyor with whom she traveled in the Mideast. The presence of Sawyer in her text was problematic for Bird Bishop, threatening both her control of her narrative and her maintenance of propriety. While she could not completely remove his presence in her narration, Bird Bishop did make use of several rhetorical techniques to marginalize his presence as much as possible. Because of her need to remove Sawyer from her narration, and since she was in actuality providing cover for his clandestine surveying of areas outside British control, Bird Bishop's relationship with Sawyer is not completely clear. Her surviving letters indicate that she met up with him after her trip to Tibet and traveled with him from Baghdad to Teheran, then caught up with him again somewhere in southern Persia to survey the region controlled by the Bakhtiari tribes.[70]

Initially, *Journeys in Persia* makes Sawyer a shadowy presence and does not explicitly indicate when he is present and when Bird

Bishop is traveling without him. He is merely identified in a foot-note as "an officer, with whom I was then unacquainted . . . [who] kindly offered me his escort" (1: 45). Bird Bishop is clearly reluc-tant to admit Sawyer into her text. On occasion, he is limited to the single initial "M——." Eventually, he becomes an irritating but disembodied call in the morning "to boot and saddle."

In the second volume of *Journeys in Persia*, where she recounts how her camp had to deal with hostile Bakhtiari tribes, Sawyer loses his European identity and starts appearing in the narration under the name "the Agha," which Bird Bishop's glossary identi-fies as "a master." This identification is perhaps purposely confus-ing since Bird Bishop does not explicitly identify him as European and, on first reading, there is an assumption that he is one of the several guides or an Arab official. A reader might be reading along for quite awhile before the sentence—"The Agha did not return, and for a day and night I [Bird Bishop] was the only European in camp"—brings one up short and signals that "the Agha" was a fel-low European (2:69). Similarly, the only sign that Sawyer left her company on 9 August in Burujerd[71] is the following comment made after reaching town: "Happy thought, that no call to 'boot and sad-dle' will break the stillness of to-morrow morning!" (2:125), a comment which could either mean she could now sleep in or that the source of the background call is finally gone. Most probably, her original journal discussed continuing difficulties with Sawyer, but she eliminated as much reference to him as possible in prepar-ing her text for publication in order to maintain her own primary position in the text.

In her introduction to the first volume of *Journeys in Persia*, Barr explains that "due to the clandestine nature of Major Sawyer's mis-sion, Isabella felt obliged to all but ignore his presence" during her journey.[72] It is likely, though, that even if Sawyer's surveying activ-ities were not secretive, she would still have moved his presence to the background of her narrative. Sawyer's appearance was difficult to handle because he threatened her dominant narrative position in her book and she wished to keep the focus on her role in the jour-ney; additionally, as a white male widower, his company suggested scandal. Only by reducing him to a morning call, an initial, or by transforming him into a non-European, could Bird Bishop retain both control and propriety in her book.

Her involvement with Sawyer on this trip also indicates how closely she was now working with the Foreign Office, a relationship which posed later practical publication problems because her book had to be cleared by them and she was not allowed to include specific information or maps which would indicate where Sawyer was working.[73] Rather than a map, she was forced to provide a list of itineraries with approximate distances in miles or hours in an appendix. Such censorship suggests that her travel with Sawyer was carefully monitored by the British government.

But while not explicitly mentioned, Sawyer did affect Bird Bishop's writing. His presence during the first part of the Persian travels apparently dampened Bird Bishop's enthusiasm for traveling. Privately, she described his presence as an "abridgement of my liberty" in a letter and stated, "I should much prefer to travel alone."[74] Possibly as a response to her uneasiness over Sawyer, the first three hundred pages of *Journeys in Persia* are restrained in their descriptive power. (Admittedly, loss of papers and letters in the mail also contributed to the sparseness of the prose.) After she comes to an understanding with Sawyer and is in her own camp with full control of her own workers, her descriptions tend to linger more over the landscape than in most of the first volume, suggesting that Sawyer is not as dominating a figure as before and she can direct her full attention to the countryside.

When she leaves Sawyer, her resumption of control of her journey is signaled by an account in which she challenges the judgment of the guide and moves the camp because she suspects the water supply is polluted:

> On arriving at the beautiful crystal spring which the guide had indicated as the halting-place for Sunday, I found that it issued from under a mound of grass-grown graves, was in the full sun blaze, and at the lowest part of the plain. The guide asserted that it was the only spring, but having seen a dark stain of vegetation high among the hills, I halted the caravan and rode off alone in search of the water I hoped it indicated, disregarding the suppressed but unmistakably sneering laughter of the guide and *charvadars*. (1:347)

Bird Bishop found her spring high in the hills and "had the amusement of shifting the camps to another place" (1:347). In her explanation of how she made her decision to change camp, she shows her ability to read the clues of the landscape and draw conclusions, a higher level of inductive reasoning than the guide's, who, she suggests, is relying only on memory of past visits to the area. This small victory of deduction over the guide was especially sweet since just two pages earlier she described having to stand by and watch Moslem women being whipped with her own whip because they came to her camp (1:345). Thus, her delight in causing the guide discomfort by having a woman prove him wrong is more than a personal rejoinder to an irritating member of the party. It also serves as a tension relief for the emotional stress of traveling in a culture in which the inferior status of women is continually emphasized and where she had to follow Sawyer.

Finally, at the end of her travel, Sawyer's participation has been figuratively incorporated into her own persona. As she approaches the end of her journey, Bird Bishop contemplates the apparently endless passage she has traversed:

> I felt as if I should *always* be sleeping in stables or dark dens, *always* uttering the call to "boot and saddle" two hours before daylight, *always* crawling along mountain roads on a woolly horse, *always* planning marches, *always* studying Asiatic character, and *always* sinking deeper into barbarism! (2:392–93)

On the surface, the emphasis on "always" indicates a complaint underscoring the hardship she has endured. But beneath this surface grumbling, this passage serves as a recap of what she has done, and now it is she, not Sawyer, who voices the morning call, she who plans the marches. And this "barbarism" she sinks into is not a reference to the "Asiatic character" but to the rough masculine ways of the male explorer represented by Sawyer, whose role she has adopted, and one which she has claimed for those women who would follow.

Maintaining Distance

In addition to supplanting the male explorer figure (represented by Sawyer) with her own persona, in *Journeys* Bird Bishop also establishes a strong narrative presence with the creation of a particularly confident voice. She projects the voice of a businesslike, nononsense, experienced traveler who has to put up with much from weather and local customs but is determined to proceed unperturbed because she is adding to a body of knowledge about the geography and nature of an unexplored area. She knows exactly what she needs on her travel and comes well equipped with letters of introduction to British government officials. Her narrative begins with the first order of business, which is to obtain a native servant and translator. Although she brought along a Persian citizen with her from India, she rejects him during the voyage as being too Europeanized, "a man of truly refined feeling and manners, but hopelessly out of place" (1:4). She feels he would be out of place because he is a gentleman and, thus, inadequate for camp roughness. The message is clear that Bird Bishop's endurance is greater than that of an urban dweller, even a man. She requires as a traveling companion an unusually rugged individual. An underlying consideration may also be that a servant too familiar with European customs would remind her that she was not conforming to the behavior expected of a lady and Bird Bishop needed to be free from such reminders while traveling. Gentility was something she would later incorporate in her narrative, not a condition she wished to work under.

Following a pattern she uses in many of her travel books, Bird Bishop settles on a companion who embodies some sort of uncivilized aspect. In this travel, she chooses a man she calls Hadji and gives his credentials: speaks six languages, escorted horses presented to Queen Victoria, been ten times to Mecca. His appearance is particularly pleasing (although he later proved uncooperative). Unlike the rejected dandy in "snowy collar and cuffs," Hadji is "a big, wild-looking Arab in a rough *abba* and a big turban, with a long knife and a revolver in his girdle," not, as Bird Bishop comments, "a lady's servant" (1: 5). Hadji is one of several native men Bird Bishop hires who serves as a reflection of aspects of Bird Bishop's personality which she cannot acknowledge directly in her narration and still claim the title of lady. Rather, she cultivates and admires the foreign and what she perceives as wild, that is, non-British, in those with whom she chose to travel.[75]

Despite her initial fascination with native servants, Bird Bishop tends to keep them and others at a distance in her text. Barr concludes that her "instinct was to fly from the threat of any intimate personal entanglement," while complaining that the presence of others was emotionally exhausting.[76] Indeed, social functions made her ill with headaches and nervous attacks. Such reactions may be explained by Bird Bishop's intense self-consciousness when in the presence of other Europeans. However, besides this personal reaction, there was also the narrative problem of how to present the presence of others.

We have seen the rhetorical strategies Bird Bishop used to marginalize Sawyer's presence in *Journeys*. More generally, most women travelers had to exercise some care in identifying the presence of others, especially if the people mentioned were likely to read or hear of the account. The general assumption for women writers is that, when possible, they will praise hosts or companions in deference to the expectation identified by Virginia Woolf as being the "Angel in the House." If the writer wished to escape this convention, she had the option of not identifying the others with whom she had contact. Wollstonecraft and Martineau, for example, practiced selection in whom they identified on their travels.

The issue of whom to identify became more complex when the woman was unchaperoned and traveling with groups of native men, as were Bird Bishop and Kingsley. Victorian women travel writers had to be careful how they presented this situation so that their reputations at home would not be damaged. In *A Lady's Life,* Bird Bishop allows her concern for and romance with a man she calls "Mountain Jim" (who died shortly after she left), to be apparent in her text. He was a colorful local character and was easily identified as Jim Nugent. While this relationship obviously increased the sales of this book (her most popular publication), such attention undermined her dignity as a professional traveler. Possibly in response to public speculation over her involvement with Nugent, in her later books Bird Bishop kept descriptions of her relationships with others at arm's length. At times, she will mention encountering someone who has been robbed or is in need of medical attention. When this happens, she generally describes the situation, provides care if she can, and then moves on, neither making any further mention nor attempting to tie up loose ends in her text, suggesting in her movement and distancing a commitment to maintaining a focus on herself in her travels.

Rather than people, her personal attention is reserved for her horses, of which she had a series, named Birdie, Gyalpo, Screw, and Boy. Each one was a vividly described distinct character whose presence helped differentiate each major stage of her travels. While we may speculate over the underlying psychological implications of a woman's passion for horses, it should be pointed out that horses are a safe object for affection and a way of distracting readers from awkward questions about both European traveling companions such as Sawyer and the many young male native servants she employed.

Resisting Feminine and Exotic Discourse

In addition to strategies of avoidance and distraction as means of maintaining the conventional respectability of her persona, Bird Bishop also resisted situations where she would be expected to behave in a conventional feminine manner that could undercut her scientific authority. A common role for women travelers, especially to

the Mideast, was that of nurse, or more precisely, a purveyor of
British medicines. The presence of a woman in dangerous places
could be made more palatable to British conventions by emphasizing her role as ministering to the illness of others, and indeed many
women in the Mideast used nursing activities to give their travel
an appropriate service rationale. An extension of the nurturing role
women were expected to assume, this would be perceived as a natural behavior for women. While Bird Bishop is supposedly traveling
for the humanitarian purpose of establishing medical missions in
addition to reporting back her observations of the landscape, she
also resists the assumption that her primary duty is nursing and she
is sufficiently confident of her own authority in her travels to complain of this expectation.

Although Bird Bishop was better trained than many British
women who had established a tradition of passing out drugs while
traveling, she repeatedly states that she is not a real "Hakim" as she
is repeatedly overwhelmed by requests for aid at each camp stop,
not to mention calls to provide such veterinary care as sewing up
horses injured in the periodic horse fights. Obviously, her medical
supplies could not satisfy the number of requests she records and
she seems to have been gathering local herbs and making her own
compounds to refill the pharmaceutical bottles. While she is committed to providing help, especially for the eye infections she felt
she could effectively treat, she refuses to place much weight on her
service. Unlike Duff Gordon, who happily saw herself as a medical
savior to "her people," Bird Bishop had no desire to allow this
common feminine duty to form a significant part of her narrative
identity in the book; she was an explorer/naturalist, not a nurse.

Even as she traveled for the cause of medical missionaries, then,
Bird Bishop actively resisted being either medic or missionary.
Most nineteenth-century women's travel accounts in the Mideast
suggest some kind of pilgrimage, but Bird Bishop resists this trope.
(Even Martineau's *Eastern Life*, for example, has been described as
a pilgrimage toward atheism.)[77] Although in *Journeys in Persia*
Bird Bishop is traveling in lands which, considering her religious
upbringing, would resonate with Biblical connotations and her
avowed purpose for traveling is at least tinged with religious motivation, there are fewer Biblical references than might be expected.
Occasionally, she makes a comment which, in linking Biblical quotations to what she observes, clarifies or challenges European understandings of Christian texts; however, she does not dwell on or
pursue such connections. For example, she observes that the mule
caravan's lodgings, where the travelers camped out in cave-like

rooms built into the walls of the manure-encrusted stables, was probably more like Christ's birthplace than the clean pastoral image of a crib of straw in a barn like those which compose European Christmas scenes. But such observations pass quickly. She merely states, "Such must have been the inn at Bethlehem, and surely the first step to the humiliation of 'the death of the cross' must have been the birth in the manger, amidst the crowd and horrors of such a stable" (1:82–83). This observation may have been quite disrupting to Bird Bishop as the daughter of a minister, but the text continues to focus on her own discomfort in such lodging and any further religious implications remain unspoken. The accompanying illustration merely shows unoccupied windowless niches in the walls, helpful in understanding the layout of the stables, although it is also a picture which does not call attention to the potentially disrupting speculations made in the text about Christ's birthplace. This drawing presents a sanitized picture and avoids visually representing the crowd of people and animals trying to bed down for the night described in her text and which she suggests characterized the Biblical context (1:82). In another situation, she comes upon a mysterious "manna" being gathered from leaves in Armenia (*Journeys* 2:351), but makes no attempt to link this manna with the Biblical manna from heaven. She merely describes the phenomena and its use objectively, then moves on. Bird Bishop is not interested in challenging conventional understandings of Christian texts or in showing herself involved in a spiritual quest. Rather, such observations are simply sidelights to the important task of traveling and reporting back information to geographic societies, information which will be valued in case of future involvement of the British empire in Mideast affairs. Her focus is now professional and is centered on her task.

As an additional divergence from conventional feminine discourse, Bird Bishop chose to emphasize daily hardship and discomfort to a greater degree than most women travel writers in order to establish the difference and authority of her observations. In general, *Journeys in Persia* is filled with an unusually large number of complaints. These are not complaints made for political or ideological purposes, such as voiced by Trollope, but are the grumblings of an obviously wet, cold, and disgusted woman who is being hindered in her progress. As such, they are curiously refreshing, making the upbeat tone of the earlier *Golden Chersonese* seem forced. While women travel writers generally did not dwell on negative aspects of the travel experience, Bird Bishop was an exception. She did not enjoy a series of nights spent in crowded stables in winter and had no hesitation in describing a village as "a compound of foul, green ditches, piles of dissolving manure" (1:81) where they slept in a building with floors "deep with the manure of ages" (1:82), and were given tea made with water from a "broken ditch full of slimy greenish water" (1:83). The experience was such that she admitted to having "a lingering prejudice against sharing a den with a quantity of human beings, mules, asses, poultry, and dogs" (1:94). At the same time, she gives no indication that she regrets her decision to make this journey. She states that "though I exercise the privilege of grumbling at the hardships, I ought not to complain of them, though they are enough to break down the strongest men," and admits, "I really like the journey" (1:147). Here she is making it quite clear that she was undergoing an ordeal beyond the tourist experience, and thus earned the "privilege" of complaining as a serious explorer/naturalist who was going into areas which were "blank on the maps" (1:146).

She also quickly lost patience with previous travel descriptions that emphasized the exotic. Indeed, whereas conventionally a book on traveling through the Mideast would promise to British readers a warm, erotically-charged atmosphere, the first two hundred pages of *Journeys in Persia* are concerned with tramping through snow, dealing with freezing conditions, and staying in a series of huts and stables, each seeming worse than the one before. Scenes which were described as "favourable" by others, she found to be "absolutely hideous and uninteresting" (1:101). One city, Kerrind, she observed "is either grotesquely or picturesquely situated" (1:93), and the impression is that Bird Bishop, out of a sense of general annoyance, is more likely to side with the grotesque. She was distancing herself now from the aesthetic travel description. It is almost as if she is finding relief in the outpouring of what normally would not be expressible by women writers but which, as a professional, she could now indulge.

In addition to voicing complaints and irritations which generally had been left out of women's writing, Bird Bishop also showed herself to be physically engaged both with rough travel and with serious risks. During her later travels, she went further and further into central Asia, even to Tibet. In her accounts, she generally is on horseback; occasionally she walks by her horse when footing is treacherous. Sometimes, as in Persia, she has to be helped off her mount because she is frozen and exhausted. But her complaints of discomfort are usually directed more to the evening lodging than discomfort while traveling.

Even though she does record serious mishaps which Martineau, sensing the taboo against women (or at least ladies) being in dangerous situations, would hesitate to mention, the general impression Bird Bishop gives in her writing is dignified and composed. When mishaps do occur (and she was frequently thrown from her mount), it is stated matter-of-factly and distanced through use of the passive voice: "I was thrown from my horse into soft mud" (*Journeys* 1:173). Fear or comments about how the situation could have been worse are avoided.

Her description of one particularly dangerous spill in *Among the Tibetans* works simultaneously to show her own courage while rhetorically reducing the immediacy of danger. Avoiding any charges of poor judgment, Bird Bishop indicates that others in the party recommended that she cross the Shayok river in Tibet on a heavy-bodied horse. But the current proved to be too strong for the animal, and in an effort to make the bank, the horse "fell short and rolled over backwards in the Shayok with his rider under him" (76). This left Bird Bishop trapped under the horse in the water. There was, she reports,

> [a] struggle, a moment of suffocation, and I was extricated by strong arms, to be knocked down again by the rush of the water, to be again dragged up and hauled and hoisted up the crumbling bank. I escaped with a broken rib and some severe bruises, but the horse was drowned. Mr. Redslob [the local missionary], who had thought that my life could not be saved, and the Tibetans were so distressed by the accident that I made very light of it, and only took one day of rest. . . . Such risks are among the amenities of the great trade route from India into Central Asia! (76–78)

The physical stress and injuries received by Bird Bishop are downplayed here. When she is trapped under the horse, she distances herself from the climax of the mishap by using the third person pronoun rather than the first person used in the rest of the passage. Additionally, emphasis on her own danger is deflected by such comments as "the horse drowned" and concern over the effect of her accident on others. The situation might have been elaborated upon more. But whatever feelings of terror or later pain that could have been mentioned are bypassed in the narrative in favor of bringing to the forefront Bird Bishop's courage and endurance, strengths which required her to need but "one day of rest" to recover.

In many ways Bird Bishop's long travel career defied the conventional view of the physical and mental capabilities of women travelers, yet she remained essentially noncontroversial and acceptable to the scientific community. This allowed even the most traditional and masculine-oriented scientific societies to view her as a potentially valuable member. Over her writing career, Bird Bishop's goals became more focused as the range of her travel became more ambitious. While she was able to expose her armchair readers to more of the trouble and dirt of travel and to present her narratives as essentially solitary endeavors even when others accompanied her, she also kept her emotional responses in check and presented a dignified and controlled persona.

Although women would soon be edged out of scientific societies, Bird Bishop showed them that a woman was not physically limited in her fieldwork and that she could venture anywhere a man could so long as she had control over her transportation. The sheer length of her travels also indicated that a woman did not have to be part of an expedition or very wealthy to contribute to a scientific endeavor. These lessons would serve Kingsley as she, too, attempted to bootstrap her way into the scientific community via her travels in West Africa.

5

Mary H. Kingsley:
In Pursuit of Fish and Fetish

IN SOME WAYS, MARY H. KINGSLEY'S *TRAVELS IN WEST AFRICA: CONGO Français, Corisco and Cameroons* (1897) presents a culmination of a tradition of women's naturalist travel writing which arose to take advantage of a new sphere of activity, one which had not yet been firmly identified with a particular gender. Additionally, her travels ended the era of naturalist exploration that operated separately from organized scientific projects. In Clare Lloyd's *The Travelling Naturalists,* for example, Kingsley is presented as ending an era of naturalist exploration.[1] After the late eighteenth century, as government involvement with the direction of scientific research and exploration increased, who would speak in the name of science became more and more narrowly defined and, in the process, more masculine-identified. By the time of Kingsley's travels, the Victorian doctrine of "separate spheres" for men and women had not only become fixed, but (especially after *Origin*) had received scientific endorsement as deep-seated fears of women's emancipation became one of the bases for predictions of a degenerative trend in evolution.[2] This had an impact on women whom, for various reasons, felt professional loyalty to scientific institutions and who wished to be accepted by professional societies. I believe the tenor of the time required these women to present in their narratives the contradictory positions of supporting the separate spheres doctrine, while simultaneously carrying on activities that challenged such beliefs. In particular, Kingsley's writings display the tension resulting from the contradictory pressures of such a narrative position.

As traditional with Victorian naturalists, Kingsley worked in more than one area of specialty. She was an independent field naturalist with loose connections to the British Museum, who helped support her travels by collecting freshwater fish and other small specimens for biologists in Britain. She discovered new species of fish (which were named after her). Additionally, she engaged in the study of West African religious beliefs, especially those that were related to women's lives, information that was generally not available to male anthropologists. She was seen as expert enough by James Frazer, considered a founder of modern anthropology, to be cited as a source for his *The Golden Bough* (although she was less than enthusiastic about Frazer's work). Contemporary criticisms could not dismiss her work; it was too solid. Rather Alfred Lyall in the *Edinburgh Review* had to categorize her work as having lesser value because she was a collector naturalist, rather than a theorist who worked from data collected by others.[3] As with Bird Bishop, Kingsley quickly became entangled in the colonial politics of the area and eventually transferred her energies to focus on questions of colonial governance. However, also like Bird Bishop, she worked within the constraints of the scientific societies, eventually establishing a reputation solid enough to found a professional society devoted to African studies. In the process, Kingsley created the image of the woman naturalist explorer in the British mind. It was, admittedly, a caricature, but it was a caricature she formed for her own purposes, and one which defined what a woman explorer was like. At the same time, Kingsley's travel narratives are disruptive of many nineteenth-century discipline norms that drove scientific methodology, especially in anthropology and ethnology, but even in zoology. As Julie English Early put it: "Decidedly captivating and decidedly odd, Kingsley was clearly adept at performing herself, but also at performing science. Kingsley's critics perhaps registered only imperfectly that the self-performance that brought her a popular audience was intrinsic to her critique of disciplinarity."[4]

Along with the need to reckon with evolutionary speculation over sexual roles in Victorian science, Kingsley also had to deal with beliefs about race more explicitly than earlier women travelers. In her writing, both gender and race became interconnected as she took on male exploratory roles in her travels which needed to be presented narratively as feminized or otherwise discursively destabilized through humor. At the same time, as Alison Blunt[5] and Dea Birkett[6] indicate, Kingsley's assumed racial superiority as a European traveling in colonized Africa superseded her home-based sense of gender inferiority; and this position gave her unusual authority and access to traditionally masculine activities, while it also restricted her ability to identify with African women in her writing. As a result, she often took contradictory stands on issues of racial superiority, attempting, for example, simultaneously to validate native African culture and legal structure and to defend British imperial practices.

Like Bird Bishop, Martineau, and Wollstonecraft, Kingsley used the travel writing genre as a means of obtaining authority through personal experience, then parlayed these credentials to bolster her entrance into scientific discourse. Her narrative also shows some similar motifs found in Martineau's and Wollstonecraft's travels. She, too, was a solitary traveler who presented herself narratively as traveling alone for the purpose of further knowledge and who used her access to the domestic sphere and domestic images to validate her own travel expertise. Her goals were similar in that she wished to obtain scientific authority and, thus, her rhetoric needed to reflect the changing image of science in nineteenth-century Britain.

As noted earlier, in order to compare and evaluate writing anxiety and authorial tension in different historical periods, attention should be paid to the social limitations and economic pressures under which each individual writer worked. In this regard, Kingsley occupied a social position similar to Wollstonecraft and Martineau. While initially there was a tendency for critics to see her as occupying a privileged position in Victorian society as the niece of Charles Kingsley (a highly influential author and Canon of Westminster), more recent biographical research has shown that her hold on gentility was more tenuous.[7] Her travel writing and lectures made a major difference in her income and she had hoped they would finance her future travel.

While Martineau and Wollstonecraft are primarily known for non-travel writings, Kingsley's reputation rests on her *Travels in West Africa*, an account of her 1895 excursion to Gabon and Cameroon, during which she collected small animal specimens, especially freshwater fish, and observed native religious beliefs. Her purpose, as she stated, was to collect "fish and fetish."[8] This work, along with her later *West African Studies* (1899), shows the strong contradictions and anxieties of a woman who is working within a masculine scientific discourse and yet outside it, maneuvering around and making use of a feminine discourse in ways which support male authority without undermining her own authoritative stance. She downplays her personal danger through satiric self-deprecation and paints images of tropical Africa as domestic and, thus, a natural locale for a woman traveler. Beneath this appearance of control, there are also revelations of severe depression and suicidal thoughts as Kingsley, at times, feels driven to tempt fate, knowing the odds of her survival in Africa are slim. She presents herself as a sort of martyr, or perhaps a sacrifice, both for scientific endeavors and for the future of developing colonial Africa.

As such, her account forms part of a pattern of Victorian women's search for a vocation under the auspices of science and through the instrument of travel. Since many proponents of science distanced their organizations from women's active involvement in the 1890s, it was difficult for women to find inclusion in scientific endeavors. This situation is apparent in the intense tension and striking contradictions in Kingsley's narration. Kingsley has in many ways been an elusive writer, one not easily fitted into a modern critic's sense of women and colonialism, as Sara Mills readily admits. While she conforms to conventional expectations for feminine and colonial discourse and can be supportive of the status quo, at the same time she subverts both. Mills concludes that "Kingsley's text, rather than being a 'feminine' text or a 'colonial' text or for that matter a 'feminist' text, seems to be caught up in the contradictory clashes of these discourses one with another. No stable position can finally be given to the text."[9] Eva-Marie Kröller concurs, pointing out that "[f]rom a feminist perspective, Kingsley's befuddled pose may at times be exasperating. . . ."[10] Yet, at the same time, Kingsley is a highly original and lively writer; her humor is on the level of Mark Twain in its moments of dark self-denigration and like Twain, she was at odds with Christianity and thought most missionary activities in Africa did more harm than good.[11]

Also, more than any other woman traveler, Kingsley formed the public image of the Victorian spinster traveler as a naturalist. She gave several public talks, almost performances, purposely playing up for humorous effect the contrast between an old-fashioned decorum and dress and the swamps, mud, and crocodiles she encountered. Two extant cartoons drawn by audience members during a debate she led in Cambridge in 1899 indicate the contrast between her activity in Africa and her presentation at home.[12] Labeled "Anticipation" and "Realisation," the first shows a young woman in military attire and short skirt, a pistol in one hand and a saber in the other, suggesting an unconventional and aggressive "New Woman" explorer, consistent with the view of Kingsley which a reader might form from her activity in Africa. The second figure, "Realisation," expresses the audience member's disappointment with the conventional appearance which Kingsley was careful to cultivate in public to offset the nonconformist elements of her travel. This is a sketch of an old bespectacled woman engaged in specimen collecting, hunched with a butterfly net over the shoulder, poking at a large beetle with a walking stick, and wearing an ankle-length skirt.[13] The appearance of conventional femininity, which this cartoon points to, was very important for Kingsley to maintain in public; yet her

Mary Kingsley. From *West African Studies* (London, 1899).

accounts also reveal that the privacy afforded by being outside European gaze was an immense liberation since she could discard the socially constructed feminine facade and assume a male explorer persona in the jungle, a role indicated by the first drawing.

While Kingsley's work was both popular with a general audience and treated with respect within scholarly circles, her position in Victorian intellectual history became obscured and was diverted into British imperial propaganda when she was declared a martyr after her death at the age of thirty-seven while serving as a volunteer nurse for Boer prisoners of war in 1900.[14] Rudyard Kipling wrote a memorial for her and mentioned her in one of his lesser poems, "Dirge of Dead Sisters" (1902), dedicated to "the Nurses who died in the South African War." In this poem Kingsley appears as "Her that fell at Simon's Town in service on our foes."[15] While not well known in the U.S., Kingsley achieved a place in British girls' literature as a self-sacrificing heroine, similar to Florence Nightingale, and as a representative figure of the female explorer.

MacDonald Educational published a children's biography of Kingsley, *Mary Kingsley the Explorer*, in 1975 as part of their Starter series of reading primers.[16] In this series, Kingsley joins Joan of Arc and Anna Pavlova as the only female representatives of a historical spectrum of people ranging from Hannibal to Cousteau. She is "the Explorer" as Jesse James is "the Outlaw," Thomas Edison, "the Inventor," and Cousteau, "the Diver," an ironic emblematic figure of what she actually satired in her African accounts—the daring penetrator of the wilderness.

Her martyrdom led to an unusual postmortem recognition, as the Royal African Society (a society she helped develop) was founded in her name in 1901. The *Journal of the African Society* bore Kingsley's image on the title page until the 1923/24 issue, when it was replaced by an image of the African continent.[17] Although Kingsley spoke out against women's admission to professional societies and against women's suffrage in general, the Royal African Society admitted women from the time of its foundation.[18] Through this society, Kingsley obtained a level of recognition which was denied to Wollstonecraft, Martineau, and Bird Bishop. However, to achieve this, she had to distance herself from increasingly vocal feminist movements during her lifetime.

"HAVING ONCE BEEN MADE A FELLOW BY THE COUNCIL": WOMEN AND THE RGS

Shortly before Kingsley first left for Africa, women, as mentioned earlier, began to be admitted to the Royal Geographical Society as full fellows. Although twenty-two women, Bird Bishop among them, were allowed to attach the letters F.R.G.S. (Fellow of the Royal Geographical Society) to their names,[19] this was out of a membership of over three thousand. Such a change in membership rules offered greater respect and recognition for women travelers. However, in 1893, this decision was rescinded as a result of a concerted effort by a few members, who also attempted to unseat those who had just been admitted. While this action has been discussed from the viewpoint of Bird Bishop's involvement, here I will return to the topic in order to discuss its broader relationship to a growing anti-"New Woman" movement.

An anonymous letter in the *Times* on 29 May 1893 signed "A Bona Fide Traveller," made this unseating attempt public and called on members to prevent the move against women's membership. This letter forced those who did not want women as members to defend their views in responding letters. Part of the rationale for the rescindment was that women by definition were incapable of adding to scientific knowledge. On 31 May, Curzon stated in a letter to *The Times*,[20]

> We contest *in toto* the general capability of women to contribute to scientific geographical knowledge. Their sex and training render them equally unfitted for exploration; and the genus of professional female globe-trotters with which America has lately familiarized us is one of the horrors of the latter end of the 19th century. In our teeth are thrown the names of one or two distinguished ladies, such as Mrs. Bishop, whose additions to geographical knowledge have been valuable and serious. But in the whole of England these ladies can be counted on the fingers of one hand; and in the entire range of modern geography I question if history will preserve the names of half that number.[21]

After this somewhat self-fulfilling prophecy from Curzon, *Punch*, which since its founding had delighted in attacking folly committed in the name of science, represented the attempt to oust the women members and the defeat of that attempt in two comic verses. The first was published on 10 June 1893:[22]

TO THE ROYAL GEOGRAPHICAL SOCIETY[23]
["Sir," said Mr. Pickwick, "you are a fellow."]

Ye Admirals, who brave for us the battle and the breeze,
What meaneth all this hitching of your trousers?
Why are timbers to be shivered, what makes you ill at ease,
Ye briny, tarry, glim-destroying dousers?

Has Britain lost an ironclad, that makes you pipe your eye?
Have reefs been found improperly projecting?
Has a hundred-tonner burst and blown a company sky-high,
Whose remains will take a week in the collecting?

Has France destroyed our commerce? Has Russia burnt our towns,
That ye rage in all this nautical commotion?

Has a Dutchman, curse his broomstick, gone and anchored in the
Downs?
Has a Yankee fleet outfought us on the ocean?

Then an Admiral made answer, and gloomy was his face,
And his voice was like the booming of a 'cello,
"Avast there with your fooling; there's a lady in the case,
A lady whom they want to make a Fellow.

"A lady an explorer? a traveller in skirts?
The notion's just a trifle too seraphic:
Let them stay and mind the babies, or hem our ragged shirts;
But they mustn't, can't, and shan't be geographic."

And still the salts are fuming, and still the ladies sit,
Though their presence makes these tars, who women trounce, ill
For no woman, bless her petticoats, will ever budge a bit,
Having once been made a Fellow by the Council.

As *Punch's* poem indicates, the presence of women was primarily
challenged by naval members such as Admiral Cave and Admiral
M'Clintock who associated exploration with military culture. Attempts to unseat those women who had been installed failed and
Punch followed on 17 June with "The Admirals' Doom," satirical
lyrics set to the tune of "The Admiral's Broom," celebrating the
Earl of Mayo and Sir John Lubbock (also president of the Anthropological Society) as ones who did

> ". . . let those hectoring admirals know
> Science slays not chiv-al-ree!
> They fancy they'll get their way,
> But the Twenty-two shall stay.
> When they swear they'll sweep out the ladies—like black sheep,
> 'Tis a game more than three can play!"
> Then he [Mayo] blazed away at those Admirals gay,
> 'Till he made their jibs to fall;
> Then he hoisted the flag of the women (a "Red Rag"),
> And cried to his merry Fellows all—
> "This vote is a proof," cried he,
> "That science from poor prejudice is free,
> And that women who *do* know, and globe-trotting bravely go,
> Are fit 'Fellows' for you and for me!"
>
> Chorus of chivalrous F.R.G.S.'s—
> For *she's* a jolly good Fellow,
> And so say *most* of us!

Despite these public encouragements, by the time Kingsley returned from her second African trip, it was evident that a backlash had begun.[24] While the twenty-two women who had been admitted were allowed to stay, no more women would be admitted and this remained the situation until November 1912. As Kingsley worked on her travels, she had to take this regression in women's professional access into account.

This particular occurrence with the RGS was also mirrored in a growing anti-suffragette movement. The 1890s New Woman movement was part of the fin-de-siècle revolt against traditional values which differed from previous woman's movements in its emphasis on personal self-determination, not just political rights.[25] The movement to counter this increased social independence for women was led by Eliza Lynn Linton. Lynn Linton wrote a series of articles in the *Fortnightly Review* from 1887–89 on the history of women from classical Greece to the nineteenth century arguing that women's involvement in political activity led to national decline.[26] She concluded, "The rule of women becomes the precursor, as it is the signs of general decay. Society becomes disorganized, undisciplined, individualized, and falls to pieces."[27] She joined Mrs. Humphrey Ward in signing "An Appeal Against Female Suffrage," published in the *Nineteenth Century* in June 1889. In 1895 she found in women travelers a symbol of this disturbing trend; she heaped scorn on "globetrotting adventuresses" who traveled to remote areas, especially female missionaries who, in their attempt to improve the condition of women in other cultures (especially in the Mideast), were making "all women as restless and discontented as themselves."[28]

BECOMING A NATURALIST

As with all the women travelers in this study, I am emphasizing the interest and achievement of women in nineteenth-century scientific endeavors and examining the strategic maneuverings they performed in order to be taken seriously in a masculine intellectual world. I assume therefore that Kingsley was genuinely interested in her scientific activities. While this may be a given when discussing the writings of a man, it tends to be challenged in women's work. Birkett, for example, in her biography of Kingsley, contends that Kingsley's naturalist activities were a mere front to make her look more respectable. According to Birkett, Kingsley came back from her first trip with "an impressive collection of fish, flies, beetles,

Engravings of fish named for her, from Mary Kingsley's collection. From *Travels in West Africa* (London, 1897).

plants and geological specimens that she used as a disguise for her wonderfully self-indulgent 'skylarking' on the Coast. She was, she would argue, 'collecting,' a respectable pastime for a middle-class spinster, and could show her specimens to prove it."[29] I do not suggest that Kingsley did not have mixed motives in her travel: collecting was a way of justifying travel. But there is no evidence that her activity was simply a facade. Intelligent collecting requires knowledge of the field and a sense of what to look for. Kingsley had sufficient knowledge to properly choose, preserve, and transport specimens that had not been described before in Britain.

There is every indication that Kingsley had the sort of childhood that can produce a naturalist. Such scientific interests ran in her family, as is often the case, as evidenced by her father's ethnology and travels and the abundance of interest in natural history shown by a couple of her uncle, Charles Kingsley's, books: *Water Babies* (1863) and *Glaucus: Or the Wonders of the Shore* (1855). Additionally, her home life did not display the well-regulated routine valued in Victorian society that served to reinforce behavior proper for women. Her father, George Kingsley, was frequently gone for years at a time, leaving financial control of family affairs to his younger brother, who had his own marriage problems. Kingsley's mother, like some madwoman in the attic, stayed holed up in a house with bricked-up windows, going slowly insane. Instead of a parent, Kingsley had her father's large collection of travel and science books and a collection of travel souvenirs. Isolated, ignored, and self-educated, she was at liberty to follow her own inclinations.

Chance, rather than a planned regime, gave Kingsley her exposure to science and travel. When her father was home, she seemed to view him as much a nuisance as a parent, because he took over the library. She recounted one incident when both father and daughter simultaneously wanted to read Norman Lockyer's *Solar Physics* (she hid it).[30] The *in loco parentis,* Henry Kingsley, was author of twenty-one books including *Ravenshoe* (1862) and *Geoffrey Hamlyn* (1859), based on his experiences gold mining in the Australian outback, and he was another source of information about foreign flora and fauna. Her mother apparently kept several pets, as indicated by one visitor's complaint that all the chairs were occupied by cats.[31] Kingsley, herself, identified with animals. Even in Africa, she sought comfort by taking household cats to bed with her. With no close supervision as a young girl and inspired by George Craik's *Pursuit of Knowledge under Difficulties*, and a magazine called the *English Mechanic*, a mass-circulation science journal found in 1865 for a largely working-class readers who exchanged views and information in its pages,[32] she experimented with machinery and kept fighting cocks.

She also took science lessons from a neighbor, C. F. Varley, an electrical engineer.[33] When her brother Charles entered Cambridge, the family was moved in order to be closer to him, which placed Kingsley, at the age of twenty-four, in contact with the academic life centered around the pioneering women's college, Girton.

To substantiate her dismissal of Kingsley's collecting, Birkett also states that she "seldom fished" and that most of her specimens were obtained from the field by Africans for payment.[34] Despite this portrayal of the use of native collectors as some sort of cheat, Kingsley's collecting procedure was fairly standard. Male naturalists did (and still do) the same thing.[35] Natives usually know their environment better than strangers and know where to look.[36] The quickness to suspect that, if a woman is involved, somehow procedures will not be properly followed, even if men are doing the same thing, is simply a version of the belief that women are incapable of scientific rigor. However, even in Birkett's generally antagonistic biography, there are indications of Kingsley's serious involvement in methodical collecting. Birkett mentions that Kingsley would carefully record what she observed during long walks in West Africa, that she even managed to ship a driver ants' nest to the British Museum. When Birkett opened one letter from Kingsley to Albert Günther, the taxonomist she was corresponding with at the British Museum, "a stem of pressed grass and a moth, with a note attached reading 'moth mimicking bird's dropping,' fell out."[37] The energy she spent recording, collecting, and shipping, and her awareness of the importance of camouflage and mimicry according to Darwinian theory, all suggest that Kingsley's scientific interests were as genuine as those of any other Victorian naturalist. Even today, despite such assessments as Birkett's, Kingsley is one of the few women travelers who are acknowledged to have been scientific. In one book on traveling Victorian naturalists, Kingsley is the only woman mentioned in depth.[38] More recently, Kingsley has attracted increasing attention, especially from geographical societies who have found in her writings and professional activities indications of the difficulties of understanding both women's roles in the implementation of Victorian imperialism and women's membership in scientific societies.[39]

Escaping to Africa

In terms of the rigid Victorian class standards that dictated much of nineteenth-century social life, Kingsley was born into a difficult position.[40] The family was not wealthy and Kingsley's father, George, while he held a medical degree, did not sustain a practice but seemed devoted to a rather ingenious dilettante way of life. He made his way as a professional companion/traveler, accompanying healthy globe-trotting aristocrats as a personal physician. Although George Kingsley was both a member of the Linnaean Society and the Royal Microscopic Society and was involved in numerous projects at his employers' massive libraries, he seldom brought any of his projects to completion. [41]

Kingsley's birth was not planned and she was nearly illegitimate; she lied about her age to cover up the fact that she was born only four days after her parents' marriage. While the date of her birth could be hidden, however, Kingsley's mother, Mary Bailey (formerly George's housekeeper and the daughter of an innkeeper), still represented a social fault which was not forgivable in Victorian society, especially since she had a pronounced cockney accent which Kingsley picked up and could never shake. Most probably, as a result of this forced and socially unequal marriage, Kingsley's father stayed abroad as much as possible and her mother isolated herself in illness. Uneasy in her class identification, Kingsley had to form her own place in society and eventually support herself and her brother Charles, who was well educated but lacked drive and, like his father, tended not to complete projects. Later on, completing their father's book, a project which Charles, as the male heir, was expected to assume, became a continual area of conflict between the two siblings. She eventually took it over and finished it.

Although Kingsley seldom explicitly voiced complaints about the unfair treatment she received as a woman, the lack of access to education did rankle, especially since Charles did little with his schooling. She said the only education her father paid for was her German lessons so she could help with his work in ethnology, while $2,000 was spent on her brother.[42] This inequity was pointed to by Virginia Woolf in her essay on women's education in *Three Guineas*.[43] Kingsley also received some medical training so as to provide nursing services for family members. As her parents aged (they were both in their mid-thirties when Kingsley was born), her life became centered on caring for them. Her mother's mental state worsened and she became paralyzed after a stroke in 1890. Her father was finally forced to stay home as an invalid. The stress on Kingsley was enormous. A friend and independent scholar, Lucy Toulmin Smith, recommended demanding study as a means of finding mental relief, so Kingsley studied Latin, Arabic, and Syrian. In these endeavors she was aided by other intellectually oriented women (in addition to Smith) who were her neighbors in Cambridge: Hatty Johnson, Clara Skeat, Agnes Smith Lewis, and Violet Paget Roy.[44]

In 1892, everything suddenly changed when her parents died within ten weeks of each other, leaving Kingsley with her brother. Kingsley was expected to be her brother's housekeeper and to nurse other family members, but when Charles went off to Asia, she left on her first trip to Africa.

USE OF PUBLIC ACCOMMODATION

While Kingsley never groveled before male authority figures to the extent that Mrs. Trollope did, she did carefully acknowledge male figures in her writing more so than did the other travel writers of this study, a gesture that suggests she was honoring a well-entrenched separate spheres ideology. Closer examination of the biographical accounts, however, complicates such readings. References to male family members do conform to traditional role expectations for women. Kingsley, as was expected of a Victorian daughter and sister, did what she could to support the public reputation of her father and brother. She initially justified her traveling as a duty in continuing her father's work and submerged her own autobiographical writing in a biography of her father. Similarly, she dedicated *Travels* to her brother, although his contributions were minimal. (He failed to even finish compiling its index.)

Her relationship with Henry Guillemard, a friend of her father's, who was supposed to be her editor, is also typical of her care always to praise the men with whom she worked. The preface to *Travels* begins typically with Kingsley downplaying her abilities:

> To the Reader—What this book wants is not a simple Preface but an apology, and a very brilliant and convincing one at that. Recognising this fully, and feeling quite incompetent to write such a masterpiece, I have asked several literary friends to write one for me, but they have kindly but firmly declined, stating that it is impossible satisfactorily to apologise for my liberties with Lindley Murray and the Queen's English. (vii)

This is a conventional beginning within the tradition of feminine discourse: Kingsley is making excuses for writing directly under her own name. She then continues to acknowledge Guillemard's help, but something changes enroute as she establishes her narrative persona even in the midst of downplaying her own writing:

I am therefore left to make a feeble apology for this book myself, and all I can personally say is that it would have been much worse than it is had it not been for Dr. Henry Guillemard, who has not edited it, or of course the whole affair would have been better, but who has most kindly gone through the proof sheets, lassoing prepositions which were straying outside their sentence stockade, taking my eye off the water cask and fixing it on the scenery where I meant it to be, saying firmly in pencil on margins "No you don't," when I was committing some more than usually heinous literary crime, and so on. (vii–viii)

In the passage, Kingsley starts praising Guillemard while at the same time clarifying and delineating the limits of his contributions. In the process, she indicates how limited his services actually were. While Kingsley states that the work would have been better if he *had* edited it, this is also a diplomatic way of stating he *did not* edit the work. This point is important when we realize that Guillemard and Kingsley actually struggled over control of *Travels*. Guillemard originally did edit the book. He attempted to rewrite her prose, substituting more formalized and Latinized language (what Kingsley called "Guillemardese").[45] He, in turn, would later refer to her writing as the "undammable logorrhea of Kingsleyese."[46] After eight months, Kingsley called off the arrangement. She wrote to Guillemard privately, telling him,

Your corrections stand on stilts out of the swamps and give a very quaint but patchy aspect to the affair so that I do not know my way about it at all. I never meant you to take this delicate labour over the thing but only to arrange it and tell me point blank if I was lying about scientific subjects. I would rather have the rest of the stuff published as it stands. I have no literary character to lose at present and no ambition to gain one.[47]

There is no indication of these struggles in the preface, nor of Kingsley's rejection of Guillemard's desire to separate the popular material from material on fish and ethnology.[48] These conflicts were kept private. Kingsley finally instructed her publisher not to show Guillemard her appendix with its identification of fish and an Eboe story.[49] The friendly tone projected in the preface thus masks a bitter struggle over control of the text.[50]

While Kingsley's preface to *Travels* shows clearly designed strategies of public accommodation rather than confrontation with authority figures, femininity is not emphasized. Kingsley did feel the need to substantiate and clear the scientific material with an established authority. (Guillemard was the geographical editor for the

Cambridge University Press.) But rather than show a passive obedi-
ence to authority, she presents her own language as energetic, unconventional, and active, like a herd of cattle whose dangling
prepositions may be lassoed, but which will be only marginally
controllable.

Also raised in the preface is the unconventional viewpoint which
will shape her account, as Kingsley indicates that her conformity is
only superficial, a trade-off to balance a deeply held identification
with a non-European culture. Kingsley does continue in her preface
to proclaim, like Martineau, that she is writing scientifically from
"personal experience and very careful observation," in anticipation
of the usual attacks made on travel observations as being too subjective (viii). However, she also prepares the reader for a perception
centered on African, not British interests, and for a viewpoint
which she does not expect her readers to share. She asks her readers
to "make allowances for my love of this sort of country, with its
great forests and rivers and its animistic-minded inhabitants, and
for my ability to be more comfortable there than in England" (ix).
In taking this stance, Kingsley is doing something very different
from the other naturalist travel writers discussed in this study. Others, such as Bird Bishop, have declared a preference for traveling
rather than being in England, but Kingsley is identifying specifically with West Africa in preference to Britain, not just as a place
but also as a culture. And although European ethnocentricity and
racism do confusingly intrude into her text, her acknowledged
choice of what would be seen as an inferior culture and race is still
very unusual for the time, even more so for a woman who would be
expected to support the imposition of the home culture in the colonies. Kingsley anticipates disagreement with her stance, but does
not back off from it. As she concludes in her preface, "Your superior culture-instincts may militate against your enjoying West Africa, but if you go there you will find things as I have said" (ix).

The preface, then, has set the stage, announcing a strategy of accommodation that resists passivity, and a careful balance of public
acknowledgments to male authorities, while maintaining private
control. Additionally, she uses personal experience to substantiate
an authoritative position and a voice that intends to speak for Africa
as a legitimate and rich culture.

As her account continues, other male authorities make their appearance and are praised. Again, however, such strategies of accommodation are not what they may initially appear to be. Whereas
Kingsley's praise for Guillemard hid an editorial struggle, traditional feminine obeisance was also used to support unpopular

causes and to highlight individuals who, she felt, were unfairly treated by institutions. A primary example of this can be seen in her repeated references in *Travels* to Robert Hamill Nassau as the leading authority on African fetishism. Nassau was an American Presbyterian medical missionary in West Africa; he had worked on the Mpongwé language and collected ethnological observations, but he was also very controversial. He assimilated himself into African society and refused to dismiss an African nurse and church member from his household who had had an illegitimate child.[51] Kingsley, who felt for the most part that missionaries were destroying African culture and causing more harm than good, singled out Nassau for praise because she wished to side with those supporting native culture against missionary conversions. Caroline Alexander, after examining in detail the missionary logs and correspondence in the Nassau controversy, suggests that Kingsley's attention to Nassau helped bolster his reputation with the missionary board, eventually leading to institutional support for his work on African fetishism.[52]

As Kingsley did not hesitate to back individuals who she perceived were moving toward self-government in British African colonies, neither did she hesitate to become involved in politics. For a while, she did have political influence as a spokesperson for trading interests in West Africa, as she hoped that a colonial relationship based on trade would be less destructive to native cultures than the control from Britain and missionary boards typical of Crown Colony governance.

However, Kingsley felt more secure picturing herself as a behind-the-scenes manipulator. Unafraid to speak her views of colonial governance in lectures, she nevertheless refused to take power directly. Rather, she maintained the appearance of conforming to traditional women's roles by publicly speaking out against women's suffrage, not supporting women's membership in scientific societies, and diminishing her own travel exertions in contrast to the hard work expended by women who cared for their families. This was, however, a cultivated façade and these positions should not always be taken at face value.

Besides the authority figures who could be acknowledged or thanked with various levels of nuance, there were also more mythic figures in the background of Kingsley's text. One figure among the many who made up much of Kingsley's childhood reading was Richard F. Burton. Burton played an enormous role in shaping Kingsley's early self-identification and fantasy. This common experience for young women of closely identifying with male figures from history or literature poses difficult problems later on when their social roles become rigidly defined and the imaginative life of childhood cannot be pursued in adulthood. Charlotte Brontë's fascination with Lord Nelson, for example, is also evidence of strong male hero identification. In Kingsley's text, Burton's influence can be seen in her sympathy for Moslem religious beliefs as a better religion for Africans than Christianity, her references to Allah, and her support for polygamy. What is particularly interesting in Kingsley's travels is that her text indicates that she had found a way to fulfill those male explorer roles with which she identified. She, like Bird Bishop, traveled to a place where European gender expectations were not known and where she could define herself, so long as she did not carry this newly formed identity back to Britain and accepted more conventional behavior restrictions at home.

TAKING ADVANTAGE OF GENDER BLURRING

The jungle provided for Kingsley what may be called an "area of transition," a mental construct of a territory where identity is fluid and the individual is free to form his or her own identity separate from social and cultural expectations. Kingsley presented herself as solitary, traveling only with natives, whom, she explained, had never seen a European woman and who had no expectations about her behavior being any different from any other European rubber trader. While away from European eyes, Kingsley obtained a level of privacy that was liberating.

The means of communication between natives and traders also promised an additional layer of shielding from gender expectations. Kingsley claimed that the trade language used in the region did not make gender distinctions, and she reported that on one occasion a native's message led a European trading agent to expect the arrival of a male trader, only to have a well-drenched Kingsley show up. The agent's mistake is presented humorously and Kingsley declares in rather drawing-room-tinted language that she was quite embarrassed: "Had there been any smelling salts or sal volatile in this subdivision of the Ethiopian region I should have forthwith fainted . . . but I well knew there was not, so I blushed until the steam from my soaking clothes . . . went up in a cloud . . ." (*Travels* 502). Yet there is a certain amount of pride buried in the reporting, as with the mock complaint that she was always called "sir" (*Travels* 502). The situation is reported because it serves as an affirmation of the removal of limitations, of getting away with something through an unexplored loophole in the socially constructed rules. It is with the same sort of subversive glee that she informs French officials, who are trying to prevent this lone unaccompanied woman from traveling up a dangerous river, that the Royal Geographical Society's *Hints for Travellers* does not list husbands among the traveling equipment recommended for jungle travelers, implying that as an explorer she is exempt from such constrictions (*Travels* 167).

The first response of her publisher, George Macmillan, to the manuscript of *Travels* was that it sounded masculine, apparently referring to the fact that conventions of feminine discourse were being transgressed. Kingsley simply professed to not comprehend what Macmillan was referring to: "I do not understand what you mean by 'story being told by a man.' Where have I said it was?"[53] In the same letter, the issue of gender and authorship arose—how was she to be identified? She responded,

> Of course I would rather not publish it under my own name, and I really cannot draw the trail of the petticoat over the [African] Coast of all places—neither can I have a picture of myself in trousers or any other little excitement of that sort added. I went out there as a naturalist not as a sort of circus, but if you would like my name, will it not be sufficient to put M. H. Kingsley?—it does not matter to the general public what I am as long as I tell them the truth as well as I can—I have written it all with my eye on the "Coast" [West African traders] who will of course know I was a lady and will also be the only people who will know the value of what I say, and I do not wish to appear ridiculous or unladylike before them.[54]

The title page ended up with the name "Mary H. Kingsley," not the androgynous initials, but also without the less dignified title of "Miss." Kingsley did not wish to be presented with an emphasis on her femininity. She was trying to present her work as part of a larger male-identified community of naturalists, explorers, and traders. In this letter, it is apparent that she is quite aware that the ways her audience could perceive her are both limited and unsatisfactory. She is rejecting both the less authoritative feminine portrayal which would result in a "trail of petticoats" and the trousered-woman-rebel portrayal, which would distance her from mainstream cultural politics or scientific organization, and thus, from having any political or scientific influence.

One element of Kingsley's prose which Macmillan would either consciously or unconsciously have tagged as masculine in tone is her description of her own movement in her travels. Kingsley's presentation of herself is probably one of the most physical in women's narratives. Whereas Wollstonecraft mentions learning to row in Norway, Martineau tends to place herself in the position of a quiet dignified observer. Bird Bishop, although an active rider, still gives the impression of ladylike stability and upright posture, even when she is crawling up a mountain. Kingsley, in striking contrast, falls down holes and hillsides, tips canoes, gets muddy, stumbles and describes her own movements as having all the grace of a pratfall. Contemporary reviewers made comparisons to Jerome K. Jerome's boating mishaps, and Mark Twain's physical humor also comes to mind.

Part of this emphasis on physicality is the result of Kingsley's mode of travel. Most other travel accounts show the narrator being transported via couch or boat for longer distances. But Kingsley describes herself as either walking (at a time when Europeans, both male and female, were carried by bearers) or navigating her own canoe. This presentation would be particularly novel for readers of this time period when any focus on a gentlewoman's physical efforts was seldom presented. Heroines of novels usually stayed in the home within a domestic space and those few walking scenes which do appear in literature, such as Elizabeth Bennet's lone three-mile cross-country trot in Austen's *Pride and Prejudice* (1813) with her dirty stockings, suggested poor country manners to Mrs. Hurst and Miss Bingley.[55] Only characters with lower class positions such as Tess in Hardy's *Tess of the d'Ubervilles* (1891) would be shown regularly engaged in activities resulting in blisters on the feet. Yet Kingsley, whose primary means of transportation was walking, describes herself walking such long distances as to become quite unpresentable.

At one point, she worries as she approaches a German trading post about the response of the European trader to her appearance, "mud-caked skirts, and blood-stained hands and face," and carefully washes herself before she makes an appearance, debating to herself: "Shall I make an exhibition of myself and wash here [among native men and women], or make an exhibition of myself by going unwashed to that unknown German officer who is in charge of the station?" (563). Although she does wash in the open creek before approaching the European, it apparently was not successful because he still wanted her to have a bath. She refused, noting the lack of doors or shutters in the building, and commented, "Men can be trying!" (*Travels* 563). Kingsley's point was that when she was among Africans, her cleanness did not matter; it was only when she knew she would be viewed within the context of European culture that she became self-conscious to the point of refusing a European bath because of lack of privacy, even though she had already bathed in the open air.

As with Bird Bishop, traveling outside the influence of British social convention afforded Kingsley the opportunity to direct her own travel by controlling the very means of her transportation. And Kingsley lays great stress on this in *Travels*, pairing her pride with being helpful in an auxiliary fashion with gaining a form of independence: "I can honestly and truly say that there are only two things I am proud of—one is that Doctor Günther has approved of my fishes, and the other is that I can paddle an Ogowé canoe" (200). For Wollstonecraft and Martineau, most travel was by boat or carriage during which they were accompanied by groups of people, but both also featured scenes involving a lone woman rowing. And Bird Bishop's early writings display her joy in the freedom of traveling by herself on horseback for long distances. Kingsley, too, in managing a native canoe in the swamps, was searching for a means of independence equivalent to that possessed by the native population: "it is quite impossible to see other people, even if they are only black, naked savages, gliding about in canoes, without wishing to go and glide about yourself" (197). Beneath her emphasis on the technical control and management of a canoe is a sense that she is taking advantage of the lack of social supervision to grab control of her life. She describes with some nervousness that others termed her efforts "recklessness" (196), and points out that her first attempts were made when no one from the missionary settlement was looking and there was "no one to keep me out of mischief" (197). Amidst the fears of watchers, Kingsley presents herself as calmly going about her "studies." In response to cries of "You'll be drowned," Kingsley retorts, "Gracious goodness! . . . I thought that half an hour ago, but it's all right now; I can steer" (198). This exchange, of course, places Kingsley in the position of holding to a steady calmness in contrast to the fears of her hostess, "a sweet and gracious lady" (199).

Having performed so many unladylike actions, Kingsley attempted to defuse a possible backlash against her explorer role and accusations of unfemininity by carefully emphasizing her maintenance of feminine clothing during her travel. This anticipation of the charges of wearing pants was so worrisome, carrying with it all the emotive connotations of degradation and the New Woman movement, that Kingsley clung almost irrationally to the claim that she wore a skirt during her treks and that she would never consider any other traveling costume.

While Bird Bishop did everything she could to make pants ap-

pear skirt-like so she could ride astride, Kingsley did not feel sufficiently secure in her femininity nor gentility to attempt any variety
of bloomers or heavily lace-draped divided skirts. In her best
known sketch, and one which has been used as a sort of defining
moment for all nineteenth-century women travelers, Kingsley describes falling into a jaguar pit trap onto the points of spears. She
survives, she claims, because her voluminous heavy skirt protected
her from any harm.

> It is at these times you realise the blessing of a good thick skirt. Had I
> paid heed to the advice of many people in England, who ought to have
> known better, and did not do it themselves, and adopted masculine gar-
> ments, I should have been spiked to the bone, and done for. Whereas,
> save for a good many bruises, here I was with the fulness of my skirt
> tucked under me, sitting on nine ebony spikes some twelve inches long,
> in comparative comfort, howling lustily to be hauled out. (*Travels* 270)

It is a little difficult to determine just how seriously Kingsley intended such a claim to be taken. But then she later reaffirmed the
importance of feminine dress, declaring,

> I hasten to assure you I never even wear a masculine collar and tie, and
> as for encasing the more earthward extremities—well, I would rather
> perish on a public scaffold. (*Travels* 502)

She also mentioned using stays (at least when visiting Europeans),
lacing them up with a shoestring when they broke.

The message of the "blessing of a good thick skirt" was reem-
phasized when she was contradicted by Lady MacDonald, a friend
who had sailed with her on one trip. MacDonald claimed (probably
truthfully) that Kingsley wore pants under her skirt, removing the
skirt when having to wade through rivers and swamps, then securing the pants' legs around her ankles to keep leeches off.[56] In response, Kingsley carefully dressed in outdated conservative
fashions whenever she gave lectures in Britain. All approved studio
photos showed her in full black mutton-sleeved dress with umbrella
and gloves. Frank comments that those photographs suggest that
Kingsley "is doing her utmost . . . to seem like the last person one
would accuse of having traveled in West Africa" (222). While her
books are illustrated by photographs of West African natives (some
of which she probably took), unlike Bird Bishop, whose first book
had a woodcut of her with a horse in a long divided skirt and who
later featured a photograph of herself in native costume, Kingsley's
illustrations do not feature herself, and since she only traveled alone

with uninterviewable natives, no one could dispute her accounts. Apparently, this situation was either engineered by Kingsley or taken advantage of when field photographs became damaged, and the opportunity to travel free from social censure became one of the appeals of West Africa.

The *Daily Telegraph* attempted to link her with the New Woman feminism by writing shortly after she arrived back in England, "It is a curious and a novel feature of the modern emancipation of woman—this passion on the part of the sex to emulate the most daring achievements of masculine explorers."[57] In response Kingsley worked with Sarah Tooley of the *Young Woman*, a magazine which promoted marriage as the best role for women, to emphasize the most conventional aspects of Kingsley's life for public consumption.[58]

UTILIZING RACE AND GENDER DIFFERENCES

As Kingsley resisted her contemporaries' efforts to peg her as representative of women's movements, so her work continues to resist modern critics' attempts to see her as either a feminist hero or a champion of colonial emancipation. Although, in some ways, she can be seen as both if one looks at her actions and the main focus of her writing; at the same time, she also made comments which could brand her as both racist and sexist. She was an independent woman who was against women's activities outside the home and a supporter of self-governance who also supported British imperialism. These stances are clearly contradictory and the question may not be how *could* she hold these positions, but rather *why* did she need to?

We have seen that during the later part of the century the discussion of women's roles became increasingly polarized. The reversal of membership policy in the RGS also occurred in other societies such as the Ethnological Society, as T. H. Huxley, a major spokesman for Darwinian evolution, justified colonialism and the subordinate position of women on the basis of inherent differences. In 1864, Huxley described the structural differences between male and female brains (and races) and concluded: "On the whole [the cerebral convolutions] are simpler in women than in men, and in the lower races the convolutions have a greater simplicity and symmetry than in the higher."[59] The next year he added in his essay "Emancipation—Black and White" that "in every excellent character, whether mental or physical, the average woman is inferior to the average man, in the sense of having that character less in quantity and lower in quality."[60]

As women's legal and educational situation improved, the debate moved from the treatment of women as a group to focus more intensely on individual women's lives. Rather than a lessening of the separate spheres ideology, with increased legal rights and acceptance of women in the workplace came a renewed insistence on separate spheres as the ideal and natural position for women. Darwinian and anthropological studies led August Strindberg in January 1895 to conclude that "between the child, woman, and the inferior races there exists a not negligible analogy,"[61] and evolutionary theory seemed to suggest that the division between men and women needed to widen for human society to evolve.[62] As British society nervously viewed the coming fin de siècle, the position of public women became more difficult to justify, and the more a woman identified with a progressive science, the more contradictory were the beliefs she was asked to hold.

Jordanova's and Laqueuer's studies of shifts in medical paradigms in the construction of sexual differences suggest that marginal groups (identifiable by sexual or racial differences) are generally contrasted with the dominant (male European) group in two ways. In one paradigm, the marginal groups are aligned in a linear hierarchy beneath the dominant groups, similar to the Great Chain of Being. In this paradigm, the marginalized groups are described as being more childlike and less developed than the more powerful group. The other paradigm perceives outsider groups as different, subject not to lesser but to different expectations; this paradigm often results in polarized categorizations and can be seen as the basis for the late Victorian idea of separate spheres for men and women. Neither paradigm places the marginalized group in a very good position, but the expectations may be different according to which paradigm is in operation. While such divisions make it easier to talk about rhetorical choices, the actual arguments of individual authors may not be consistent within these categories.

When viewing issues of gender and race, Kingsley made use of both paradigms according to whichever argument worked best in her favor. When evaluating her own position, she made use of a linear hierarchy. Despite her own achievements in collecting and observation, she emphasized that she worked under male direction. She made the collections and anthropological observations but had male authorities verify their importance and make the identifications (and name the fish after her).[63] Later on, Kingsley would oppose women's membership in professional societies (even in ones she helped form) and she was against woman's suffrage. While she is on record as saying that women were quite capable of physical endeavor, this was done to praise women working in the home. Kingsley wished her achievements to be listed among those of men, not women. In a sense, her accomplishments were made while, in the eyes of the outside world and within her area of transition, she was a man.

In regard to the African native population, however, Kingsley used the argument of difference. Referring to the Abolitionist slogan, "Am I not a Man and a Brother?" she stated that the Negro was a man but not a brother, that she believed in separate evolutionary origins. Surprisingly, this argument allowed her to maintain a level of tolerance very unusual for her time. She argued that African natives were not unintelligent. Rather their culture and their environment required a different type of intelligence and, therefore, European culture should not be imposed upon Africa; that polygamy was a sensible system considering the work load most African women had with rubber processing and childcare; that alcohol was an excellent trade item, no different than alcohol available in London, and usually more watered down, and that it was easy to transport and did not rot in the jungle. She also pushed for home rule for the Crown Colonies, insisting that native laws were as intelligent and workable as any other laws.

Kingsley tried to connect these two paradigms or at least tried to present them as essentially the same. She attempted to explain that missionary teachings failed because missionaries did not realize "the difference between the African and themselves as [one] being a difference not of degree but of kind" (*Travels* 659). She then tried to tie this reasoning to the separate spheres ideology as she understood it.

> . . . I feel certain that a black man is no more an undeveloped white man than a rabbit is an undeveloped hare; and the mental difference between the two races is very similar to that between men and women among ourselves. A great woman, either mentally or physically, will excel an indifferent man, but no woman ever equals a really great man. (*Travels* 659)

Apparently, Kingsley attempted to appeal to the conventional belief that men's and women's spheres should be separate because they are different, and she used a similar reasoning to argue for cultural tolerance. At the same time, she reserved the highest achievement potential for men and left unspoken the analogous conclusion that the highest cultural achievement was European.

This explanation of male superiority is based on the supposedly scientific rationale that justified keeping women at lower levels of scientific endeavor. This rationale is linked to a definition of professional science (advanced by Whewell among others) which emphasized the intuitive genius of individual men who advanced a scientific field through perception of general theories. While the logic is difficult to follow, this rationale allowed women and non-Europeans access to most types of intellectual pursuits, while reserving the recognition of genius to certain great European men.

One explanation for this acceptance of general limitations among independent women may be that women who were forced to seek independence through work still tended to hold onto the ideology of separate spheres as an ideal which external situations prevented them from achieving. Although successful, their culture told them that they were placed in their situation unfairly, that a vocation should be an alternative choice only when marriage and home life were not available. Although happy with their economic freedom, they still clung to a belief that all this worry and stress and enfranchisement would not have been necessary if the right man had been available or if men were fulfilling their proper social roles.

Another consideration which should be taken into account is a general social retreat in the later part of the 1890s from an earlier progressive movement. The trial and conviction of Oscar Wilde for homosexuality in April 1895 (while Kingsley was still in West Africa) signaled an end to the late Victorian revolt against conventional gender roles.[64] Politically, this change in the country's mood was reflected in a change in government during the summer of 1895. The Liberal government resigned to be replaced by the government of Lord Salisbury, who represented "jingoistic patriotism and expansive imperialism."[65] After this, Lynn Linton predicted that now women would accept their limitations and return to "their womanly delicacy of thought and sphere."[66] When Kingsley returned to England on 30 November 1895, she found a definite change in social levels of tolerance toward women's activities outside the domestic sphere.

IN DEFENSE OF TRAVEL AND WRITING

Kingsley's *Travels* was clearly written in England for the British public, yet initially she was not sure how to present herself. In a letter to Lady MacDonald, she wrote that "personal experiences get in your way sadly" and that the "amount of expurgation my journals have required has been awful,"[67] suggesting a fair amount of self-censorship was required. Most of the book is in the form of a narrative with some dated journal-like entries, which are generally used to focus attention and to underline the immediacy of a particular adventure. Anticipating criticism that her book does not follow the expected journal format, Kingsley turns the tables on that argument by suggesting that real scientific field journals would not be publishable in their original state because of the very nature of field work. Rather than apologizing for losing the authenticity readers associated with the journal convention, Kingsley first apologizes for using any diary extracts at all, then follows with an explanation for why they were not used more:

> I must pause here to explain my reasons for giving extracts from my diary, being informed on excellent authority that publishing a diary is a form of literary crime. Such being the case I have to urge in extenuation of my committing it that—Firstly, I have not done it before, for so far I have given a sketchy *résumé* of many diaries kept by me while visiting the regions I have attempted to describe. Secondly, no one expects literature in a book of travel. Thirdly, there are things to be said in favour of the diary form, particularly when it is kept in a little known and wild region, for the reader gets therein notice of things that, although unimportant in themselves, yet go to make up the conditions of life under which men and things exist. The worst of it is these things are not often presented in their due and proper proportion in diaries. Many pages in my journals that I will spare you display this crime to perfection. For example: "Awful turn up with crocodile about ten—Paraffin good for over-oiled boots—Evil spirits crawl on ground, hence high lintel— Odeaka cheese is made thus:—" Then comes half a yard on Odeaka cheese making. (100)

In giving her defense for her "literary crime," she points out that travel is generally exempt from the rules of literature, since "no one expects literature in a book of travel"; thus unconventionality is allowed. Kingsley indicates (as Bird Bishop had also argued) that journal entries also capture the "unimportant" daily details of life in isolated areas which would otherwise be forgotten. When Kingsley touches upon the issue of "proportion" in what she called her "bush diaries"; however, we are also given a hint of what she (and by extension other scientists) were really concerned with: the data collected for later theorizing, which is of greater value than the narrative account. Such explanations serve as a reminder to the reader that Kingsley was traveling for scientific study, not just to produce another popular travel account.[68]

While Kingsley thus presents herself as a scientific traveler, still the very act of traveling to such an isolated area was not easily justified when the traveler was a woman. Kingsley's defense of her travel activities employs some strategies used by Martineau in her American travel accounts. Thus, she does not explicitly present herself as having prepared for travel by studying or as representing a particular government or religious organization. David Livingstone, in contrast, refers to both the RGS and the London Missionary Society in his preface, then begins his account of his journeys in South Africa with an autobiographical sketch of those studies which prepared him for his research.[69] Rather than open with such a sketch, Kingsley, like Martineau, gives the impression that the opportunity simply presented itself:

> It was in 1893 that, for the first time in my life, I found myself in possession of five or six months which were not heavily forestalled, and feeling like a boy with a new half-crown, I lay about in my mind, as Mr. Bunyan would say, as to what to do with them. (*Travels* 1)

Nothing of her years of reading Burton, Du Chaillu, and deBrazza are mentioned.[70]

Later on, additional excuses are presented: continuation of father's work, Günther's directions for fish collecting, the demands of science, the needs of Africa. Each reason she presents varies in its level of abstraction, utilitarianism, and inward needs—reflecting the shifting expectations for women's endeavors. The most self-effacing reasons were given in her later *West African Studies,* where she felt compelled to distance herself from *Travels*, "a word-swamp of a book," by nearly blaming her publisher for the idea ("George Macmillan lured me"). She was also concerned that the book made her look braver than she should be.[71] In her preface, she explained that rather than being "an intrepid explorer," she was rather "the prey of frights, worries and alarms," dependent on the toleration of others, not just for her writing but also for herself, "with half-a dozen colds in my head and a dingy temper" (*West* vii). In their increasing conventionality, these later protests suggest that the popular reaction against women's reform movements in 1899 placed Kingsley in a position that made defending *West African Studies* more difficult than *Travels*.

When Kingsley does refer to the advancement of science as a reason for her travels, science becomes personified and patriarchal. In *Travels*, she does indicate that a practical purpose, the fish-collecting needs of Günther, dictated itinerary: "My reasons for going to this wildest and most dangerous part of the west African regions were perfectly simple and reasonable. I had not found many fish in the Oil Rivers, and . . . my one chance of getting a collection of fishes from a river north of the Congo lay in" the Ogowé (*Travels* 103). This reason, however, is apparently not sufficiently forceful and is not stressed in her accounts. Rather, she speaks of the larger goals of science in ways which through personification transform the word "science" making it authoritarian and demanding as a proper noun. This personification allows her to serve in a respectful, nonthreatening auxiliary position within her text without the loss of authority inherent in being bound to the wishes of a particular male authority. Thus, she presents herself as merely obeying Science, that is, fulfilling a feminine duty. That abstraction, however, while it gives the appearance of being an outside force, actually represents her own nonsocially acceptable drives. Rather than saying she is obsessed with jungles or that she follows a personal resolution to understand tropics, that portion of her personality is isolated and transformed into the proper noun "Science." So, Kingsley can say she followed such dictates as, " 'Go and learn your tropics,' said Science" (*Travels* 1).

This "Science" then makes its demands, and, at times, calls for its sacrifices. At one point, albeit tongue-in-cheek, Kingsley imagines taking the call for scientific sacrifice literally, becoming herself a specimen for future scientists. Initially, she reflects that the mud of the mango swamp is deep and dangerous; then musing further, considers that

> sinking into it means staying in it, at any rate until some geologist of the remote future may come across you, in a fossilised state, when that mangrove swamp shall have become dry land. Of course if you really want a truly safe investment in Fame, and really care about Posterity, and Posterity's Science, you will jump over into the black batter-like, stinking slime, cheered by the thought of the terrific sensation you will produce 20,000 years hence, and the care you will be taken of then by your fellow-creatures, in a museum. But if you are a mere ordinary person of a retiring nature, like me, you stop in your lagoon until the tide rises again; most of your attention is directed to dealing with an "at home" to crocodiles and mangrove flies, and with the fearful stench of the slime round you. What little time you have over you will employ in wondering why you came to West Africa, and why, after having reached this point of absurdity, you need have gone and painted the lily and adorned the rose, by being such a colossal ass as to come fooling about in mangrove swamps. (*Travels* 89)

On the self-mocking surface she presents herself as a "colossal ass" for taking such risks and making a commitment to an area of study whose members have been only reluctantly supportive of her efforts, for having bucked social conventions and tried to be a scientific explorer in a culture which ties such endeavors to a cult of masculinity. But beneath this self-mockery lies a sense of desperation. And this desperation does at times become apparent in the text as Kingsley reveals herself as depressed to the point where losing herself in the dangerous swamp is a temptation. She frankly admitted to her feelings of alienation and loneliness in a letter writing, "[t]he fact is I am no more a human being than a gust of wind is. . . . It never occurs to me that I have any right to do anything more than now and then sit and warm myself at the fires of real human beings."[72] Indeed, Kingsley seems almost inclined to make her sacrifice. She continues in this letter to describe her state of mind at this time as being "dead tired and feeling no one had need of me any more, when my Mother and Father died within six weeks [sic] of each other in '92, and my Brother went off to the East, I went down to West Africa to die." I argue, though, that, in addition to the loss of her parents, Kingsley was fighting off a depression linked to the frustration of having no place, no role for herself in 1890s society or science. She felt isolated from the very pursuit of science she was committed to, an isolation reflected in her reference to herself as "the human atom."[73] In her travels, her profession, and in her life, Kingsley was a solitary figure, always feeling somewhat apart from human life.

The only relief from her black moods was in those occasions when she could simply lose herself in the wildness of the African landscape. In two scenes in her book, she described metaphorically situations in which suicide is a temptation and she is brought out of her depression, not by her commitment to science, but by the call of duty in the concern for others. On one occasion, she is looking over rapids at night, surrounded by fireflies, and she finds peace in the loss of self-consciousness associated with the feminine sublime, but not in the form of poetic reflection, however, rather in something darker:

> The majesty and beauty of the scene fascinated me, and I stood leaning with my back against a rock pinnacle watching it. Do not imagine it gave rise, in what I am pleased to call my mind, to those complicated, poetical reflections natural beauty seems to bring out in other people's minds. It never works that way with me; I just lose all sense of human individuality, all memory of human life, with its grief and worry and

doubt, and become part of the atmosphere. If I have a heaven, that will
be mine, and I verily believe that if I were left alone long enough with
such a scene as this . . . I should be found soulless and dead; but I never
have a chance of that. (*Travels* 178)

Kingsley dismisses those by now clichéd "poetical reflections" as
inadequate to describe the pull the wilderness has for her. Instead,
the sparsely inhabited African landscape attracts her because the reminders of "grief and worry" at home can be escaped. Bird Bishop
also sought escape in isolated lands, but expressed her travel as a
relief from illness and the suffocation she felt among European
crowds. While Bird Bishop stayed abroad as much as possible, this
was not an option for Kingsley. She had less personal freedom than
Bird Bishop and had to return to Britain.

Despite her humorous asides then, Kingsley was more inclined to
despair than Bird Bishop, and the tenor of her travels is closer to
that of Wollstonecraft. This loss of "all sense of human individual-
ity" and escape from the stress which threatens to overwhelm her,
the simple loss of consciousness, is an allusion to suicide, to the
possibility of being "found soulless and dead." Kingsley, a "redundant" woman and near bastard, hoped to lose herself by merging
with an impersonal nature, but her memories and commitments prevented her from making a conscious self-sacrifice. Any hope contained within Christian ideas of an afterlife, such as would have
sustained Bird Bishop, is dismissed here by the lifelong atheist who
never had any crisis of belief. This dark reverie implies a request
for a reason to continue. She answers this herself by interrupting
her train of thought with the report of a shriek in the night as one
of her men gets burned in a campfire mishap. This account suggests
that she is brought away from the temptation of suicide by her duty
to care for others. The nurturing role of women established in the
separate spheres ideology is thus presented as her main, if not sole,
anchor to life.

Kingsley is similarly tempted to lose herself while climbing in
the Cameroon mountains. Feeling exhausted after a long climb, she
looks over a crater wall and becomes lost in the sight of rising
mountain peaks.

The space around seemed boundless, and there was in it neither sound
nor colour, nor anything with form, save those two terrific things [the
peaks of Cameroon and Clarence]. It was like a vision, and it held me
spellbound, as I stood shivering on the rocks with the white mist round
my knees until into my wool-gathering mind came the memory of those

anything but sublime men of mine; and I turned and scuttled off along
the rocks like an agitated ant left alone in a dead universe. (578)

As an atom and as an ant, Kingsley has no identity unless she is
involved in the service of a larger duty. Her desire to lose herself
in a transcendental identification with a non-human world and to
disregard the teachings of Christianity are cloaked in the proper
nurturing responses which would be accepted in a racist understanding of "her" Africans as child-like.

While such a portrayal is a common nineteenth-century racist response to Africans, it may also be understood as part of a rationale
that, in its reference to women's nurturing role, provides an acceptable motive for travel. As Blunt points out, the paradoxical expectations of women in late nineteenth-century Britain meant that while
Kingsley was seen as transcending "the standards of other women,
she was primarily praised for conforming to ideals of feminine conduct."[74] Eventually, however, that nurturing duty she invokes becomes broadened to a commitment to all of Africa, a place where
she was not reminded of her awkward class position and gender inferiority.

CIRCUMVENTING THE MALE EXPLORER CONVENTION

As a result of previous writings about tropical Africa by such explorers as Richard Burton, Henry Morton Stanley, Paul Du Chaillu,
Livingstone, and deBrazza, the British audience had come to expect
certain conventions in the writing of exploratory travel books. In
the late nineteenth century, there arose what Pratt terms "imperial
stylistics," designed to paint peak moments which symbolize a
masculine and British force conquering a foreign land.[75] These conventional moments involved establishing records by climbing new
peaks, killing new or larger animals, and confronting threatening
tribes against backgrounds of suggestive impenetrable mystery.

As an avid reader of exploration narratives since her childhood,
Kingsley was well aware of such conventions and, initially, had
problems finding where she fit in. In a letter to another woman traveler, she wrote,

> I am really beginning to think that the traveler—properly so called—the
> person who writes a book and gets his FRGS etc., is a peculiar sort of
> animal only capable of seeing a certain set of things and always seeing
> them in the same way, and you and me are not of this species somehow.
> What are we to call ourselves?[76]

As this passage indicates, Kingsley was quite conscious of the problems posed by her narrative position. She was also conscious of holding views at odds with conventional perceptions of Africa.

In *Travels,* Kingsley found ways to refer to the explorer conventions, not to identify with them but to subvert them. As Pratt points out, she made use of the themes of "the monarchic male discourse of domination and intervention" and, through irony and comic inversion, she questioned and parodied the power they presented.[77] As my expansion on Pratt's analysis of *Travels* will show, Kingsley challenged the masculine explorer (and related big game hunter) conventions through her own non-confrontational responses to big game; her privileging of subjective naturalist, rather than quantifiable academic, responses to nature; her demystification of the tropics through domestic imagery; and through an approach to mountain climbing unmotivated by conquest.

Many explorer-naturalists came from a country squire background (such as Darwin), and considered themselves sportsmen in addition to scientists, bagging game for both scientific study and sportsman records. Some accounts of British gentlemen's travels emphasized what to modern readers seems a horrifying accumulation of slaughtered endangered species and, for much of the nineteenth century, collecting was synonymous with hunting. For very practical reasons, Kingsley made no attempt to gather big game. As a single individual with limited resources (unlike the men, she did not receive economic support from government organizations or societies in her travels), she restricted herself to easily transportable specimens for the British Museum, creatures such as fish and insects, which would not require a host of bearers to transport the carcass or carry and care for guns.

In challenging the explorer conventions, she raises questions over the validity of such discourses, and proposes alternative ways of seeing wildlife, all while engaging in humorous self-depreciation. On one occasion, she describes seeing a herd of five elephants, which she could only watch. She observes ironically,

> I am certain that owing to some misapprehension among the Fates I was given a series of magnificent sporting chances, intended as a special treat for some favourite Nimrod of those three ladies, and I know exactly how I ought to have behaved. I should have felt my favourite rifle fly to my shoulder, and then, carefully sighting for the finest specimen, have fired. The noble beast should have stumbled forward, recovered itself, and shedding its life blood behind it have crashed away into the forest. I should then have tracked it, and either with one well-directed

shot have given it its quietus, or have got charged by it, the elephant
passing completely over my prostrate body; either termination is good
form, but I never have these things happen, and never will. (*Travels* 258)

Such general categorizations of what is supposed to happen invite
the suspicion that they really don't happen in quite the way the big
game hunter-explorers present the events. In other words, explorer
heroes often lie. Her comment that, "I never have these things happen" also suggests that, as a writer, Kingsley will not allow such
things to happen in her book.

Showing that she knows "good form," Kingsley recalls from her
reading that she should dodge around trees, "working down wind
all the time, until they [the elephants] lose smell and sight of you,
then to lie quiet for a time, and go home" (*Travels* 258). As she
obediently moves around a tree and lies down in accordance with
these remembered instructions, the elephants ignore her. Her observation of the calmness of the elephants is thus at odds with the common presentations of travelers such as Du Chaillu (who traveled in
the same area as Kingsley), for whom African animals were uniformly fierce and menacing. Since no danger presents itself, Kingsley decides to move in closer, "until I was close enough to have hit
the nearest one with a stone, and spats of mud, which they sent flying with their stamping and wallowing came flap, flap among the
bushes covering me" (*Travels* 258).

In presenting this feat, Kingsley is offering her readers an example of bravery greater than the traditional bravery involved in shoot-
ing the creature, but without directly challenging previous accounts
by male explorers. Having obtained an unusually privileged viewing position, Kingsley carries on scientifically with the observation
that the elephant's trunk is carried differently when going upwind
than down, for some unknown reason, leaving the observation open
to speculation. She adds flippantly, mimicking the voice of imperialistic administration, that the reason is probably due to "arrested
mental development, I suppose," then explains in a footnote that
this is "[t]he usual explanation for anything you do not understand
in a native of Africa's conduct" (*Travels* 259). But the reader is
quickly distracted from dwelling on this criticism of assumed European superiority by Kingsley's falling over one of her men who,
unbeknownst to her, had also come to watch the elephants, and then
falling yet again down another hillside.

Kingsley's desire to find a place in the study of science posed its
own problems as the realm of scientific studies was being divided
into specialist areas, sometimes more for political reasons than for

the needs of the discipline (as with ethnology and anthropology). At different times, Kingsley called herself a naturalist, an ichthyologist, and an ethnologist. When she visited Nassau in West Africa, her interests and references identified her as scientific and in his journal he referred to her as an "English scientist."[78] Her nature descriptions, however, place her within the older naturalist tradition and, at times, she implicitly criticizes the more quantifiable academic expectations which, she suggests, fail to comprehend field conditions. In one passage, she momentarily sets aside the qualitative attention to nature associated with the natural history tradition of Gilbert White in order to perform the measurements required by the newer more analytic approaches to observation. First, Kingsley presents her immediate response to the vegetation:

> At the sides of the path here grow banks of bergamot and balsam, returning good for evil and smiling sweetly as we crush them. Thank goodness we are in forest now, and we seem to have done with the sword-grass. The rocks are covered with moss and ferns, and the mist curling and wandering about among the stems is very lovely. (*Travels* 562)

Such descriptions, however popular, were not as valued as measurements that suggested scientific rigor. In her own collecting and measuring, usually of smaller creatures which could be easily preserved in alcohol and transported, she acknowledges those expectations. On the walk mentioned above, Kingsley interrupts her observations to measure a large but uncooperative worm:

> I have to pause in life's pleasures because I want to measure one of the large earthworms, which, with smaller sealing-wax-red worms, are crawling about the path. He was eleven inches and three-quarters. He detained me some time getting this information, because he was so nervous during the operation. (*Travels* 562)

While Kingsley obtains her measurement, the "operation" is not done with emotional detachment. She sympathizes with the worm and, in doing so, suggests that the exactitude required in the measurement (eleven and three-quarters inches in contrast to an approximate foot) is more a matter of maintaining a certain form than in gaining information.

Other creatures she feels obligated to collect require that she display unladylike determination. Kingsley handles this by claiming fear, and then going in to do the job (much as she did with the canoe). She describes having "sensational meetings with blue-green snakes, dirty green snakes with triangular horned heads, black cobras, and boa constrictors" (*Travels* 161). Yet she is hardly put off by the experience:

> I never came back to the station without having been frightened half out of my wits, and with one or two of my smaller terrifiers in cleft sticks to bottle. When you get into the way, catching a snake in a cleft stick is perfectly simple. Only mind you have the proper kind of stick, split far enough up, and keep your attention on the snake's head, that's his business end, and the tail which is whisking and winding round your wrist does not matter. . . . (*Travels* 161)

Although the British public had been entertained with tales of big game hunting and record sizes (and even those who collected for scientific purposes had become fixated on size), Kingsley made no attempt to take on large game. When she came across large and dangerous animals, she let her readers know that she generally retreated. On one occasion, she remarks on being caught in the forest during a wind storm; after crawling out from a dunking in a stream, she finds herself suddenly very close to a large leopard up on the bank. Instead of dwelling on the danger, she sympathizes with its responses to the storm and describes the leopard as a personality who is so annoyed and bewildered by the weather conditions that she claims, "that depraved creature swore, softly, but repeatedly and profoundly" (*Travels* 544–45). As she beats her retreat (while occasionally marking its position), it is the animal's view of the situation which remain with her, "his observation on the weather, and the flip-flap of his tail on the ground," rather than a fear of attack (*Travels* 545).

Instead of taking on big game, she pokes fun at past journalistic descriptions and the demands for measurement. When, after sighting several crocodiles, she asks a native whether there "are many gorillas, elephants, or bushcows round here," he replies, "Plenty too much," a response she agrees with (*Travels* 244). Having presented this critical view that such wildlife is something to be avoided rather than hunted as coming from native knowledge, she then recalls a typical picture of the male explorer from her youthful readings:

> . . . soon there rises up in my mental vision a picture that fascinated my youth in the *Fliegende Blätter*, representing "Friedrich Gerstaecker auf der Reise." That gallant man is depicted trampling on a serpent, new to M. Boulenger, while he attempts to club, with the butt end of his gun, a most lively savage who, accompanied by a bison, is attacking him in

front. A terrific and obviously enthusiastic crocodile is grabbing the tail of the explorer's coat, and the explorer says "Hurrah! das gibt wieder einen prächtigen Artikel für *Die Allgemeine Zeitung*." (*Travels* 244)

Kingsley wishes to distance herself from this view of exploration and adventure as fodder for yet another splendid sensational newspaper article. She wants to be seen as scientific, but not in the competitive sportsman sense associated with the word "explorer." And in the process of distancing herself from this big game association, she also challenges the disciplinary association of size measurements with scientific rigor. She was advised by a "scientific friend" to "Always take measurements, Miss Kingsley, and always take them from the adult male" (*Travels* 244–45). Kingsley remarks at this point that she has been negligent in her duty (with a mock guilty conscience), but she will not go back for measurements since "the men [her guides] would not like it [measuring crocodiles], and I have mislaid my yard measure" (*Travels* 245). On another occasion, after describing a couple of evening run-ins with leopards in villages (during which her general response is to throw household stools and water pitchers at the animals), she gives "for the benefit of sporting readers whose interest may have been excited by the mention of big game," the size of the largest skin she had measured in addition to a few other big measurements, all the while noting that "experienced bushmen" (such as herself) know how difficult it is to preserve large things in the tropical climate (*Travels* 546–47). Her implication being that excitement over large-sized specimens is more indicative of (male) amateurs than experienced field scientists such as herself.

While there are reminders that Kingsley is a working scientist, her text is also shaped in such a way as to make her behavior as palatable and as nonthreatening to her readers as possible, and her readers recognized and praised her for this. Besides the previously discussed presentation of conventional dress, Kingsley also used domestic references and self-mockery to add enough feminine discourse in order to counterbalance the unconventional aspects of her writing and traveling. It should be remembered, as Catherine Barnes Stevenson states, that Kingsley was "caught in an impossible situation."[79] In order to win an audience for her ideas, she could not alienate her politically conservative readership by seeming too radical. At the same time, while the use of conventional feminine references would seem to undermine her presentation of herself as a serious scientist, Kingsley used a feminine discourse indirectly in ways that challenged many masculine explorer conventions in an effort to create a space for women naturalists in the field.

In many descriptions, the previously mentioned challenges to requirements for measurement are combined with domestic imagery. These descriptions serve, on the one hand, to present her travel as a continuation of the woman's sphere or to show that the jungle is a proper place for a woman. Yet they also serve to subvert the general emphasis on the strangeness and exoticism in jungle descriptions which often work to distance readers' sympathetic responses to native peoples. Kingsley's descriptive techniques involve the personification of animals and plants in such a way as to identify them with British village experiences, in contrast to the hyperbole common in journalistic celebrations of masculine scientific exploration. When a crocodile attempts to enter her canoe, for instance, Kingsley avoids playing the situation up. Rather, her description downplays the danger, while poking fun at popular newspaper phrasing: "On one occasion, . . . a mighty Silurian, as *The Daily Telegraph* would call him, chose to get his front paws over the stern of my canoe, and endeavoured to improve our acquaintance" (*Travels* 89). Kingsley comments in a footnote, "It is no use saying . . . I was frightened, for this miserably understates the case" (*Travels* 89). But this crocodile was not conventionally bloodthirsty: "This was only a pushing young creature who had not learnt manners" (*Travels* 90). Thus scientific demands are appeased and the danger is de-emphasized by placing the invading crocodile within the realms of domestic manners. The crocodile is merely wishing to "improve our acquaintance," but has not yet "learnt manners."

Similarly, plants are presented as the sort of village characters one might find in such idyllic English novels as Elizabeth Gaskell's *Cranford* (1851–53).[80] Palms may look beautiful but they behave badly and are guilty of gossiping, and this is the reason for disruption of telephone communication: "these gossiping palms—the most inveterate chatterer in the vegetable kingdom is a cocoanut palm—talk to each other with their hard leaves on the wire . . . so that mere human beings can hardly get a word in edgeways" (108). Additionally, the mangrove trees are feminine and, despite their visible prop roots, are usually properly clothed:

> At high-water you do not see the mangroves displaying their ankles in the way that shocked Captain Lugard. They look most respectable, their foliage rising densely in a wall irregularly striped here and there by the white line of an aërial root, coming straight down into the water from some upper branch as straight as a plummet. (*Travels* 88)

Such descriptions domesticate the wildness of the jungle. Kingsley is indicating that here too there are rules and order. Amidst these stereotyped feminine plants, the jungle's sense of decorum is strict. Crabs behave according to their own sense of correct manners, which leads to their downfall.

> It seems to be crab etiquette that, even when a powerfully built, lithe, six foot high young man is coming at you hard all with a paddle, you must not go rushing into anybody's house save your own, whereby it fell out many crabs were captured." (*Travel* 111)

Even in African nature, Kingsley suggests, there are codes of conduct. This is a place which does not need to be tamed. Rather the British need to understand the order which is already present.

At one point, the entire jungle scene appears to be a cross between a carefully tended English garden and a parlor.

> The climbing plants are finer here than I have ever before seen them. They form great veils and curtains between and over the trees, often hanging so straight and flat, in stretches of twenty to forty feet or so wide, and thirty to sixty or seventy feet high, that it seems incredible that no human hand has trained or clipped them into their perfect forms. Sometimes these curtains are decorated with large bell-shaped, bright-coloured flowers, sometimes with delicate sprays of white blossoms. (*Travel* 129)

And where the exoticism cannot be denied, it becomes aestheticized in a particularly feminine manner:

> . . . added to this there is also the relieving aspect of the prevailing fashion among West African trees, of wearing the trunk white with here and there upon it splashes of pale pink lichen, and vermilion-red fungus, which alone is sufficient to prevent the great mass of vegetation from being a monotony in green. (*Travel* 129)

As the language of fashion and dress generally associated with women magazines feminizes the scene, these descriptions serve to counter images of danger and savagery generally associated with jungles. So great is the confusion between the jungle and domestic articles through her telling that Kingsley, and even the natives, seem to confuse the two worlds. When she explains why the word for umbrella and a particular tree are the same, she finds herself muddled in a linguistic confusion over the role of association in word formation. She explains that the leaves of the engombie-gombie trees growing in a cluster at the top of the straight stem give an umbrella-like appearance to the affair; so the natives call them and an umbrella by the same name, but whether they think the umbrella is like the tree or the tree is like the umbrella, I can't make out. I am always getting myself mixed over this kind of thing in my attempts "to contemplate phenomena from a scientific standpoint," as Cambridge ordered me to do. I'll give the habit up. "You can't do that sort of thing out here—it's the climate," and I will content myself with stating the fact, that when a native comes into a store and wants an umbrella, he asks for an engombie-gombie. (*Travels* 141)

Language and meaning become confused in Wonderland-type puzzles, as Kingsley presents herself as trying once again to follow scientific guidelines and report the "phenomena." However, the fieldwork does not always correspond with what is supposed to happen. The nineteenth-century anthropological guidelines for reporting on "primitive" culture are based on the assumption that native cultures remain pure, consistent, and unaffected by trade influences. Here, although she cannot make the expected report on native language usage, Kingsley brushes off the problem by first saying she gets mixed up and then claiming the climate is at fault, rather than suggesting that the experts at Cambridge may be wrong.

In this cozy village atmosphere, where the jungle is not a wilderness but part of an orderly world, the African natives become, not half-clothed savages, but the sort of people one would meet while walking down a rural path in an English village. Coming across "an old gentleman with a bundle of bamboos," she greets him and notices that he is watching a large lizard. Finding that they share an interest in collecting, Kingsley gives him "tobacco and a selection of amiable observations, and he beams and we go on down the road together, discussing the proper time to burn grass, and the differences in the practical value, for building purposes, of the two kinds of bamboo" (*Travels* 118). This, Kingsley implies in her narration, is how one should engage in anthropology: find common ground, have a nice chat, and listen sensitively. This, and a desire to be polite, is more effective than a distant "scientific standpoint."

When a social faux pas is committed, it is Kingsley, not an African, who is responsible for the breach in manners. While walking on a steep hillside overlooking a village Kingsley recounts how,

I slipped, slid, and finally fell plump through the roof of an unprotected hut. What the unfortunate inhabitants were doing, I don't know, but I am pretty sure they were not expecting me to drop in, and a scene of great confusion occurred. My knowledge of Fan dialect then consisted of Kor-kor, so I said that in as fascinating a tone as I could, and explained the rest with three pocket handkerchiefs, a head of tobacco, and a knife. . . . I also said I'd pay for the damage, and although this important communication had to be made in trade English, they seemed to understand. (*Travel* 134)

Such encounters emphasize the social order among Africans and the similarity of their culture to the most traditional aspects of British culture. When Kingsley interacts with Africans, it is with sympathetic curiosity. She assumes that they have developed a culture with reasonable and workable laws and codes of conduct and that, while there are problems which are not the result of European colonization (such as the practice of killing twin children), similar situations can be found in all cultures.

While Kingsley presents West Africa in a way which normalizes African culture and her presence in it, she also allows her audience to perceive her as outside the norm and yet forgive her for it. By emphasizing her own eccentricity for preferring Africa, she sets herself apart. Thus, in regards to African forest life, she confesses, "Unless you are interested in it and fall under its charm, it is the most awful life in death imaginable. It is like being shut up in a library whose books you cannot read, all the while tormented, terrified, and bored. And if you do fall under its spell, it takes all the colour out of other kinds of living" (*Travel* 102). Kingsley's narratives, in effect, do take her readers under her spell as she asks them to understand African culture in ways that go beyond the data recording, creating what Early calls, "a multivoiced narrative of mutual misperceptions and perceptions, alternative scales of value, and, always, a sense of the provisional and partial nature of any 'truths.' "[81]

CLIMBING MT. CAMEROON

If *Travels* can be said to have a plot, then the climb of Mt. Cameroon is probably its climax. Here Kingsley challenges the male explorer convention of mountain climbing records which was a focus of geographic research and calls into question the nineteenth-century rhetorical convention of surveillance. This surveillance convention was well established in African travels by such male explorers as Mungo Park, Richard Burton, and Henry Morgan Stanley.[82] In general, women's travel writing is not as concerned with describing sweeping viewpoints as men's. While Martineau and

Bird Bishop do manage to fit a few promontories into their travels, such tropes tend to be highly gendered. The scarcity of such rhetorical techniques in women's writings has caused Pratt to conclude that the appearance of such viewpoints is a distinguishing difference between men and women's travel narratives.[83] One reason for the limited number of examples may be the association of this trope with the discourse of discovery and exploration, a narrative position which was not easily available to women. The climbing of Mt. Cameroon in *Travels,* however, is a prominent exception to this generalization and Pratt describes Kingsley's manipulation of a conventional masculine discourse as resulting in "a monarchic female voice that asserts its own kind of mastery even as it denies domination and parodies power."[84] Generally, according to Pratt, the use of this convention implies a close relationship between control (and imperial power) and visual surveillance, similar to Foucault's description of the use of the Panopticon in eighteenth-century prisons.

When Kingsley climbs Mt. Cameroon, she seems to be fulfilling an expectation that, as an explorer, she needs to climb, survey the view and announce the achievement of some sort of record. Yet, in fulfilling this expectation, she also questions its entire rationale. Chapter 24 (like many of the chapters) is rather melodramatically titled—"Ascent of the Great Peak of Cameroons"—and is captioned, "Setting forth how the Voyager is minded to ascend the mountain called Mungo Mah Lobeh, or the Throne of Thunder, and in due course reaches Buea, situate [*sic*] thereon" (548).[85] Instead of moving right into the preparations for ascent, however, Kingsley begins by praising German colonial structure in Africa and, in particular, supporting individual German colonial officials who had recently been subjected to reprimand. In doing this, Kingsley is following her general rhetorical strategy of first acknowledging the help of men who allowed her to travel and speaking in their favor.[86] After this obligatory praise, she returns to her "own trivial experiences."[87] Despite the heroic subtitle, the emphasis on the importance of her climb is now humorously undercut as the climb is presented merely as a "temptation," a temptation she really has no reason to give into: "Now it is none of my business to go up mountains. There's next to no fish on them in West Africa, and precious little good rank fetish [religious rites], as the population on them is sparse—the African, like myself, abhorring cool air" (*Travel* 549). This raises the question of why she should attempt the trip, a question that also undercuts the conventional expectations raised by the title. At the same time, it also identifies Kingsley with the Africans, who now seem more rational than mountain-climbing Europeans.

Continuing with the mock analysis of her rationale, she points out,

> Nevertheless, I feel quite sure that no white man has ever looked on the great Peak of Cameroon without a desire arising in his mind to ascend it and know in detail the highest point on the western side of the continent, and indeed one of the highest points in all Africa. (*Travel* 549–50)

Most resident Europeans, "coasters," being "stronger minded" or ill, resist this temptation. Kingsley, however, has for the moment aligned herself with the white male explorers, even while she is establishing that such climbing serves no worthwhile purpose. Having weakened her narrative position, while she has also established the importance of this particular peak as the highest point in the region, Kingsley then gives the expected listing of the mountain climbers and her place among its European male explorers. The first person to reach the summit was Richard Burton, "accompanied by the great botanist, Gustav Mann" (*Travel* 55). [88]

Notably, at no point here does Kingsley refer to herself as the first European woman to make this climb, although this would have been acknowledged as a greater record. In this genealogy of Mt. Cameroon climbers, Kingsley assumes a male identify in placing herself as "the third Englishman to ascend the Peak and the first to have ascended it from the south-east face" (*Travel* 550). [89] Moreover, she allows nationality to take precedence over gender, befitting her sense of herself as a European male while traveling and in order not to challenge male achievement. Of course, readers would immediately recognize her climb as an achievement in terms of gender. But by not explicitly acknowledging it as such, Kingsley again avoids direct challenge to male authority.

After establishing the existence of the mountains within the context of European exploration and her own place within that genealogy, Kingsley switches to a diary format to emphasize both the immediacy of her narration and the placement of it as a historical record, important enough to be worthy of a day-by-day account. Yet the content of her entries is less focused on the climb than on the practical and unheroic difficulties with which she has to cope.

Her difficulties with the road to the summit, for example, provide a humorous contrast between the view of the landscape from a distance and her immediate practical experience as a climber. The adventure begins with a sketch on the beauty of the scenery, then moves to an awareness of the presence of butterflies and gradually to a comment that, noble and lovely as the road may be, it is best appreciated from a butterfly perspective because "for of all the truly awful things to walk on, that road, when I was on it, was the worst" (*Travel* 553). The aesthetic appreciation of the butterflies in the opening is then countered with a list of travel problems increasing in their severity: The road was unfinished, footing was difficult, and the rains increased. Umbrella in hand, Kingsley initially attempts to maintain the safe comfortable domestic allusions while, at the same time, she establishes the risk and difficulty of the endeavor. As she moves on into a torrent of warm water, for instance, she describes the feeling as "like that of a cucumber frame with the lights on, if you can . . . forget the risk of fever which saturation entails" (*Travel* 555).

As she climbs, rather than focusing her attention on the goal ahead (as a conventional climbing narrative would), her attention is continually distracted by the needs of her crew. The situation worsens as she continues her climb: her crew are frequently drunk or hung over, they run out of water, the men get separated and lost. She drops the domestic imagery and decides that the expedition is not worth risking the health of the men in the storm. Continuing on her own, she reaches the summit only to find that the visibility is so poor she cannot see anything.[90] Consequently, there is no sense of achievement or of having wrested some power from nature. She simply finds some trash left by the previous German climbers, bows to their achievement, and leaves her calling card, not as any permanent marker or proof of her accomplishment, but rather "as a civility to Mungo [the mountain], a civility his Majesty will soon turn into pulp. Not that it matters—what is done is done" (*Travel* 594). Disappointed with the whole experience, she concludes,

> Verily I am no mountaineer, for there is in me no exultation, but only a deep disgust because the weather has robbed me of my main object in coming here, namely to get a good view and an idea of the way the unexplored mountain range behind Calabar trends. (*Travel* 594)

The trip down is a little more dramatic than the climb as Kingsley is preoccupied with keeping ahead of an approaching storm. The whole expedition, however, dissolves in the rain and mist, becoming an undignified scramble as Kingsley slips down a hillside. This slide is described as yet another pratfall, a ploy of self-negation, nervously used whenever Kingsley feels she has once again gone too far subverting convention:

Unfortunately, I must needs go in for acrobatic performances on the top of one of the highest, rockiest hillocks. Poising myself on one leg I take a rapid slide sideways, ending in a very showy leap backwards which lands me on the top of the lantern I am carrying to-day, among miscellaneous rocks. There being fifteen feet or so of jungle grass above me, all the dash and beauty of my performance are as much thrown away as I am, for my boys are too busy on their own accounts in the mist to miss me. After resting some little time as I fell, and making and unmaking the idea in my mind that I am killed, I get up, clamber elaborately to the top of the next hillock, and shout for the boys, and "Ma," "ma," comes back from my flock from various points out of the fog. (*Travel* 596–597)

Having failed to find any validity or place for herself within this conventional masculine discourse, she shows her heroism in repairing the damage this now ridiculous expedition has caused. She finally regroups, finds her way back to camp and dries out her now drenched camp. After dosing the men with rum and herself with the ever present domestic symbol of a cup of tea, order is restored (at least for the moment).

Thus, in Kingsley's hands, the purpose of mountain climbing, achieving a record, becomes a meaningless, even suicidal, extravagance in comparison to the danger and disorder it causes. Nevertheless, she refuses to romanticize her position by ignoring practicalities. Moreover, while the self-deprecatory comments and humor may distract the reader from her less agreeable message, that message is clear enough: the lives of her crew are more important than a citation in a recordbook at home. This leaves the impression that those famous explorers, whom she had admired and who were heroes of British imperialism, were also very self-serving. For her, as a woman, the mountain top gives no sweeping sense of power and domination. Indeed, she sees less from such a position than she does in the forests and swamps among the African people.

Making Use of Travel: Influence and Later Years

When Kingsley returned home, she set about establishing a market for her writing and making political use of the publicity she would attract after publication. Through judicious use of lectures and newspaper accounts that she coordinated within a month after returning to England, Kingsley prepared her readers for *Travels*. She translated a relatively short stay in West Africa into a position of authority, speaking out on the controversial issues of liquor in

Africa and the Hut Tax.[91] Soon after publishing *Travels*, she was
elected fellow of the Anthropological Society and joined the British
Empire League and the Folklore Society. By using her influence to
promote the career of Matthew Nathan, who was eventually appointed Acting Governor of Sierra Leone, she attempted to gain behind-the-scenes power over colonial policy. She was responsible for
the earliest plans for indirect rule in West Africa based on native
African government and legal structure. Finally, her influence has
been linked to the use of indirect rule in Nigeria and the Congo
Reform Movement as well.

The traders she supported lost power after the revocation of the
Royal Niger Company's charter to govern Niger, and the transfer-
ence of territorial governance to the British government. Kingsley
then applied to nurse in the Boer War through the recently formed
Colonial Nursing Association (which she had championed). Her
reasons for volunteering are unclear. It is likely that she was attempting to regroup her resources and gain more onsite experience
in another imperialistic hot spot, but she also considered traveling
to Nigeria and Lake Chad afterwards.[92]

Less than two months after Kingsley's senseless death from en-
teric fever in 1900 (the result of her nursing activities) and her military burial, Alice Stopford Green took up the idea for an African
society which Kingsley had shelved because she felt that she
"dared nòt show a hand in it for ladies *must not* be admitted."[93]
Kingsley had also argued in 1899, in language reminiscent of Wollstonecraft and Martineau, that women should not petition for membership in scientific societies because "if we women distinguish
ourselves in Science in sufficiently large numbers at a sufficiently
high level, the great scientific societies . . . will admit [us]" otherwise "we shall form . . . our own [society] of equal eminence."[94]
From the publicity surrounding Kingsley's death, Green saw that
the time was ripe to transfer the praise for Kingsley into momentum
for the establishment of the long planned organization which
Kingsley had earlier felt to be too unconventional an idea to risk
posing.

The eulogies which followed the announcement of Kingsley's
death generally emphasized a feminine devotion to duty which
played well in anti-feminist imperialistic Britain. While one obituary accurately presented her death as a "loss to science, to the literature of travel, and, above all, to the West African colonies,"[95]
others claimed she embodied traditional feminine traits. E. Clodd
referred to her life as one "of self-sacrifice which nurtured no hope
of recompensating glory in a vision of the martyr's crown."[96] The

Morning Leader headlined their obituary as "Mary Kingsley: Her Charms as a Woman, Nurse, Cook, and Conversationalist Told by One Who Knew Her," an article which declared that "Mary Kingsley the woman will hold a much more important place than Mary Kingsley the traveller" because of her devotion to duty.[97] Such responses to Kingsley's death made it easier for Green to establish the African Society (later the Royal African Society) since its journal's masthead read, "founded in memory of Mary Kingsley," with a classical rendition of her profile as the emblem on the title page.[98] Green's description of Kingsley in the new journal emphasized the traditionally feminine reputation that Kingsley had so carefully nurtured. Green described her as "a skilled nurse, a good cook, a fine needlewoman, an accomplished housewife" and continued with a portrait which countered any suggestion that Kingsley was part of an organized woman's movement:

> [I]t was her special gifts as a woman that gave to her work its unique and original character: in them lay her strength and her authority. She thought it may be truly said, through her heart: and it was in good measure the maternal instinct of protection and helpfulness that vivified her intelligence.[99]

In a sense, by continuing to maintain this facade of femininity, Green was following Kingsley's advice in one of her last letters to her: "Set yourself to gain personal power—don't grab the reins of power—but [while] they are laying on the horses [*sic*] neck, quietly get them into your hands and drive."[100]

6

Conclusion

BEATRIX POTTER'S DECISION TO REFOCUS HER EFFORTS TO GAIN independence toward the realm of children's literature rather than microscopic botany marked an end of an era. It indicated that science had become professionalized to the point where women (and natural historians) were edged out. Scientific patrimony was established; women were actively discouraged from scientific areas of study and those working within the old tradition of natural history became like younger sons, tolerated but not accorded the full status of "scientists." They were merely amateurs, outside the professional lineage whereby established scientific practitioners trained and mentored their male successors, only passing professional status onto each generation those selected students who received their teacher's blessing.

What happened then to women's involvement in those disciplines which grew out of natural history? This question is at least partly answered in Phillips's study of women's interest in science during the eighteenth and nineteenth centuries. Phillips sadly concludes with Emily Davies's founding of Girton College, Cambridge in the 1870s, an act that opened university education to women while it simultaneously encouraged the study of classics rather than sciences. Her decision to move the first three women students away from consideration of the natural sciences tripos signaled what would become a general policy as the Bryce Commission in 1894–95 discouraged girls from taking science classes.[1] While there was increased interest in science at the turn of the century and some club activity among women in Oxford, the jobs, however, were not available, as there was strong social pressure for women to be trained in homemaking.[2] This became educational policy by 1918 and in her conclusion to her study of women's scientific involvement Phillips states:

> Just as the research field was about to become highly specialized and politically and strategically important—in other words, just as science

222

was posed to become a respectable profession—women were finally excluded. Science, after all, was soon to be a serious matter. Women had other jobs to do.[3]

This regression of opportunities for women's scientific involvement was paralleled by the systematic dismissal of women in the scientific societies and other organizations with roots in natural history. Like Kingsley, travel writer Amelia Edwards (along with Reginald Poole) managed to found a society, the Egypt Exploration Fund, for the study of Egyptology in 1880, only to be "inched out of the decision-making processes of the society."[4] Her health broken by the work she had put into the society, Edwards died leaving behind a bequest for the first English chair in Egyptology in 1892.

Similarly, after a period of openness, participation in the Royal Astronomical Society was blocked to women until 1915. Honorary women members were allowed after 1835, but only three were actually admitted during the nineteenth century: Caroline Herschel, Mary Somerville, and Anne Sheepshanks.[5] After the turn of the century, in this field too, resistance to women membership became more unified. This is apparent in the case of Agnes Clerke who was a popularizer of astronomy but one who worked very closely with the professional astronomers of her time, used the objective language of science, and synthesized recent advancements in research so it would be more accessible to astronomers in different areas of study. Her 1885 *Popular History of Astronomy During the Nineteenth Century* was very successful, was reprinted in 1902, and is still valued as a source on the history of nineteenth-century science, but as Bernard Lightman explains, her continuation of natural theological interpretations in her work brought her into conflict with some professional astronomers. When in 1903, she and Margaret Huggins were elected as honorary members of the Royal Astronomical Society, Richard A. Gregory, assistant editor of *Nature*, wrote a series of attacks on her credentials in *Nature* which specifically attacked her gender. In one review he wrote:

In preparing a statement of the position of fact and theory in any branch of science, great care must be exercised, and not a single assertion should be made without substantial reason for it. A cynic has said that it is a characteristic of women to make rash assertions, and in the absence of contradiction to accept them as true. Miss Clerke is apparently not free from this weakness of her sex.[6]

Women were just too rash to be considered capable of scientific work.

Even if women were university-educated, they met a cool reception at societies' meetings. Women were able to acquire degrees at women's colleges but were then stymied at attempts to attend professional meetings and fieldwork opportunities were very limited. Some women participated in fieldwork by doing record keeping and/or illustrations; a handful just went out and did their work independently with little or no support.[7] The situation was so bad during the Edwardian period that at the 1913 meeting of the British Association of Anthropology, Dr. Margaret Murray was firmly discouraged from attending lectures and one woman tried to attend talks by hiding from the men's sight.[8]

Opportunities opened a bit in the 1920s. And then there were periods of opportunity and blockades as war moved men in and out of civilian life. There was some marginal work by individuals from 1935–60 and the continual quiet spousal activity such as that of Mary Nicol Leakey, the great-great-granddaughter of John Frere, a major British geologist/archeologist of the early nineteenth century, who had established herself in the field by the early 1930s. She was the supportive record-keeping, accurate part of a spousal team.[9] Her scientific ancestry, however, is generally obscured by that of her husband, Louis Leakey and, for the most part, the historical record has been silent on the role of such spousal team members.

In such an atmosphere as that presented at the turn of the century, the hopes of Wollstonecraft and others like her that science would provide new professions for better-educated women died. So well established was the identification of science as a particularly masculine way of thinking that it was generally accepted that the mind was sexed. Debates over comparative intellectual capabilities of men and women continue today; at times, feminist critics have even propagated this belief that science is an inherently male-identified way of thinking. As a result, the history of women in science must then continually be unearthed and reassembled to challenge such assumptions. This necessitates not only an examination of those women who did find their way into the laboratories and the history of science texts, but also those working in the field and publishing in such fringe areas as travel accounts, popularizations, gardening texts, and children's literature. Here, I predict, we will continue to find other attempts by women, with varying successes, to work within an established profession, to reshape that profession and, possibly, to create new disciplines, as nonfictional writing gave women a staging ground from which to maneuver their charges into masculine-dominated activities. The scholars gathered in such anthologies as *Natural Eloquence* is the start of just such an examination of more "popular" writings with an eye to how women had to make their contribution indirectly to scientific study.

The question may naturally be raised whether these travel accounts constitute what we call "science." The claim that Wollstonecraft was a scientist would, I suspect, be derided. And admittedly, I have been using a much broader definition of science than would be accepted today. Yet texts which have been accepted as part of science history today do not immediately strike one as scientific either, as arguments are based on speculation, and the scientific discovery may not be that apparent as it is hidden among several incorrect conclusions which are presented as equally valid and are reached by a logical process which is as valid as that used for the conclusions we accept. Great discoveries develop from often very muddled sources as different scientists examine, challenge, and clarify masses of observations into general rules. The codifying of science history is one of going back to establish and clarify the lines of scientific genealogy, a process which often presents a misleadingly unambiguous story of an eureka-type event which provides a foundation for what Thomas S. Kuhn calls "normal science." It is a process of historiography that asks questions not originally posed by the historic figures who are examined. Establishing individuals as being part of the scientific development of a paradigm requires that we go back and examine pre-paradigm work which reflects many views and try to find that starting point for an accepted paradigm—a difficult task.

Contributing to this process, however, requires that the practitioner be capable of attracting "an enduring group of adherents away from competing modes of scientific activity."[10] The one who could gets in the history books. As seen in the case of Martineau, a nineteenth-century woman simply did not have the social status to become equivalent to Comte or Spencer; her social position was too entrenched in the auxiliary service roles, her influence too closely bound to her martial status and the prevailing ideas of sexual propriety.

Thus, these studies of women's involvement on the margins of science must necessarily be accounts of potentials missed or modified. Yet they were read and they did contribute to the history of science, although seldom acknowledged as such, and they did see themselves as being "scientific" in the questions they asked and the way they organized and examined their observations. Moving from the 1790s to the 1890s, we have seen these writers' continual focus on the importance of trained observation rather than an accumulation of data, a resistance to objectivity without sensitivity, and a reiterated argument that women belong in the "field"—out in the world and in the discipline.

Looking over the rhetorical approaches used by Wollstonecraft, Martineau, Bird Bishop, and Kingsley, we can see that those women who did manage to edge their way a little into scientific work did so by modifying the explorer identity to include women. They tended, like Martineau, to bring a modulated voice into the exploration, one which tried to understand other cultures and societies; they might place more emphasis on endurance than feats of strength as did Bird Bishop or subtly subvert the competitive nature of exploration by undercutting its importance, as did Kingsley. If they were faced with issues that threatened to become erotic or challenge the status quo, they sidestepped issues, were silent, or praised in ways which challenged indirectly. All of these techniques required that they work away from other Europeans who could give conflicting evidence about how they work, and possibly damage the veneer of gentility upon which they depended to maintain their authority.

To function as natural historians though after Wollstonecraft, women travelers found it best not to have family duties and to make it clear that they were not needed in the domestic sphere. Maintaining an intellectual reputation and a family in the nineteenth century would have required a more secure economic and social position than these women had. Rather, maternal duties could be directed as needed to the care of native workers as in the case of Kingsley; but once scientific authority was established, there was an avoidance of maternal roles by the traveler if they threatened to undercut the scientific authority of the traveler as can be seen by Bird Bishop's refusal to allow herself to be typecast as a nurse.

In general accounts of natural history, an impression is often left that natural history was eventually replaced by professionalized science. This, however, is not quite accurate. There are many organized societies that focus on a particular group of organisms. There are, for example, botanical societies: the orchid society, the succulent society, the bromeliad society, the African violet society—organizations of enthusiasts who are more than hobbyists; they are growers, collectors, experts in propagation and cultivation who publish papers in their own journals but are outside the academic world. They are paralleled by similar organizations devoted to animal breeding. And then there are mineralogy, paleontology, and archeology societies. While science in its proper, modern sense is concerned with theoretical, broad issues, natural history, functioning through such organizations, still maintains a base of knowledge about particular species and their habitats. Its practitioners still retain a sense of place and a feeling for the individual organism missing in modern scientific work. I need look no further than my own parents and their work in science teaching and with plant and mineralogy societies to see that natural history is still operating on the margins of academic science.

But what then can we learn from the careers of Wollstonecraft, Martineau, Bird Bishop, and Kingsley? Have the travel narratives examined in this study contributed to women's scientific work in the twentieth century? Can we trace influences to the present? What do these rhetorical strategies tell us about the obstacles women scientists in the field face when they write? In many ways, the rhetorical situation has changed. There is still a need for popularizers, and a few scientists do write for the general public, but this appears to be more likely among men. Travel accounts are still popular and, in fact, there has been a resurgence of interest in this genre. However, for the most part, we don't see the sort of use being made of the genre that was prevalent in the eighteenth and nineteenth centuries as science no longer looks to such accounts for field data the way Charles Darwin did. In a couple of areas, however, there does seem to be a continuation of this tradition: in anthropology and ethnology, particularly primatology.

Kingsley took the travel genre as far as she could, making it a vehicle for advancement into professional scientific status within the gender constraints of the end of the nineteenth century. Today, the travel account, while still popular, has not been as usable as it was during the expanding colonization of Britain as national interests are not viewed as being crucially affected by frontier exploration. It is possible though to see some continuation of natural history–oriented travel in the twentieth century in the popular writings of women working in scientific fields in places far from Europe and their treatment in films and the popular press: the anthropology accounts of Margaret Mead in the 1940s and 1950s; the zoology work of Joy Adamson with lions; Alison Jolly's twenty-year study of lemurs in Madagascar; Shirley Strum's work with baboons; Cynthia Moss's fourteen-year study of elephants; and, most strikingly, the work of Louis Leakey's "ape ladies," women primatologists Jane Goodall, Dian Fossey, and Biruté Galdikas, who have spent most of their lives following individual chimpanzees, gorillas, and orangutans. As with the travel writers we have examined, these women also have based their scientific reputations on their ability to work in distant, isolated areas, far from other Europeans and they emphasize their abilities to use careful observation in the field.

Their narratives, however, are not travel accounts per se, but descriptions of a particular place where they are doing their fieldwork. However, as they stress their distance from "civilization" and solitude, as they are in a sense exploratory and a continuation of natural history, they are working within the tradition established by Wollstonecraft, Martineau, Bird Bishop, and Kingsley. They have also faced some of the same type of challenges in their authorial presentation of their work and in the presentation others have made of their presence in the field.

Leakey purposefully sought out women for primate study because he believed that compared to men, they were tenacious, tougher, more sensitive, and intuitive, and that they would proceed with less heavy-handed manipulation of their object of study. This is the reputation of women in the field that had been established by such women as Bird Bishop and Kingsley. He also sought out women who had not been part of the scientific establishment since the long-term study of individual animals smacked too much of the popular science genre of animal biography; it was too anthropomorphic and has been avoided in scientific training. Goodall and Fossey had no academic training in primate behavior before being recruited by Leakey. Goodall had worked as a waitress and secretary. Fossey had been an occupational therapist. Only Galdikas had a graduate degree and training in data recording. All three were shepherded into Ph.D. programs to provide sufficient scientific credentials to "practice" science; however, they still faced scientific criticism for their field practices, their less-than-frequent publications, and their use of popular appeal (and the tourist industry) to raise funding for their research. Goodall has also been criticized for not being quicker to take a more outspoken role in primate conservation, for being like Martineau, Bird Bishop, and Kingsley, less assertive about feminist issues, although her success is probably related to her being more reserved about political issues.

And their narratives, too, have made use of trade-offs, as they try to manipulate gender expectations to their best advantage in order to popularize and gain support for their fieldwork. In the eighteenth and nineteenth centuries, women's presence in the field and the development of an authoritative voice required full control of how the public perceived these women naturalists. This meant the solitary stance was the most effective narrative technique. And by seeing how effective this narrative technique was—indeed, how necessary it was—we gain some insight into the difficulties modern women scientists have working in the field. For modern women primatologists, these efforts to establish an authoritative voice have not always been controllable as they were for earlier women natural history travelers since they do not have the sort of isolation needed to circumvent gender expectations. As Donna Haraway and James Krasner point out, in the case of women primatologists popularized by the *National Geographic*, "the camera remains firmly in the hands of men,"[11] subject to male mediation. *National Geographic* continues the close nineteenth-century connection between science and travel literature. The woman scientist in these situations, in distant, wild, non-European lands, "does not hold the camera; she is still the one photographed for millions to view."[12] This loss of privacy is tellingly underscored in a complaint made by Bob Campbell, the *National Geographic* photographer who covered Fossey. He seemed mystified that she was not interested in "keeping up" her appearance while working in the field, and complained that:

> Off the mountains . . . with rest, makeup, and feminine clothing, Dian could transform herself into a startlingly attractive woman. But in Rwanda she did not often make the change. I had great difficulty with her looks in the field—in many situations where there was no possibility of preparations, she looked terrible.[13]

This comment is particularly interesting when we remember Bird Bishop's uneasiness with Sawyer's presence in Persia and her need to separate their camps so she would not be made so conscious of her rough ways, of ignoring her appearance in the field. Kingsley, too, was made aware of her appearance when she encountered a European man, an issue she could otherwise ignore. Most of the time, however, these travelers could control when and how they were seen, and control how their appearance was presented to their public. This is no longer the case. Distance is no longer the guarantee of isolation if you are not your own photographer. Bird Bishop and Kingsley realized the great advantages brought by full control of both narrative and photographic image—an option no longer available in the twentieth century if the goal is to gain public recognition and funding.

Maintaining a fairly conservative private life was important to Martineau, Bird Bishop, and Kingsley, especially considering how it affected Wollstonecraft's reputation. And this lesson apparently still holds true today. Goodall, the first and most successful of the three in gaining both public support and scientific respect, was single when she started her work and then was able to present a life which seemed traditionally stable with a European husband and children. As one biographer put it:

Jane's own family drama unfolded along with the chimps': on National Geographic specials, we watched the infant [chimpanzee] Flint take his first uncertain steps right along with Jane's toddling son, Grub. . . . Jane was always one of "us": her Westernness stands out like a porcelain teacup on a rough-hewn tree stump. Hers was the story with the familiar, fairy-tale elements: the intrepid blonde marries a baron and produces a golden-haired son. Hers was the choice we felt was most comfortable and, well, respectable.[14]

Her later divorce is generally passed over. Goodall is a teacup, a recognizable "lady" who maintains an air of decorum and largely because of this ability not to unsettle or disturb her audience, of knowing how to shape and package her appeals for primate care, she is the most effective of the three. Like Bird Bishop and Kingsley, she absorbed the message that one must keep to the image of a lady in a good thick skirt even when she is actually wearing pants. The story is familiar because it is a story, a rhetorical, now made visual, strategy developed over the centuries by women who sought to negotiate their way around gender constraints while working in the field.

When Fossey defined herself as being alone, she meant being without a (European) man.[15] As she remained single and sought isolation, she has received the harshest biographic treatment, often characterized as sadistic, degenerate, and simply too aggressive and obsessive.[16] Her murder has been excused as something she brought on herself for insisting on being in the wrong place for a woman and for becoming as Galdikas put it, "very, very African."[17] Galdikas has also attracted concerned commentary suggesting that she too had gone too native, especially after her second marriage to a Indonesian, an act which attracted racially tinged attention as he was shown as being more primitive and closer to the orangutans under study. Both women found that they had to adapt to a different culture to gain authority in that culture; this was necessary to run their research stations. However, both have had difficulties translating these behaviors back to their home cultures—a difficult feat and one that Kingsley found required some posing once back in England. These modern scientists, however, are working afield in one place for much longer periods, require more funding, and thus the balancing acts are even more difficult to maintain.

As with previous naturalist travelers, the actual fieldwork also tends to fade into the background as the narratives are biographical, but they also pick up some themes common in exploratory narratives. The distance from European settlements and isolation from

Western culture is continually emphasized. This isolation in Goodall's case is translated into dedication to her subject. Fossey, in *Gorillas in the Mist*, presents herself in terms of traditional explorers into the dark primitive wilderness: "I spent many years longing to go to Africa, because of what that continent offered in its wilderness and great diversity of free-living animals."[18] In Fossey's work, this emphasis on wilderness and isolation backfires as it is seen by biographers as a possible contributor to instability and comparison has been made to Kurtz in Conrad's *Heart of Darkness*.[19] For Galdikas, this theme of isolation has been used to underscore her vulnerability in an effort to evoke a sympathetic response from readers. However, whereas Wollstonecraft was able to control her projection of vulnerability and carefully balance it with intellectual strength, Galdikas has not been able to keep such controls and biographers have dwelt on her body erotically, painting such images as menstrual blood leaking through pants because no tampons were available[20]—a really rather silly claim which ignores the fact that native women also cope with menstrual flow as have all women for centuries without such supplies. In this case, it seems that Victorian prudity did allow women some freedom since they could simply ignore such inquires (especially from men) and they could rest assured that no publisher would print such material.

The physical presence of the women also raises problems for these scientists. Whereas Bird Bishop did complain of her hardships, she never admitted to being vulnerable. Galdikas attempts to gain audience appeal by emphasizing her struggles, but she comes across as being too vulnerable and ends up being continually eroticized in her biographers' treatments.[21] As noted above, Fossey was faced with continual demands that she conform her appearance to that expected by a Hollywood-focused audience as if the world was not ready to see a woman sweat. Again, Goodall has come off the best and has managed to keep some distance with an air of propriety.

All three, however, have made use of maternal imagery in promoting their studies. They focus on the mother and child relationship among primates and caring for orphaned young animals has been made the focus of their research centers. This has been effective for practical reasons of animal conservancy, but it also works because nurturing the young is considered to be the proper role of women. Resisting such stereotypes is difficult; Strum had to fight *National Geographic* editors to avoid maternal encoding with her baboon studies.[22] However, beyond the practical use of such a focus, Goodall in particular has made use of her observations of other-child interactions for sociobiological arguments, drawing parallels between primate behavior and human behavior. This is a theme that our travel writers skirted clear of or used only gingerly. They sensed that the heavy use of such images could backfire on them, and put them in a defensive position regarding their own work. And making such parallels has also made it difficult for Goodall as continued observations of chimpanzees have produced dark themes of interspecies violence apparently counterdicting the earlier romanticized portrayal of primate behavior.

Although the use of the travel narrative to advance scientific careers for women is something that did not continue long into the twentieth century, the cultural burden with which women need to negotiate, to shift, to subvert, still exists. Women working in the field pursuing science-oriented professions must continually take note of how they present themselves just as much as women natural history travelers did. Not to do so, not to learn from the strategies of earlier women naturalists, could seriously undermine the success of a field project. Science is still not a gender-free endeavor and while the rhetorical situation has changed, and become more challenging as technology is more intrusive, the need to negotiate gender expectations still exists.

Notes

CHAPTER 1. NEW OPPORTUNITIES: WOMEN, SCIENCE, AND TRAVEL

1. Some of these were considered accurate enough to use to illustrate W. P. K. Findlay's 1967 *Wayside and Woodland Fungi*. (See "Beatrix Potter and Charles McIntosh, Naturalists" by Mary Noble in *A Victorian Naturalist: Beatrix Potter's Drawings from the Armitt Collection* by Eileen Jay, Mary Noble, and Anne Stevenson Hobbs [London: Warne, 1992], 55).

2. The details of Beatrix Potter's mycological studies can be found in Noble, 55–135. Also see Margaret Lane, *The Tale of Beatrix Potter* (Glasgow: Fontana-Collins, 1968).

3. Barbara T. Gates, *Kindred Nature: Victorian and Edwardian Women Embrace the LivingWorld* (Chicago: University of Chicago Press, 1998), 137.

4. Ann B. Shteir, "Botany in the Breakfast Room: Women and Early Nineteenth-Century British Plant Study." In *Uneasy Careers and Intimate Lives: Women in Science, 1789–1979*, edited by Pnina G. Abir-am and Dorinda Outram (New Brunswick: Rutgers University Press, 1987), 34.

5. Ibid., 34.

6. Ibid., 34.

7. Ibid., 38.

8. Marilyn Bailey Ogilvie, "Marital Collaboration: An Approach to Science." In *Uneasy Careers and Intimate Lives: Women in Science, 1789–1979*, edited by Pnina G. Abir-am and Dorinda Outram (New Brunswick: Rutgers University Press, 1987), 110–11.

9. Debra Lindsay, "Intimate Inmates: Wives, Households, and Science in Nineteenth-Century America." *Isis* 89(1998): 631–52.

10. Since specimens had a monetary value as collectible items in the eighteenth and nineteenth centuries, generally the names of the owners, not the finders, were recorded. Laborers could gain a supplemental income from collecting and, once in a while, as in the case of Mary Anning and Hugh Miller, they became local heroes, but were not acknowledged in the scientific societies unless they became Fellows. The difficulties this poses for science history is discussed in Stephen Jay Gould and Rosamond W. Purcell's *Finders, Keepers: Eight Collectors* and Hugh Torrens's "Mary Anning (1799–1847) of Lyme. 'The Greatest Fossilist the World Ever Knew,' " *The British Journal for the History of Science* 28 (1995). Those with higher class standing and education could start as collectors and hope to advance in scientific circles with worthwhile collections. This interesting class distinction between collectors is dramatized in A. S. Byatt's novella "Morpho Eugenia" (which was filmed under the title *Angels and Insects*). Among travel writers, this was the procedure used by many, including Charles Darwin, Mary Kingsley, and Henry O. Forbes. For a discussion of Darwin's status as a collector on the *Beagle* see Janet Browne's *Charles Darwin: Voyaging*, the first volume of her proposed two-volume biography of Darwin.

11. Hugh Torrens, "Mary Anning (1799–1847) of Lyme: 'The Greatest Fossilist the World Ever Knew," 266.

12. Bernard Lightman, "The Voices of Nature: Popularizing Victorian Science," *Victorian Science in Nature,* ed. Bernard Lightman (Chicago: University of Chicago Press, 1997), 190.

13. Ibid., 191.

14. Gates, 440.

15. Flora Tristan, "Women Travelers," in *Flora Tristan; Utopian Feminist: Her Travel Diaries and Personal Crusade,* ed. and trans. Doris Beik and Paul Beik (Bloomington: Indiana University Press, 1993), 3.

16. Barbara T. Gates and Ann B. Shteir, eds., *Natural Eloquence: Women Reinscribe Science* (Madison: University of Wisconsin Press, 1997), 6.

17. Shteir, "Elegant," 240.

18. Ibid., 242.

19. Gates, 71–74.

20. Ibid., 48.

21. Ibid., 81.

22. Ibid., 74.

23. Ibid., 74.

24. Anne McClintock, *Imperial Leather: Race, Gender and Sexuality in the Colonial Contest* (New York: Routledge, 1995), 166.

25. Robin Gilmour, *The Victorian Period: The Intellectual and Cultural Context of English Literature, 1830–1890* (London: Longman, 1993), 111.

26. Janet Browne, *Charles Darwin: Voyaging* (New York: Knopf, 1995),181.

27. Ibid., 181–182.

28. Ibid., 368.

29. Pnina G. Abir-am and Dorinda Outram, eds., *Uneasy Careers and Intimate Lives: Women in Science, 1789–1979,* (New Brunswick, NJ: Rutgers University Press, 1987), 3.

30. See as a contrast, Susan Morgan's introduction to Marianne North's *Recollections of a Happy Life* (Charlottesville: University Press of Virginia, 1993).

31. Shirley Foster, *Across New Worlds: Nineteenth Century Women Travellers and their Writings,* (Hemel Hampstead, England: Harvester, 1990), vii.

32. As a result, although two authors traveled in the United States (Martineau and Bird Bishop), American travel will not be a central focus of the study.

33. Gillian Thomas, *Harriet Martineau* (Boston: G. K. Hall, 1985), 49–50.

34. An example of the drawbacks of thematic organization can be seen in Dea Birkett's *Spinsters Abroad: Victorian Lady Explorers*, whose focus on biographical and rhetorical similarities makes it difficult to distinguish one traveler from another.

35. John Lowes's study of Coleridge's sources of inspiration, *The Road to Xanadu,* and John Christie's study of the influence of travel writing on Thoreau, *Thoreau as World Traveler,* are fairly typical of older literary studies which focus on travel writings as influences on a particular literary work. In studies such as these, the travel narrative is seen as a form of sub-literature or marginal non-literary material which could be transformed by the creative genius of the canonized author into a work of literature, rather than be literary in its own right.

36. Marion Tinling's *Women into the Unknown: A Sourcebook on Women Explorers and Travelers* provides short biographies on some forty women travelers and then lists another 370 or so more authors in the appendix. Admittedly, not all of Tinling's authors were writing in the nineteenth century, but that period claims a large percentage of the works listed.

37. She advocates these writers' approaches to different cultures as alternatives to standard ethnological scholarship. Her approach is unusual because she looks at travel writing as an anthropologist, viewing these narratives as early field studies, precursors to ethnology. Pratt calls for a closer study of these narratives that she feels were more successful in fusing objective and subjective observations than modern anthropological theory. She notes similarities between modern ethnological writings and travel writing traditions in the continuance of recurring tropes and the use of the organizational duality of personal narration and generalized descriptions.

38. Mary Louise Pratt, "Fieldwork in Common Places," in *Writing Culture: The Poetics and Politics of Ethnography*, ed. James Clifford and George E. Marcus (Berkeley: University of California Press, 1986), 49.

39. While there have been several studies of the links between scientific and literary writings—Gillian Beer's *Darwin's Plots,* George Levine's *Darwin and the Novelists,* and Peter Morton's *The Vital Science*—little work has been done on the links between science writings and travel narratives.

40. I had completed writing most of this study before Morgan's publication.

41. Anna Forbes wrote her *Insulinde: Experiences of a Naturalist's Wife in the Eastern Archipelago* (1887) as a self-identified spouse, a mere helpmate with and sufferer of her husband's scientific (i.e., collecting) pursuits. Her *Insulinde* followed her husband Henry's *A Naturalist's Wandering in the Eastern Archipelago* (1885). It was reprinted as *Unbeaten Tracks in Islands of the Far East: Experiences of a Naturalist's Wife in the 1880s* in 1987, seemingly picking up Bird Bishop's title for her travel book on Japan, *Unbeaten Tracks in Japan* (1880). Morgan discusses the political implications of this title change in *Place Matters* (60). And while Marianne North was well-respected for her botanical studies and was an independent traveler, her wealth and class insulated her from the shaping effect of market expectations; additionally, her work was published posthumously and this also changes the rhetorical context of her travel account.

42. Pratt, *Imperial Eyes,* 5.

43. Ibid., 4.

44. Sara Mills, *Discourses of Difference: An Analysis of Women's Travel Writing and Colonialism* (London: Routledge, 1991), 18.

45. Ibid., 18.

46. Ibid., 29–30.

47. Ibid., 28.

48. Ibid., 28–29.

49. Ibid., 30.

50. The woman is identified as Lillian Zoe Smith. While Pratt's study does discuss the illustration used on the cover of her book, the cover illustration of Mills's book is not specifically alluded to in her study. The two books are both published by the same publisher, Routledge.

51. Dorothea Barrett's *Vocation and Desire: George Eliot's Heroines* gives a helpful examination of the different feminist approaches to George Eliot. Nicholas McGuinn's "George Eliot and Mary Wollstonecraft" attempts to explain George Eliot's response to Wollstonecraft's *A Vindication of the Rights of Woman.* McGuinn argues that Eliot had to cautiously moderate her response to Wollstonecraft so as to not upset her male readership.

52. Julia Swindells, *Victorian Writing and Working Women: The Other Side of Silence* (Minneapolis: University of Minnesota Press, 1985), 6.

53. Nancy Fix Anderson's biography of Lynn Linton, *Woman Against Women in Victorian England,* focuses on this paradoxical element of her life.

54. Peter J. Bowler's "Holding Your Head Up High: Degeneration and Orthogenesis in Theories of Human Evolution" is especially helpful in giving background to this particular approach to Darwinism and its effect on women's issues.

55. Lawrence Buell, "American Pastoral Ideology Reappraised," *American Literary History* 1 (1989):14.

CHAPTER 2. MARY WOLLSTONECRAFT: "A NEW GENUS"

1. Mary Morris, ed. *Maiden Voyages: Writings of Women Travelers,* (New York: Vintage, 1993), xxii.

2. This also seems to be the way Rousseau understood the activity. His seventh walk (promenade) of *Reveries* deals with love of botanizing and abandonment of self-absorption in the "immensity of this beautiful order" (108). Rousseau also perceived this activity as purely intellectual with no application which would sully the activity with mercantile pursuits. He praises Linnaeus for rescuing botany from its earlier pharmacological associations (110), a view which is ironically very much at odds with actual use of botanical identification to establish plantation economies. Finally, in Rousseau's case he became so depressed that he stopped writing *Reveries*, leaving it unfinished, turning instead to botany, an activity to which he devoted his last two months of life (Katz 106).

3. Mary Louise Pratt, *Imperial Eyes: Travel Writing and Transculturation,* (London: Routledge, 1992), 15–18.

4. Ibid., 144.

5. Quoted in Lisbet Koerner, "Linnaeus' Floral Transplants," *Representations* 47 (1994): 147.

6. Ibid., 151–54. Such attempts were similar to that used by Lysenko to improve agriculture in Stalinist Russia.

7. Pratt, 29–30.

8. For a discussion of such eighteenth century dualisms, see for example Ludmilla Jordanova's *Sexual Visions: Images of Gender in Science and Medicine between the Eighteenth and Twentieth Centuries.*

9. Virginia Sapiro, *A Vindication of Political Virtue: The Political Theory of Mary Wollstonecraft,* (Chicago: University of Chicago Press, 1992), 58–59.

10. 324; quoted in Sapiro, 57.

11. *"On Poetry,"* 141–42; quoted in Sapiro, 58–59.

12. Wollstonecraft did not emphasize the religious connection as much as she did the moral development of the individual. The phrase "footsteps of the Creator" would later become associated with anti-evolutionary geology as in Hugh Miller's *Footprints of the Creator* (1849).

13. *"On Poetry,"* 142; quoted in Sapiro, 59.

14. Pratt, 87–88.

15. This is especially true of the Wedgwood family who had known the Wollstonecrafts in Wales and for whom Wollstonecraft's sister, Everina, had worked as a governess (Flexner 237, 300n. 15).

16. In her day, Wollstonecraft's travels was one of her best known works (Sapiro 2).

17. Originally published as *Letters Written during a Short Residence in Sweden, Norway, and Denmark.* I will use the abbreviated title in this discussion, following Richard Holmes's lead, to avoid confusion between Wollstonecraft's actual correspondence and her travel account.

18. Anka Ryall, "A Vindication of Struggling Nature: Mary Wollstonecraft's Scandinavia," (Conference Paper. Snapshots from Abroad: A Conference on American and British Travel Writers and Writing. University of Minnesota, Minneapolis. 16 November 1997), 6–10. Grateful thanks to Anka Ryall for sharing her findings of Wollstonecraft's indebtedness to Buffon's work.

19. In *Letters from an American Farmer*, Crèvecoeur wrote that immigrants to America would be transformed by the place, "become distinct by the power of the different climates they inhabit" (70). He added, "Men are like plants; the goodness and flavour of the fruit proceeds from the peculiar soil and exposition in which they grow. We are nothing but what we derive from the air we breathe, the climate we inhabit, the government we obey, the system of religion we profess, and the nature of our employment" (71).

20. Richard Holmes, ed, *A Short Residence in Sweden, Norway and Denmark by Mary Wollstonecraft and Memoirs of the Author of The Rights of Woman by William Godwin.* (Harmondsworth, England: Penguin, 1987), 78. 287n.

21. Sylvia Bowerbank, "The Bastille of Nature: Wollstonecraft versus Malthus in Scandinavia," *Studies on Voltaire and the Eighteenth Century* 304 (1992): 826–27.

22. Ibid., 826.

23. This response seems to mark a change in her response to phrenology, since besides translating Lavater's book, she also incorporated references to reading character in faces in both *The Female Reader* and *The Cave of Fancy* (Sapiro 21).

24. Quoted in Arthur O. Lovejoy, "Buffon and the Problem of Species," *Forerunners of Darwin: 1745–1859,* ed. Bentley Glass, Owsei Temkin, and William L. Straus, Jr. (Baltimore: Johns Hopkins University Press, 1959), 101.

25. See Milton Millhauser, *Just Before Darwin: Robert Chambers and Vestiges,* (Middletown, CT: Wesleyan University Press, 1959).

26. This was after he had written the essay stating his ideas in 1844, having reread Malthus in 1838. His reading of Wollstonecraft might have also been promoted by Harriet Martineau, a close friend of his brother, Erasmus.

27. "Star fish" is probably Wollstonecraft's translation of *stella marina*, the star of the sea. The confusion over the jellyfish and the starfish goes back to Pliny's identification of what was probably some sort of medusa form of a jellyfish, but which was read as referring to both jellyfish and starfish. See C. G. Jung on the Medusa in *Aion: Researches into the Phenomenology of the Self*, trans. R. F. C. Hull (Princeton: Princeton University Press, 1968), 126–29.

28. Janet Browne, *Charles Darwin: Voyaging,* (New York: Knopf, 1995), 484–85.

29. Lynn L. Merrill, *The Romance of Victorian Natural History*, (New York: Oxford University Press, 1989), 195.

30. Pratt, 74

31. Ibid., 102.

32. See Eve Katz's "The Problem of the Environment in *Les Reveries du promeneur solitaire.*"

33. Mitzi Myers, "Mary Wollstonecraft's *Letters Written . . . in Sweden*: Toward Romantic Autobiography." *Studies in Eighteenth-Century Culture* 8 (1979): 166.

34. Virginia Sapiro has encountered similar problems with the past use of Wollstonecraft's life and also notes that this is a continual problem in feminist theory (2–6).

35. Janet Todd sees in the critical treatment of Wollstonecraft a reflection of

the assumptions made in early feminist criticism. See *Gender, Art and Death*, pages 1–10, 154–59.

36. Orrin N. C. Wang, working from de Man's study of Shelley uses this phrase to describe limitations of past readings of Wollstonecraft's *Vindication* (129).

37. Eleanor Flexner, *Mary Wollstonecraft: A Biography* (Baltimore: Penguin, 1972), 264–65.

38. Ibid., 265.

39. Moira Ferguson and Janet Todd, *Mary Wollstonecraft* (Boston: Twayne, 1984), ii.

40. C[harles] Kegan Paul, *Mary Wollstonecraft: Letters to Imlay* (1879; reprint, New York: Haskell, 1971), v–vi.

41. Janet Todd, *Gender, Art and Death,* (New York: Continuum, 1993), 4.

42. See Claire Tomalin, *The Life and Death of Mary Wollstonecraft*; Eleanor Flexner, *Mary Wollstonecraft*; Moira Ferguson and Janet Todd, *Mary Wollstonecraft*; Emily W. Sunstein, *A Different Face: The Life of Mary Wollstonecraft.*

43. Quoted in Claire Tomalin, *The Life and Death of Mary Wollstonecraft* (1979; reprint, New York: Meridian, 1983), 39.

44. It is also of interest to note that Johnson was involved in printing the complete works of Joseph Priestley, and thus had contacts with other members of the Lunar Society—R. L. Edgeworth and Erasmus Darwin, later Maria Edgeworth and Thomas Beddoes. See Tomalin, 72.

45. Ralph M. Wardle, ed., *Collected Letters of Mary Wollstonecraft*, (Ithaca: Cornell University Press, 1979), 164.

46. *Rights of Man* was also published as *Rights of Men* but the awkward sounding singular "Woman" of the title *Rights of Woman* gains significance as it is contrasted with smoother sounding, yet also singular, "Man" of her earlier book, as it points to the inherent sexism in the English language.

47. Wardle, 227.

48. Mary Wollstonecraft, *A Vindication of the Rights of Woman*, 1792, ed. Miriam Brody, (London: Penguin, 1992), 257.

49. Richard Holmes, *Footsteps: Adventures of a Romantic Biographer,* (New York: Viking, 1985), 87.

50. Penelope J. Corfield, "The Case of *The Cabinet,*" *Times Literary Supplement* 21 March 1997, 11. Corfield's article suggests that Wollstonecraft might have written for *The Cabinet*, a short-lived radical magazine from Norwich.

51. Tomalin, 9.

52. Her letter to Talleyrand (85–89) in the introduction of *Vindication* has been used in a recent composition text as an example of the use of a letter form as a strategy to present a particular identity and as a means to give both praise and criticism to advance an argument. See *Writers' Roles: Enactments of the Process* by Nondita Mason and George Otte (240–45).

53. Richard Holmes, Introduction to *A Short Residence*, 25.

54. Indeed, Holmes's notes indicate that Wollstonecraft did little to edit her text for publication; she did not check her quotations, supply missing information nor attempt to resolve contradictions. However, this should not weigh heavily in determining how much the work was purposely shaped for public reading. When *Short Residence* is compared to *Vindication*, it is evident that Wollstonecraft was not a heavy editor. *Vindication* contains shifts in topic and ambiguous pronoun references. When Wollstonecraft was given the chance to make corrections in preparing the 1792 second edition of *Vindication*, she made very few major changes,

not even bothering to check her quotations against the originals (Poston vii). This resistance to rewriting is consistent with her almost mystical trust in her own mental associations and her general reluctance to make too many changes in her prose. In *Vindication* at one point she brushes away anticipated criticisms of wanderings away from the topic of discussion in the text with a comment that "as it was produced naturally by the train of my reflections, I shall not pass it silently over" (106).

55. Holmes, *Short*, 279 n. 1.

56. Mary H. Kingsley, *Travels in West Africa: Congo Français, Corisco and Cameroons*, (London: Macmillan, 1897), 100.

57. Paul, xlvii. Besides the apparent attempt to feminize Wollstonecraft's writing (and thus make her respectable from a Victorian viewpoint) with the rather dilettante categorization of her travels as "a summer tour," Paul's observations are quite puzzling. First of all, *Short Residence* does contain much personal and emotional undercurrent, not to mention occasional outbursts; and, secondly, there is very little overlap between the letters that were actually sent to Imlay and the published work. It is apparent that the main concern of the actual letters during the time period of her travels is the fact that Imlay was not writing to her and what little writing he did do was not allaying Wollstonecraft's concerns over his coolness toward her and their daughter.

58. An entry in *The Cambridge History of English Literature* mentions that Wollstonecraft's "literary reputation was increased by letters written to Imlay during a Scandinavian tour" (Previte-Orton 49). The fifth edition of the *Norton Anthology of English Literature* also mentions that Wollstonecraft "used the letters she had written to Imlay to compose a book, *Letters Written during a Short Residence in Sweden, Norway, and Denmark*" (111).

59. Pratt, *Imperial*, 171.

60. James Buzard points to Addison's *Letters from Italy* (1701) and Smollett's *Travels through France and Italy* (1766) as two well-known early works presented as letters (68). Even Gilbert Imlay used such a framing device in his description of the Kentucky region (*A Topographical Description of the Western Territory of North America* [1793]) and Catherine Macaulay, whose works influenced the writing of *Vindication*, presented her arguments for women's education in the form of letters addressed to a fictional correspondent, Hortensia (*Letters on Education* [1790]). Wollstonecraft herself suggested that women found it easier to gain acceptance using the epistolary format. In one book review she noted, "Women have been allowed to possess, by a kind of prescription, the knack of epistolary writing . . ." ("*On Poetry*" 322).

61. The text was also accessible. *Short Residence*, the most popular of Wollstonecraft's writings, was translated into German, Dutch, Swedish, and Portuguese and received favorable reviews (Holmes 36). Southey wrote to his brother Tom, "Have you ever met with Mary Wollstoncraft's [*sic*] letters from Sweden and Norway? She has made me in love with a cold climate, and frost and snow, with a northern moonlight" (quoted in Lowes 161), and Coleridge's Notebook contains a note to himself to read her travels. Lowes includes Wollstonecraft's travels as among one of the influences for Coleridge's "The Rime of the Ancient Mariner" (161) and possibly "Kubla Khan" (593 n. 127).

62. Moving further afield, influences of Wollstonecraft's travels may be found in such later works as daughter Mary Shelley's presentation of her *Rambles in Germany and Italy* (1844) as a means of gaining self-control over her own loss and her use of landscape for emotional and imaginative inspiration (discussed in Fraw-

ley 58–61). Additionally Anna Jameson in *Diary of an Ennuyée* (1826) used a fic-
tionalized unnamed female narrator who is trying to forget a former lover (also
unknown) through her travels in Italy, a plot device similar to that of *Short Residence.*

63. Mary Poovey, *The Proper Lady and the Woman Writer: Ideology as Style
in the Works of Mary Wollstonecraft, Mary Shelley, and Jane Austen,* (Chicago:
University of Chicago Press, 1984), 53–54.

64. See discussion of these interactions in Gary Kelly, "Godwin, Wollstonecraft, and Rousseau," *Women and Literature* 3.2 (1975): 22–24.

65. Wollstonecraft, *Vindication,* 107.

66. Jean-Jacques Rousseau, *Reveries of the Solitary Walker,* trans. Peter France
(Harmondsworth, England: Penguin, 1979), 57.

67. Wardle, 164.

68. Holmes, *Short,* 280n. 8.

69. This movement to natural scenes as a means to seek relief from what was
witnessed during the French Revolution shows aesthetic sensibilities close to
Wordsworthian Romanticism, although Wollstonecraft's text pre-dates Wordsworth's 1799 *Prelude.*

70. Poovey, 67.

71. Kingsley, *Travels,* 578.

72. Barbara T. Gates, *Kindred Nature: Victorian and Edwardian Women Embrace the Living World,* (Chicago: University of Chicago Press, 1998), 170.

73. Poovey, 91.

74. Amy Elizabeth Smith's article, "Roles for Readers in Mary Wollstonecraft's *A Vindication of the Rights of Woman*" analyzes the number of specific
references to readers' gender in *Vindication* to show the dual nature of its intended
audience.

75. William Godwin, whom Wollstonecraft later married, described the book's
intensity and the effect on him as a reader in similar terms in his memoirs of Wollstonecraft:

> . . . perhaps a book of travels that so irresistibly seizes on the heart, never, in any other
> instance, found its way from the press . . . If ever there was a book calculated to make a
> man in love with its author, this appears to me to be the book. She speaks of her sorrows,
> in a way that fills us with melancholy, and dissolves us in tenderness, at the same time that
> she displays a genius which commands all our admiration. Affliction had tempered her
> heart to a softness almost more than human; and the gentleness of her spirit seems pre-
> cisely to accord with all the romance of unbounded attachment. (249)

76. The heading for this section is from a 1787 letter (Wardle, 165).

77. Mary Wollstonecraft, *"On Poetry," Contributions to the Analytical Review
1788–1797,* ed. Janet Todd and Marilyn Butler, vol. 7 (New York: New York University Press, 1989), 127.

78. Wollstonecraft, *Vindication,* 151.

79. Sara Mills, *Discourses of Difference: An Analysis of Women's Travel Writing and Colonialism* (London: Routledge, 1991), 3.

80. Wollstonecraft, *Vindication,* 237.

81. Ibid., 237–38.

82. Ibid., 242.

83. This imagery is also strongly suggestive of Charlotte Turner Smith's 1784
poem, "To the Moon," which Wollstonecraft was apparently familiar with:

> Queen of the silver bow!—by thy pale beam,
> Alone and pensive, I delight to stray,

And watch thy shadow trembling in the stream,
Or mark the floating clouds that cross thy way.
And while I gaze, thy mild and placid light
Sheds a soft calm upon my troubled breast;
And oft I think—fair planet of the night,
That in thy orb, the wretched may have rest. . . .

(15)

84. Wollstonecraft, *Vindication*, 200.

85. See Stuart Andrews, "Fellow Pantisocrats: Brissot, Cooper and Imlay," *Symbiosis* 1.1 (1997): 35–47.

86. John Seelye, "The Jacobin Mode in Early American Fiction: Gilbert Imlay's *The Emigrants*," *Early American Literature* 21 (1986): 204.

87. Alexander Cowie, *The Rise of the American Novel* (New York: American Book, 1948), 38–43.

88. Janet Todd concludes that in Woolf's biographical sketch of Wollstonecraft "the woman she creates is often freed from fact" (157).

89. Virginia Woolf, "Four Figures," *The Second Common Reader*, 1932 (New York: Harcourt, 1960), 145.

90. Ibid.

91. Gilbert Imlay, *A Topographical Description of the Western Territory of North America . . . The Third Edition, with Great Additions* (1797; reprint, New York: Johnson Reprint, 1968), vi.

92. Imlay's recreation of himself may have been inspired by the persona Crèvecoeur assumed in his *Letters from an American Farmer*, a text which may have also influenced Wollstonecraft's initial response to Imlay. Here Crèvecoeur, an aristocratic French-born New Yorker, an "ex-soldier-surveyor-salesman" (similar to Imlay), created the role of James, a second-generation Pennsylvania farmer, to give an account of his "trans-atlantic utopia under the wigwams" (Stone 8).

93. Ralph Leslie Rusk, "The Adventures of Gilbert Imlay," *Indiana University Studies* 10 (1923): 10–11.

94. Ibid., 14–15.

95. Oliver Farrar Emerson, "Notes on Gilbert Imlay, Early American Writer," *PMLA* 39 (1924): 416.

96. Ibid., 413.

97. Wardle, 251.

98. Wollstonecraft, *Vindication*, 225.

99. Here I will assume that *Western Territory* was indeed written by Imlay. Robert R. Hare, an editor of *The Emigrants*, is convinced that the novel and *Western Territory* are both actually authored by Wollstonecraft (vii–xi). It has been noted by Seelye that the time period involved would make this improbable; my comparison of Wollstonecraft's responses to Imlay in *Short Residence* would make it increasingly unlikely that Wollstonecraft was the author of *Western Territory*.

100. It also serves as a rebuke to Jefferson, whom Imlay regarded as having "superficial" judgment (81).

101. This suggestion that the product would interest a purchasing market concerned with human rights is followed with a dismissal of anticipated health concerns (i.e., that the sugar is bad for the teeth). Such appeals seem similar to those made to modern issue-oriented "alternative" markets.

102. Emerson believes Imlay's travels and his novel were inspirational to Coleridge and Southey's Pantisocracy plans (427–31). Some Europeans were sufficiently attracted by these reports to emigrate. The poet Tom Moore went to

America in 1803 and was greatly disappointed that reality did not correspond to the impression he had gained from "such romantic works as *The American Farmer's Letters* [probably Crèvecoeur's book, *Letters from an American Farmer* (1782)] and the account of Kentucky by Imlay," which "would seduce us into a belief, that innocence, peace and freedom had deserted the rest of the world for Martha's Vineyard and the banks of the Ohio" (quoted in Fairchild 269).

103. Rupert Christiansen, *Romantic Affinities: Portraits from an Age 1780–1830* (New York: Putnam's, 1988), 34.

104. H. Arnold Barton, *Scandinavia in the Revolutionary Era, 1760–1815* (Minneapolis: University of Minnesota Press, 1986), 211.

105. Ibid., 212. Although implementation was delayed until 1807 and slavery was not abolished in the Danish colonies until 1848.

106. Ibid.

107. Moira Ferguson, *Colonialism and Gender Relations from Mary Wollstonecraft to Jamaica Kincaid: East Caribbean Connections* (New York: Columbia University Press, 1993), 99.

108. Barton, 228.

109. T. K. Derry, *A History of Scandinavia: Norway, Sweden, Denmark, Finland and Iceland* (Minneapolis: University of Minnesota Press, 1979), 200.

110. Ibid., 187.

111. Barton, 247.

112. Ibid., 173.

113. W. R. Mead, *An Historical Geography of Scandinavia* (London: Academic Press, 1981), 141.

114. Ibid.

115. Edward W. Said, *Culture and Imperialism* (New York: Knopf, 1993), 74.

116. Paul Fussell, *Abroad: British Literary Traveling Between the Wars* (Oxford: Oxford University Press, 1980), 208.

Chapter 3. Harriet Martineau: An Investigating Observer

1. Richard R. Yeo, *Defining Science: William Whewell, Natural Knowledge, and Public Debate in Early Victorian Britain* (Cambridge: Cambridge University Press, 1993), 114. The problem of establishing authority in science after *Vestiges* is examined in Yeo's "Science and Intellectual Authority in Mid-Nineteenth-Century Britain: Robert Chambers and *Vestiges of the Natural History of Creation*," *Victorian Studies* 28 (1984): 5–31. It should be noted that, in contrast to earlier studies of science in Victorian culture, which emphasize Darwin's *Origin* as the initiating cause of tension over the purpose and methodology of science, Yeo traces signs of tension back farther to the 1830s. My assessment of the purpose of Martineau's travel writing would agree with such a historical reading.

2. Maria H. Frawley, "Harriet Martineau in America: Gender and the Discourse of Sociology," *The Victorian Newsletter* 81 (1992): 15. Frawley expands upon Martineau's use of a discourse of scientific inquiry in her recent *A Wider Range: Travel Writing by Women in Victorian England* (160–91), coming to similar conclusions as in this study about the use of travel by women to establish an authoritative position for their writing. However, Frawley does not make connections between the methodology of the American travel and the Mideast. Her study is weakened by the decision to separate the two travels into different chapters, placing the Mideast travel discussion before the American (139–50), out of chronolog-

ical order, in order to compare the responses of several women travel writers to the same geographical area. This common methodology, also used by Dea Birkett, makes it more difficult to study these writers in a socio-economic context.

3. Londa Schiebinger, *The Mind Has No Sex?: Women in the Origins of Modern Science* (Cambridge: Harvard University Press, 1989), 273.

4. The historical development of a scientific study of gender is discussed in Evelyn Fox Keller's *Reflections on Gender and Science* and Carolyn Merchant's *The Death of Nature: Women, Ecology and the Scientific Revolution.*

5. Schiebinger, 273.

6. Ibid., 274.

7. Ibid.

8. See Michel Foucault, *The History of Sexuality: An Introduction: Vol. 1* (New York: Vintage-Random, 1990) and his introductory discussion of the treatment and diagnosis of hermaphrodites in *Herculine Barbin: Being the Recently Discovered Memoirs of a Nineteenth-Century French Hermaphrodite* (New York: Pantheon, 1980). Also see Thomas Laqueur's *Making Sex: Body and Gender from the Greeks to Freud* (Cambridge: Harvard University Press, 1990).

9. "Female Education," *Monthly Repository* (1823): 77; quoted in Valerie Kossew Pichanick, *Harriet Martineau: The Woman and Her Work 1802–1876* (Ann Arbor: University of Michigan Press, 1980), 18.

10. Quoted in Gayle Graham Yates, ed., *Harriet Martineau on Women* (New Brunswick, NJ: Rutgers University Press, 1985), 159.

11. Harriet Martineau, *Harriet Martineau's Autobiography,* 2 vols., Introduction by Gaby Weiner, 3rd ed., 1877 (London: Virago, 1983), 1:399.

12. Martineau, *Auto.,* 1:400.

13. Ibid., 401.

14. See Deirdre David, *Intellectual Women and Victorian Patriarchy: Harriet Martineau, Elizabeth Barrett Browning, George Eliot* (Ithaca, NY: Cornell University Press, 1987) for a valuable discussion of the auxiliary position.

15. Martineau, *Auto.,* 1:402.

16. Barbara Caine, "Victorian Feminism and the Ghost of Mary Wollstonecraft," *Women's Writing* 4 (1997): 261–62.

17. Ibid., 262. Caine takes Martineau's view of Wollstonecraft at face value. I have argued for a more conflicted response to Wollstonecraft from Martineau.

18. Adele M. Ernstrom, "The Afterlife of Mary Wollstonecraft and Anna Jameson's *Winter Studies and Summer Rambles in Canada," Women's Writing* 4 (1997): 282.

19. Martineau, *Auto.,* 1:401.

20. Ibid.

21. Yeo, "Scientific," 271.

22. David Brewster, *Memoirs of the Life, Writings and Discoveries of Sir Isaac Newton* (2 vols., Edinburgh, 1855), 2:405, quoted in Yeo, "Scientific," 271. This biography was first published in 1831, but Yeo points to the 1855 edition to support his generalization of a change in the response to Baconian methodology.

23. Jane Marcet was a student of Humphry Davy and wrote elementary textbooks, including several on science. Her *Conversations on Chemistry, intended more especially for the Female Sex,* an early chemistry textbook, was published in 1805, but her authorship was not revealed until 1837. See Margaret Alic, *Hypatia's Heritage: A History of Women in Science from Antiquity through the Nineteenth Century* (Boston: Beacon, 1986), 176.

24. Martineau, *Auto.* 1:138.

25. Ibid., 160.

26. Susan Hoecker-Drysdale, *Harriet Martineau: First Woman Sociologist* (Oxford: Berg, 1992): 33.

27. Gillian Beer, "Darwin's Reading and the Fictions of Development," in *The Darwinian Heritage*, ed. David Kohn (Princeton: Princeton University Press, 1985), 557.

28. Yeo, "Scientific," 283. See also Yeo, *Defining Science* 194–195 on Whewell's response to the Ricardian claim of the title "science" for political economy.

29. See Linda H. Peterson's "Harriet Martineau: Masculine Discourse, Female Sage," in *Victorian Sages and Cultural Discourse: Renegotiating Gender and Power*, ed. Thaïs Morgan (New Brunswick: Rutgers University Press, 1990), 171–186 for a discussion of Martineau's valorization of what was perceived as masculine prose style.

30. Schiebinger, 275.

31. For some, such as Elise Oelsner, author of *Leistungen der deutschen Frau* [Achievements of the German Woman] in 1894, the very great intellectual achievements (such as those of Jesus, Plato, and Schiller) are the result of individuals whose lives displayed feminine values (Schiebinger 275).

32. Ibid., 276.

33. G. Kass-Simon, "Biology is Destiny," in *Women of Science: Righting the Record*, ed. G. Kass-Simon and Patricia Farnes (Bloomington: Indiana University Press, 1990), 231. See also Evelyn Fox Keller's biography of McClintock, *A Feeling for the Organism: The Life and Work of Barbara McClintock* (New York: Freeman, 1983).

34. Keller, *A Feeling,* xiii.

35. Quoted in Schiebinger, 269.

36. Harriet Martineau, "On Female Education," *The Monthly Repository* 18 (1823): 81.

37. Yeo, *Defining*, 39–48.

38. Keller, xii.

39. For historical discussions of women's involvement in science and eventual discouragement, see Evellen Richards's "Huxley and Woman's Place in Science: The 'Woman Question' and the Control of Victorian Anthropology;" Pnina G. Abir-am and Dorinda Outram's *Uneasy Careers and Intimate Lives: Women in Science, 1789–1979*; G. Kass-Simon and Patricia Farnes's *Women of Science: Righting the Record*; and Patricia Phillips's *The Scientific Lady: A Social History of Women's Scientific Interests, 1520–1918*.

40. Jack Morrell and Arnold Thackray, *Gentlemen of Science: Early Years of the British Association for the Advancement of Science* (Oxford: Clarendon, 1981),186.

41. Quoted in Morrell and Thackray, 186.

42. Martineau, *Auto.*, 2:137.

43. Patricia Phillips, *The Scientific Lady: A Social History of Women's Scientific Interests, 1520–1918* (New York: St. Martin's, 1990), 205.

44. Martineau, *Auto.* 2:137.

45. Ibid.

46. Morrell and Thackray, 161–62. This sketch was left out of Dickens' collected works at his request and has only recently been republished. (See Michael Slater, ed., *The Dent Uniform Edition of Dickens' Journalism: Sketches by Boz and Other Early Papers, 1833–39* [Columbus: Ohio State University Press, 1994], 513–51.) This ridicule did not end; the first issues of *Punch* continued in the same

vein in 1841–42 with continuing columns of the "British Association for the Advancement of Everything in General, and Nothing in Particular," "The Transactions of the Geological Society of Hookam-Cum-Snivey," "Proceedings of Learned Bodies" and a short verse "Labours of the British Association for the Advancement of Science," which was particularly concerned that the BAAS's purpose had quickly become submerged in entertainment (57).

47. Sources for biographical material on Martineau are R. K. Webb, *Harriet Martineau: A Radical Victorian* (London: Heinemann, 1960); Valerie Kossew Pichanick, *Harriet Martineau: The Woman and Her Work* (Ann Arbor: University of Michigan Press, 1980); and Gillian Thomas, *Harriet Martineau* (Boston: G. K. Hall, 1985).

48. R. K. Webb states that Martineau's childhood problems were typical of that of sensitive children "born into families whose demands are ordinary and conventional" (44), although he goes on to describe a family which does not really fit into either of these categories.

49. Martineau, *Auto.*, 1:142.

50. Significantly, she was more critical of Eliot for taking a pseudonym than she was of Eliot's relationship with G. H. Lewes. In her 6 February 1860 letter to Erasmus Darwin, she wrote, "it was not the romance of Miss Evans's pseudonym that I objected to. It might have been Betty or Molly or Lizzy, for anything I cared. The point was that she had adopted a false name,—even (to my knowledge) signing it to a legal instrument,—without consideration of the seriousness of an alias: and that when she moreover took a false sirname [*sic*] she had no right to complain to a strict investigation into what was true in her case." (See Elisabeth Sanders Arbuckle, ed., *Harriet Martineau's Letters to Fanny Wedgwood* [Stanford, CA: Stanford University Press, 1983], 186). It is unclear whether "sirname" is a spelling error or a word coinage intended to underscore the masculinity of the pseudonym.

51. Pichanick, 17.

52. *Personal Narrative of a Pilgrimage to El-Medinah and Meccah*; discussed in Ali Behdad, *Belated Travelers: Orientalism in the Age of Colonial Dissolution* (Durham, NC: Duke University Press, 1994), 39–40.

53. Some of these illustrations caused international controversy. The French king, although initially enthusiastic about her project, withdrew support when she wrote "about Egalité," and the Russian czar and the Austrian emperor ordered all copies of the series burned. As a result, Martineau was barred from traveling in Russia or the Austrian Empire. See Gillian Thomas, *Harriet Martineau* (Boston: G. K. Hall, 1985), 12.

54. Martineau, *Auto.*, 1:429.

55. Ibid., 197.

56. Ibid., 245–47.

57. Darwin had at one time hoped his brother would marry Martineau.

58. James Buzard, *The Beaten Track: European Tourism, Literature, and the Ways to Culture, 1800–1918* (Oxford: Clarendon, 1993),158.

59. Martineau, *Auto,* 2:3.

60. There is an advertisement in the back of the 1838 New York edition of Martineau's *Retrospect* for a treatise on the cholera epidemic observed in the Duane Street Cholera hospital in New York in 1834. See R. J. Morris's *Cholera 1832: The Social Response to an Epidemic* (New York: Holmes & Meier, 1976) for a history of the arrival of cholera to the United States.

61. Buzard, 150, and see 149–152 for a discussion of the use of this terminol-

ogy in European travel in the 1860s. The "unprotected female" was often a humorous figure, as illustrated in Anthony Trollope's short story, "An Unprotected Female at the Pyramids," written in 1860.

62. Frawley, "Harriet," 16.

63. Indeed, the desire to establish herself in this separate, masculine realm of discourse was problematic; identifying and reinforcing these "binary oppositions of public and private, description and narration, serious thought and light reading" would undercut the basis of her argument that "[m]orals, a feminine domain, was not just compatible with the scientific method, but that it depended upon it" (Frawley, "Harriet" 16).

64. Quoted in Barbara T. Gates, *Kindred Nature: Victorian and Edwardian Women Embrace the Living World* (Chicago: University of Chicago Press, 1998), 219.

65. Michael R. Hill, Introduction to *How to Observe Morals and Manners* by Harriet Martineau (New Brunswick, NJ: Transaction, 1989), xi.

66. Quoted in Sidney P. Moss, *Charles Dickens' Quarrel with America* (Troy, NY: Whitston, 1984), 91. This view is also apparent in *Martin Chuzzlewit* (1844).

67. See Donald Smalley's note in *Domestic Manners* (359). Trollope's manuscript was helped in reaching publication by Hall, who, welcoming corroboration of his observations, urged Whittaker to publish *Domestic Manners* (Smalley lxi).

68. Although Alexis de Tocqueville's famous travels in the United States took place from May 1831 to February 1832, before Martineau's, his book, *Democracy in America* was not published until 1835, when Martineau was already touring the United States.

69. Frawley, "Harriet," 17.

70. Richard L. Stein in *Victoria's Year: English Literature and Culture, 1837–1838* (New York: Oxford University Press, 1987) explains that Martineau calls "for a kind of subjective objectivity" here by acknowledging the personal aspect of her observations to reach beyond the superficial layer of relations which would normally distance a traveler from another culture. Additionally, her handicap requires that she use induction to fill in what she might have missed, but this methodology is also recommended for all travelers as a discipline leading to a more precise understanding (181–84).

71. As compensation for her deafness, she was careful in her travel accounts to be aware of the sounds she did hear or had others describe to her, and as a result, perhaps overcompensated for her disability by emphasizing the sounds of water, wind, and birds in her descriptions.

72. Martineau, *Auto*, 1:202; quoted in Thomas 12.

73. Oddly enough, the predominance of rocking chairs bothered her; she seemed to find them unsettling.

74. Also quoted in Marion Tinling, *With Women's Eyes: Visitors to the New World 1775–1918* (Hamden, CT: Archon, 1993), 41.

75. "Men came into the lower tier of boxes without their coats; and I have seen shirt sleeves tucked up to the shoulder; the spitting was incessant, . . . The bearing and attitudes of the men are perfectly indescribable; the heels thrown higher than the head, the entire rear of the person presented to the audience, the whole length supported on the benches, are among the varieties that these exquisite posture-masters exhibit. The noises, too, were perpetual, and of the most unpleasant kind; the applause is expressed by cries and thumping with the feet, instead of clapping; and when a patriotic fit seized them, and 'Yankee Doodle' was called for, every man seemed to think his reputation as a citizen depended on the noise he made" (Trollope 133–34).

76. Also quoted in David, 37.

77. David, 37.

78. Yeo, "Science," 30.

79. Frawley, "Harriet," 14.

80. Wollstonecraft also made general comparisons of women with slaves in *Vindication*. This analogy is analyzed in Moira Ferguson's *Colonialism and Gender Relations From Mary Wollstonecraft to Jamaica Kincaid: East Caribbean Connections* (New York: Columbia University Press, 1993), 8–33. In her autobiography, Martineau expressed particular pleasure in the mail she received from British women detailing their troubles in response to her section on women in *Society in America*, responses which indicated the success of her approach.

81. Quoted in Pichanick, 100–101.

82. Pichanick, 101.

83. "Miss Martineau's Monthly Novels," *Quarterly Review* 49 (1833): 151; quoted in Thomas 13.

84. Pichanick, 100.

85. *Times*, 30 May 1837, 5. Quoted in part in Pichanick, 101–2; Stein, 193. Stein points out that this review was written before *How to Observe* or her autobiography, yet it indicates that Disraeli suspected the existence of a preconceived methodology. Disraeli's praise of Volney and his argument that an ancient civilization such as Egypt would be a better field for abstract study may have initiated Martineau's interest in this part of the world and led to her later travel to the Mideast.

86. Martineau, *Auto.,* 2:106.

87. Although she traveled with a companion, Martineau makes little reference to her, focusing attention on herself much as Wollstonecraft did. Unlike Wollstonecraft, however, Martineau does not attempt to use her companion to personify female timidity. For the most part her companion, Lousia Jeffreys, is in the background.

88. See Buzard 181–209 on the use of the non-utilitarian response in Henry James' travels.

89. This is also seen in later anti-touristic rhetoric. See Buzard's discussion (115–30) of the incorporation of Byron in the Murray travel handbooks, the responding use of Byronic gestures and the anti-touristic satire of Frances Trollope, Richard Doyle, Dickens and Arthur Sketchley.

90. For a discussion of Victorian women writers' conscious awareness of arguments over women's capacities in different types of writing, see Dorothy Mermin's *Godiva's Ride: Women of Letters in England, 1830–1880* (Bloomington: Indiana University Press, 1993).

91. Martineau began her eight-month travel in Alexandia on 20 November 1846, traveling with Mr. and Mrs. Richard V. Yates and Joseph C. Ewart. See Buzard on a similar response to the isolation of the tourist in Egypt in E. M. Forster's later writings, 320–24.

92. A detailed examination of precisely what texts Martineau was familiar with and her position in Victorian religious thought can be found in Billie Melman's *Women's Orients: English Women and the Middle East, 1718–1918* (Ann Arbor: University of Michigan Press, 1992), 235–53. Melman initially undercuts Martineau's claims to originality, but finally concludes that "*Eastern Life* is an attempt at a secular geography of the Orient, and a history that is not a cosmogony" (252). Despite all its faults of ethnocentrism, it is "the first feminine travelogue proper that is not an account of a pilgrimage" (253).

93. Pichanick, 178. Darwin's *Origin of Species* was published in 1859. Erasmus Darwin sent Martineau a copy of his brother's book. In a letter to Erasmus Darwin dated 2 February 1860, she thanked him for it, mentioning that she was particularly impressed with "the patient power by which [he] has collected such a mass of facts . . ." (Arbuckle 185–86).

94. James Frazer's *The Golden Bough* would not appear until 1890, and most mythological studies, like the futile project, "The Key to All Mythologies," which so occupied George Eliot's character Casaubon, mined mythologies to find clues of Christian revelations rather than to show cultural dispersion. This search for clues of coming revelations seems to be the purpose of John Gardner Wilkinson's *Manners and Customs of the Ancient Egyptians* (1837–41), which was a primary reference for Martineau's book.

95. Martineau, *Auto.*, 2:278–9.

96. Melman, 245.

97. Quoted in Pichanick, 176.

98. Quoted in Peter Mansfield, *The British in Egypt* (New York: Holt, 1971), 316. Duff Gordon was a resident of Egypt for seven years (1862–69) and a distant cousin of Martineau's on her mother's side. The two families were not on speaking terms. Duff Gordon published her *Letters from Egypt* in 1865. Writing in reaction to Martineau's presentation of Egyptian life, Duff Gordon, an invalid, focused on her household life and her neighbors. Her sense of the mood of the country in her time later proved to be more accurate than official British state reports. A recent biography of Duff Gordon is Katherine Frank's *A Passage to Egypt: The Life of Lucie Duff Gordon* (Boston: Houghton, 1994).

99. Buzard, 155–64.

100. Nearly everyone prepared for their journey to Egypt by reading the same books, especially John Gardner Wilkinson's *Manners and Customs of the Ancient Egyptians* (1837–41) and *Modern Egypt and Thebes* (1843); the latter was eventually retitled *Murray's Handbook of Egypt*. See Anthony Sattin's introduction to Florence Nightingale's *Letters From Egypt: A Journey on the Nile 1849–1850* (New York: Weidenfeld and Nicolson, 1987), 12. Wilkinson helped encourage the literariness of Egyptian travel by recommending that his readers carry along a library of about 30 volumes, advice Florence Nightingale followed in her 1849 trip, a collection which included Martineau's book. This reliance on a group of travel books written in the 1830s and 1840s continued to influence Egyptian travel. A reprint of another commonly cited guide, Edward William Lane's *An Account of the Manners and Customs of the Modern Egyptians* (1836), was reportedly still being sold in Egypt as a guide in the 1980s. See, for example, Trevor Le Gassick's introduction to Naguib Mahfouz's *Midaq Alley* (New York: Doubleday, 1981), 8.

101. Buzard, 156.

102. See Ali Behdad, *Belated Travelers: Orientalism in the Age of Colonial Dissolution*, 13–14, 20–21; and Edward Said, *Orientalism*, 182. Behdad points to Gérard de Nerval's *Voyage en Orient* (1851) as the first time such moments of vacillations over certainty of epistemological mastery occur (20), however, Martineau's *Eastern Life* (1848) shows a slightly earlier indication of such responses.

103. Martineau's first draft writing habit is especially revealing here in its indications of mental pauses and almost stream-of-conscious thoughts.

104. This is particularly true in French literature. Commonly cited examples of the use of the harem are Gérard de Nerval's *Voyage en Orient*, Gustave Flaubert's *Notes de Voyages*, and Richard Burton's travels. Nerval's and Flaubert's accounts are largely imaginative.

105. Thomas, 58.

106. See Arbuckle's editorial explanation (96 n. 5) in reference to Martineau's 1848 letter to Fanny Wedgwood for identification of this heavily footnoted source referenced in *Eastern Life.*

107. Pichanick, 178.

108. Susan Hoecker-Drysdale, *Harriet Martineau: First Woman Sociologist* (Oxford: Berg, 1992), 102.

109. Yeo, *Defining,* 232–33.

CHAPTER 4. ISABELLA BIRD BISHOP: AN RGS FELLOW

1. Her books were published under both her maiden and married names. The first books were published under the name Isabella L. Bird, then, after her brief marriage to John Bishop, she was referred to as Isabella L. Bishop, Isabella L. Bird (Mrs. Bishop) and Isabella Bird Bishop. The marriage, however, did not require that she change her initials, "I. L. B.," with which she always signed the series of letters that made up her travel accounts. Sara Mills's work refers to her as Isabella Bishop-Bird. For this study, I will use the name Bird Bishop, the way she styled her name when using the letters FRGS on the title page of *Among the Tibetans.*

2. Ann Ronald, introduction to *A Lady's Life in the Rocky Mountains,* by Isabella Bishop (Sausalito, CA: Comstock, 1987), xiii.

3. Maria H. Frawley, *A Wider Range: Travel Writing by Women in Victorian England* (Rutherford: Fairleigh Dickinson University Press, 1994), 38–39.

4. Bird Bishop's death in 1904 triggered speculations in medical journals over the reason for her at-home invalidism when she was capable of acts requiring great endurance abroad. An article in *The Edinburgh Medical Journal* by Stoddart Walker published shortly after her death indicates the attention Bird Bishop's double-life attracted: "It was difficult for it [the lay mind] to comprehend how a woman who in the quiet of her home life seemed so fragile, sensitive, and dependent could possibly submit to, or even survive, the experiences of her multitudinous travels. The Invalid at Home and the Samson Abroad do not form a very usual combination, yet in the case of the famous traveler [Bird Bishop] the two ran in tandem for many years." He concluded that Bird Bishop was one of those who was "dependent to the last degree upon their environment to bring out their possibilities . . ." (quoted in Miller 98).

5. Pat Barr, *A Curious Life for a Lady: The Story of Isabella Bird* (London: Macmillan, 1970), 245.

6. Compare Bird Bishop's writings, for example, with the travel accounts of such contemporaries as Florence Dixie, Nina Mazuchelli, and Ethel Tweedie.

7. Thomas Richards, *The Imperial Archive: Knowledge and the Fantasy of Empire* (London: Verso, 1993), 14.

8. Ibid., 15.

9. Quoted in David N. Livingstone, "Climate's Moral Economy: Science, Race and Place in Post-Darwinian British and American Geography," in *Geography and Empire,* ed. Anne Godlewska and Neil Smith, The Institute of British Geographers series no. 30, (Oxford: Blackwell, 1994), 134.

10. Richards, 12–13.

11. Lhasa was finally reached by the Younghusband Expedition in 1904. Their description of the village dashed hopes of finding a hidden empire of knowledge

(Barr 203). Bird Bishop eventually was able to describe traveling in Chinese-controlled Tibet in *The Yangtze Valley and Beyond* (1899).

12. Barr, *Curious*, 219–23.

13. Richards explains that in *Kim* (1901) the India Survey is shown as "gathering knowledge for the state in regions of Tibet and India, and turning that knowledge into military intelligence useful in consolidating British hegemony in the region" (12).

14. Dea Birkett, *Spinsters Abroad: Victorian Lady Explorers* (Oxford: Blackwell, 1989), 215.

15. Barr, *Curious*, 267.

16. Birkett, 215.

17. Ibid., 214.

18. See appendix in Alison Blunt, *Travel, Gender and Imperialism: Mary Kingsley and West Africa,* Mappings: Society/Theory/Space: A Guilford Series, (New York: Guilford, 1994), 183–84, for a listing of names and election dates. Ironically, when women were admitted again in 1913, it was under the presidency of Curzon.

19. Barr, *Curious*, 268. Bird Bishop also faced delays since her book had to be cleared by the foreign office, but this did not set her publication date as far back as Curzon's since he had to rewrite sections.

20. Quoted in Barr, *Curious*, 267–68.

21. Quoted in Barr, *Curious*, 267.

22. Birkett, *Spinsters*, 214–30.

23. Blunt, 148–59.

24. Quoted in Birkett, *Spinsters*, 227.

25. Ibid., 227–28.

26. Ibid., 228–29.

27. Biographical material is from *A Curious Life for a Lady: The Story of Isabella Bird* by Pat Barr; *Victorian Lady Travellers* by Dorothy Middleton (New York: Dutton, 1965); *Spinsters Abroad: Victorian Lady Explorers* by Dea Birkett; *On Top of the World: Five Women Explorers in Tibet* by Luree Miller (Seattle: Mountaineers, 1984); and *Women into the Unknown: A Sourcebook on Women Explorers and Travelers* by Marion Tinling (New York: Greenwood Press, 1989).

28. Barr, *Curious*, 165.

29. Most biographical accounts ignore the first forty years of her life and focus instead on the writing she produced after her visit to the Hawaiian islands. Nearly all studies of Bird Bishop are dependent on Barr's biography. Barr underscores the division between Bird Bishop's home life and life on the road by describing Bird Bishop's travels first, putting off the less entertaining background information until chapter 5.

30. Birkett, *Spinsters*, 15–16.

31. Barr, *Curious*, 99.

32. Daniel J. Boorstin, Introduction to *A Lady's Life in the Rocky Mountains* by Isabella L. Bird, (Norman: University of Oklahoma Press, 1960), xvi.

33. John Murray III (1808–92) was a successful publisher of handbooks for travelers and was interested in publishing travel accounts. He maintained a long correspondence with Bird Bishop and was her primary publisher. Murray pioneered the publishing of travelers' guidebooks and travel magazines in Britain. Keeping the sucession of Murrays straight has been a challenge for scholars. The firm of Murray is a well-established publishing house founded by John Murray I (1745–93). Murray II (1778–1843) was associated with the publishing of Scott, Byron and the *Quarterly Review*. The firm still exists.

34. *Among the Tibetans* was the only publication resulting from this trip. It was brought out by the Religious Tract Society in 1894 and has not been reprinted. Despite the name of the publisher, *Among the Tibetans* is a readable travel account, not religious propaganda. From the advertisement in the back of the American publisher's edition, it would seem that popular religious publishers commonly carried books with travel and anthropological themes.

35. Barr, 334.

36. Boorstin, xv.

37. Quoted in Birkett, *Spinsters*, 166.

38. And provided an explanation of how she got to California (in the 1880 third edition).

39. Barr, *Curious*, 185.

40. Amelia Edwards, *Untrodden Peaks and Unfrequented Valleys: A Midsummer Ramble in the Dolomites*, 1873 (London: Virago, 1986), 333–34.

41. Ibid., 334.

42. Mary Morris, *Maiden Voyages: Women's Travel Writing* (New York: Vintage, 1993), 94. At least this is my interpretation of what must be going on. Unfortunately, Mary Morris' collection of excerpts from women's travel writing does not indicate the date or editions of her sources. This particular selection from Ethel Tweedie is not present in the 1889 edition which I have access to. Since Tweedie makes mention of writing five years after her book first came out in the Morris selection (which would be 1880), I am assuming that the second 1894 or the third 1895 editions are being referred to here. By 1918, Tweedie was herself adding the letters FRGS after her name, so she probably became a RGS fellow when the society opened up membership again to women.

43. Ibid., 89–90.

44. Helen Prentice was still show jumping sidesaddle in 1922. (See photograph in Anthony Austen Dent, *The Horse Through Fifty Centuries of Civilization* [New York: Holt, 1974], 160).

45. The practice of riding sidesaddle was also rough on the horse. While custom dictated that the woman ride on one side (the "near" or left side), sores developed unless the weight distribution was alternated from one side to the other. (See Dent, 152–63).

46. Edwards, xxxiii.

47. Dent, 155.

48. Sykes 288–89; quoted in Tinling, 287.

49. Morris, 94.

50. 248–49; quoted in Frawley, 108. This particular passage, which Frawley quotes from a 1880 edition, is apparently not included in the second edition of 1881. Lady Florence Dixie's *Across Patagonia* is an account of an aristocratic hunting expedition where Dixie actively participated in hunting ostriches and guanaco. In it, she celebrates the hunt but also shows distress when killing animals that had no fear of humans. Later, Dixie became a member of the Humanitarian League, writing against hunting as a sport. A feminist, Dixie wrote children's books which depicted women in strong positions and utopian novels (such as her 1892 *Gloriana: or, the Revolution of 1900*) promoting equality among sexes. She was a foreign correspondent for the *Morning Post* during the Boer War (Tinling 105–11).

51. Barr, *Curious*, 191.

52. The term "New Woman" was coined in 1894 and is generally credited to Sarah Grand, author of several feminist novels. Women writers of the 1890s have

recently received special critical attention. A helpful anthology of the fiction of this period is Elaine Showalter's *Daughters of Decadence: Women Writers of the Fin-de-Siècle* (London: Virago, 1993).

53. "Donna Quixote." *Punch* 28 April 1894, 194. Elaine Showalter in "Smoking Room" (*Times Literary Supplement* 16 June 1995) has identified this particular illustration as referring to the "Keynotes" series of feminist fiction, most specifically to George Egerton's (Mary Chavelita Dunne) collection of short stories, *Keynotes* (12).

54. Ibid., 195.

55. Quoted in Barr, *Curious*, 54.

56. A photograph of women on horseback contemporary with Bird Bishop's book in Barr's biography shows that the skirt part of the costume can drape down past the stirrup to about a foot from the ground. A modified version of the same basic riding habit is shown in an illustration in Tweedie's book ten years later.

57. Barr, *Curious*, 184.

58. Review of *A Lady's Life in the Rocky Mountains*, by Isabella Bird Bishop, *Times* 21 November 1879, 3.

59. Barr, *Curious*, 184.

60. Ibid., 184.

61. Middleton, 16.

62. Barr, *Curious*, 184–85.

63. In her Persian travel, she found that, on occasion, wearing a large Afghan camel driver's coat allowed her to avoid the hostile reaction of Arabs toward unveiled foreign women (an imposing difficulty in the Mideast which Martineau passed over), especially if she rode in a group (*Journeys* 1:213–14).

64. In the *Yangtze Valley and Beyond*, she first justifies this practice by presenting a photograph of a male European missionary in native dress before her own photograph of herself in a formal pose in "Manchu dress" (347). The loose robes were dignified yet exotic and indicated that she had achieved her status as an explorer. In contrast, male travelers such as Edward Granville Browne in his *A Year Amongst the Persians* (1893), used their photographs as the frontispiece illustration for their books, while Bird Bishop used photographs of native peoples.

65. The multiple uses of sewing as a symbol of women's work in seventeenth-to nineteenth-century women's fiction is discussed in Kathryn R. King's "Of Needles and Pens and Women's Work," *Tulsa Studies in Women's Literature* 14 (1995): 77–93.

66. Miller, 93.

67. Barr, *Curious*, 136–39.

68. Indeed, Susan Morgan characterized the book as "virtually a hymn to British imperialism," reflecting the established ideology of British colonialism in the region (*Place* 150). See her *Place Matters: Gendered Geography in Victorian Women's Travel Books about Southeast Asia*, (New Brunswick: Rutgers University Press, 1996), 148–78 for an analysis of Bird Bishop's rhetoric in the context of Malaysian colonial policy contrasted with Emily Innes's response.

69. The mention of the Malay Archipelago may be a reference to Alfred Russel Wallace's book, *The Malay Archipelago*, which was last revised in 1869.

70. Miller, 93.

71. Barr, *Curious*, 253.

72. Pat Barr, introduction to *Journeys in Persia and Kurdistan*, by Isabella L. Bird (London: Virago, 1988), 1:x.

73. Barr, *Curious*, 264.

74. Quoted in Barr, *Curious*, 220.

75. Eva-Marie Kröller in "First Impressions: Rhetorical Strategies in Travel Writing by Victorian Women" (*Ariel: A Review of International English Literature* 21 [1990]: 87–99) analyzes Bird Bishop's relationship with Ito in *Unbeaten Tracks in Japan*. She relates Bird Bishop's eventual disillusionment with her servant as an example of a process described by Birkett whereby women travel writers "claimed status and position over foreign male peoples by infantilizing them" and attempting to control them (91–92; *Spinsters* 126–27). I suspect Bird Bishop's relationship with native servants is more complicated. She does not uniformly have problems with all the people she hires, but rather is continually disappointed when the Byronic "savagery" she is attracted to is accompanied with a lack of responsibility.

76. Barr, *Curious*, 47.

77. This is suggested in Thomas, 47–51, Pichanick, 175–82, and Valerie Sanders, *Reason Over Passion: Harriet Martineau and the Victorian Novel* (New York: St. Martin's, 1986), 129–32. In contrast, Billie Melman in *Women's Orient: English Women and the Middle East, 1718–1918* (Ann Arbor: University of Michigan Press, 1992) refers to *Eastern Life* as an "anti-pilgrimage" (235–53).

CHAPTER 5. MARY H. KINGSLEY: IN PURSUIT OF FISH AND FETISH

1. Clare Lloyd, *The Travelling Naturalists* (Seattle: University of Washington Press, 1985), 135–46.

2. Peter J. Bowler, "Holding Your Head Up High: Degeneration and Orthogenesis in Theories of Human Evolution," *History, Humanity and Evolution: Essays for John Greene*, ed. James R. Moore (Cambridge: Cambridge University Press, 1989), 341.

3. Julie English Early, "The Spectacle of Science and Self: Mary Kingsley" in Barbara T. Gates and Ann B. Shteir, eds., *Natural Eloquence: Women Reinscribe Science* (Madison: University of Wisconsin Press, 1997), 224.

4. Ibid., 221.

5. Alison Blunt, *Travel, Gender and Imperialism: Mary Kingsley and West Africa*, Mappings: Society/Theory/Space: A Guilford Series (New York: Guilford, 1994), 140–41.

6. Dea Birkett, *Spinsters Abroad: Victorian Lady Explorers* (Oxford: Blackwell, 1989), 14.

7. As Katherine Frank's biography (*A Voyager Out: The Life of Mary Kingsley* [New York: Ballantine-Ivy, 1986]) points out, the Kingsley family seemed to have a perverse desire to make life difficult for both their contemporary corespondents and for later historians by continually reusing the same set of first names each generation. The men are always named Charles, George or Henry, while women are named Mary or Charlotte (7). In the case of Mary Henrietta Kingsley, she shared first and last names with her cousin, the daughter of Charles Kingsley. Fortunately, that Mary Kingsley (later Mrs. William Harrison) published her novels under the pseudonym Lucas Malet.

8. The term "fetish" here refers to the study of what nineteenth-century Europeans considered to be "primitive religion." As Anne McClintock explains, in 1760, the French philosopher Charles de Brosses used the term *fetishisme* in this sense. Marx in 1867 made use of the phrase "commodity fetishism" to describe aspects of industrial economy. The sexual connotation was acquired later when

Freud used it in 1905 to refer to erotic "perversions." See Anne McClintock, *Imperial Leather: Race, Gender and Sexuality in the Colonial Contest* (New York: Routledge, 1995), 181.

9. Sara Mills, *Discourses of Difference: An Analysis of Women's Travel Writing and Colonialism* (London: Routledge, 1991), 174.

10. Eva-Marie Kröller, "First Impressions: Rhetorical Strategies in Travel Writing by Victorian Women," *Ariel: A Review of International English Literature* 21 (1990): 96.

11. It is a shame that the full text of Kingsley's travel is not readily available. Rather there has long been a small market in the retelling of Kingsley's travels (Valerie Grosvenor Myer's *A Victorian Lady in Africa: The Story of Mary Kingsley* [1989] is a recent example) in order to condense the humorous accounts while discarding her arguments for indirect colonial rule and discussion of native African law. The comic travel account has become a British tradition and recent examples of approaches similar to Kingsley can be seen in Redmond O'Hanlon's *Into the Heart of Borneo* and *In Trouble Again.*

12. These cartoons were possibly drawn by Leonard Woolf or Clive Bell. The debate was for the Trinity College debating society, "The Magpie and Stump." The proposed motion was "That it is better for us to understand Alien Races than for Alien Races to understand us." Dea Birkett, *Mary Kingsley: Imperial Adventuress* [London: Macmillan, 1992], 154.

13. Birkett, *Mary*, 154.

14. She was actually thirty-seven, but for reasons which will be explained in the biographical account, she always gave herself a younger age and so is recorded as dying at the age of thirty-five.

15. Rudyard Kipling, "Dirge of Dead Sisters," *The Complete Verse* (London: Kyle Cathie, 1990), 180. The "Sisters" in the title of the poem refers to the British title for nurses and has no religious connotations.

16. Belinda Hollyer, *Mary Kingsley the Explorer* (London: MacDonald Educational, 1975). Many thanks to Elizabeth Hagglund for running down this text, which was unavailable in the U. S.

17. Blunt, 53.

18. Ibid., 158.

19. Birkett, *Mary*, 62.

20. Curzon viewed the presence of women as a personal affront and he traded several letters back and forth with the women's supporters in the *London Times.* This is the same Curzon with whom Bird Bishop traveled. He was the Marquess of Kedleston and a M.P. at the time of this letter writing. Later, he was presented with a gold medal by the RGS (1895) and became its president from 1911–14. A powerful figure both in the RGS and British imperial government, he was viceroy of India from 1899–1905, and secretary of state for foreign affairs from 1918–22. He was notable for his books on Persia, India, and Russia, his snobbery and his self-designation as a "superior person."

21. George N. Curzon, "Ladies and the Royal Geographical Society," *London Times* 31 May 1893: 11.

22. Incorrectly cited as 1839 in Birkett's *Spinsters Abroad*, 179 and Blunt, 160 and 164 n. 1. (There are also some minor punctuation errors which Birkett corrected, along with the date, in her later *Mary Kingsley*.) *Punch* began publication in 1841.

23. I give the entire text here. Lines 17–20 have been frequently reprinted out of context, giving the impression that "*Punch* celebrated the anti-women faction's

victory in verse" (Birkett, *Mary*, 63), when in actuality, as the full text shows, *Punch* was attacking this attempt to remove the women.

24. Birkett, *Mary*, 63

25. Nancy Fix Anderson, *Woman Against Women in Victorian England: A Life of Eliza Lynn Linton (*Bloomington: Indiana University Press, 1987), 196.

26. Anderson, 191.

27. Quoted in Anderson, 191.

28. Ibid., 207.

29. Birkett, *Mary*, 25.

30. Frank, 29.

31. Birkett, *Mary*, 9.

32. Bernard Lightman, " 'The Voices of Nature': Popularizing Victorian Science," in *Victorian Science in Context*, ed. Bernard Lightman (Chicago: University of Chicago Press, 1997), 205.

33. Frank, 37–38.

34. Birkett, *Mary*, 37.

35. See, for example, Gerald Durrell's numerous books on his experiences in animal collecting.

36. Kingsley gave a more detailed account of her study of fishing and her interactions with African women in her later *West African Studies*.

37. Birkett, *Mary*, 36.

38. Clare Lloyd's *The Travelling Naturalists* mentions Isabella Bird Bishop in passing, but devotes the final chapter to Kingsley (135–46).

39. Examples of geographical approaches to Kingsley are found in studies by Alison Blunt and Dorothy Middleton. A recent anthology on geography and women is *Writing Women and Space: Colonial and Postcolonial Geographies*, ed. Alison Blunt and Gillian Rose (New York: Guilford, 1994).

40. Biographical material is from Katherine Frank's *A Voyager Out: The Life of Mary Kingsley*; Dea Birkett's *Spinsters Abroad: Victorian Lady Explorers* and *Mary Kingsley: Imperial Adventuress*; Alison Blunt's *Travel, Gender and Imperialism: Mary Kingsley and West Africa*; Catherine Barnes Stevenson's *Victorian Women Travel Writers in Africa* (Boston: Twayne, 1982); and Dorothy Middleton's *Victorian Lady Travellers* (New York: Dutton, 1965).

41. He co-authored *South Sea Bubbles* with the Earl of Pembroke (1872). Besides his trips around the Mediterranean and in the tropics, George Kingsley traveled to North America. He came close to joining the ill-fated Custer at Little Big Horn and came across Jim Nugent (Rocky Mountain Jim), who Bird Bishop wrote about, in Colorado. Nugent had been seriously wounded and George Kingsley provided medical services (Frank 40–41).

42. Ibid., 24–25.

43. Virginia Woolf, *Three Guineas* (New York: Harcourt, 1938). Stevenson has noted that Woolf has Kingsley "speak for us" to underscore that fact that the daughters of educated families often suffer in order to educate the sons (5–8). See also Stevenson's "Female Anger and African Politics: The Case of Two Victorian 'Lady Travellers,' " *Turn-of-the-Century Woman* 2 (1985): 13.

44. I emphasize these women's influence here since Kingsley's later anti–New Woman comments have left the impression that she was somehow so male-oriented that she denied women's intellectual capacity. It is often difficult to separate the positions women authors hold privately from what they will state publicly, particularly when political considerations lead to exaggerated rhetorical stances. However, it is also naive to assume that writing situations do not affect the public

presentations. Of the women mentioned here, Lucy Toulmin Smith was a research assistant for her father. She independently published works on medieval history and literature and was the first woman appointed librarian of Manchester College, Oxford. Violet Paget Roy was daughter of Sir George Paget and married to the first professor of pathology, Charles Roy, at Cambridge. She later became the first woman governor of Trinity College Cambridge. Agnes Smith Lewis wrote on her travels to the Middle East, *Our Journey to Sinai* (1898). She and her twin sister, Margaret Dunlop Gibson, were established as leading scholars in ancient languages after they discovered the Sinaitic Palimpest, an early version of the Gospels in 1893. (Kingsley was present when they realized what they had.)

45. Frank, 227.

46. Quoted in Frank, 94. Guillemard made the comment many years later to Stephen Gwynn in a letter dated 21 November 1932. According to the *OED*, the term "logorrhea" (from the Greek for "word" and "flow or stream") was not coined until 1902, after publication of *Travels*. The word first appeared in *J. M. Baldwin's Dictionary of Philosophy and Psychology* as a clinical term referring to excessive verbiage as a symptom of a form of insanity.

47. Quoted in Frank, 228.

48. Frank, 228.

49. Ibid., 229.

50. This is not to say Kingsley did not need editorial help with her writing. As she was largely self-educated, her writing did not conform to standard grammatical conventions. When Kingsley's publisher wanted to publish a cheap abridged version of *Travels*, Lucy Toulmin Smith, friend and author of *Manual of the English Grammar and Language for Self-Help* (1886), checked the proofs (Birkett, *Mary*, 89).

51. Caroline Alexander, *One Dry Season: In the Footsteps of Mary Kingsley* (New York: Knopf, 1990), 134–37.

52. Ibid., 138. Alexander's book is a recent attempt to retrace Kingsley's route in West Africa. While Alexander's retracing attempts often failed because villages had been moved, and old trails lost (Kingsley was probably lost a good deal of the time herself), her clarification of missionary history in this region is very helpful in providing a context for Kingsley's observations.

53. Quoted in Blunt, 61.

54. Ibid., 62.

55. Jane Austen, *Pride and Prejudice* (London: Penguin, 1972), 79–82. Elizabeth Bennet made the trip, "crossing field after field at a quick pace, jumping over stiles and springing over puddles with impatient activity," because her sister was ill at Netherfield, and the horses were needed for farm work. This is presented in the novel as unusual behavior indicating Elizabeth's independence and liveliness, traits which are positive but which need to be regulated. Most Austen heroines remain within domestic spaces.

56. Frank, 64.

57. Quoted in Frank, 212.

58. Frank, 223–25.

59. Quoted in Evellen Richards, "Huxley and Woman's Place in Science: The 'Woman Question' and the Control of Victorian Anthropology," in *History, Humanity, and Evolution: Essays for John C. Greene*, ed. James R. Moore (Cambridge: Cambridge University Press, 1989), 260.

60. Quoted in Richards, 260. Surprisingly, Eliza Lynn Linton, the well-known speaker against "The Girl of the Period," and later, "The New Woman," spoke

against her proposed expulsion from the Ethnological Society in 1868 directly to Huxley with an eight-page petition. While Lynn Linton long held that "the sphere of human action is determined by the fact of sex, and that there does exist both natural limitation and natural direction" (quoted in Richards 272), she also told Huxley that "it is not fair to exclude us from the means of knowledge & of active thought, of extended views—such as we get from attending learned discussions—on the simple plea of our womanhood" (quoted in Richards 274). There maybe some parallels between Kingsley and Lynn Linton which can help in understanding the difficulty individual independent women faced in the later part of the nineteenth century despite the material progress women in general were making. Lynn Linton, too, did not fit well into Victorian society, was independent (separated from her husband) and earned her livelihood through writing. Although progressive in her own life and agnostic, she still identified with a male hierarchy. Even her autobiography, *Christopher Kirkland*, was written under a male persona. Her own life and her public opinion were in conflict and were confusing even to her contemporaries.

61. Quoted in Bram Dijkstra, *Idols of Perversity: Fantasies of Feminine Evil in Fin-de-Siécle Culture* (New York: Oxford University Press, 1986), 170.

62. Dijkstra, 171. Besides Bram Dijkstra's study of artistic representation of women in the late nineteenth century, overlapping discussions of women and evolutionary degeneration may be found in Stephen Jay Gould's *The Mismeasure of Man* (New York: Norton, 1981) and Sandra Gilbert and Susan Gubar's *The Madwoman in the Attic: The Woman Writer and the Nineteenth-Century Literary Imagination* (New Haven: Yale University Press, 1984).

63. *Travels* proudly displays plates in the appendix showing some of the fish with which Kingsley returned. Günther named *Ctenopoma Kingsleyae*, *Mormyrus Kingsleyae*, and *Alestes Kingsleyae* after Kingsley. Admittedly, tagging one's own name onto a new species is considered poor manners in taxonomic circles. Generally, the naming is done by the taxonomist rather than the collector.

64. Anderson, 218.

65. Ibid., 218.

66. Ibid., 219.

67. Quoted in Blunt, 133.

68. My reading of these lists diverges from that of Kröller who reads this passage as a deconstructing random sequence which "upsets the hierarchy of 'important' events and suggests a sequence almost as random" as that used in Roland Barthes' autobiography (96).

69. David Livingstone, *Missionary Travels and Researches in South Africa*, 1858 (New York: Johnson Reprint, 1971), 7–8.

70. Frank, 59.

71. This chapter was removed in the posthumous editions of *West African Studies*.

72. Quoted in Gwynn, 26.

73. Frank, 160.

74. Blunt, 137.

75. Mary Louise Pratt, *Imperial Eyes: Travel Writing and Transculturation* (London: Routledge, 1992), 201.

76. Quoted in Blunt, 132.

77. Pratt, 213.

78. Alexander, 126.

79. Catherine Barnes Stevenson, *Victorian Women Travel Writers in Africa* (Boston: Twayne, 1982), 147.

80. According to Frank Swinnerton in his introduction to Elizabeth Gaskell's *Cranford* (London: Dent, 1977), the taste for idyllic literature at the turn-of-the-century was encouraged by J. M. Dent in a series of books called the English Idylls. In addition to *Cranford*, the first volumes in this series were Goldsmith's *The Vicar of Wakefield*, and Mitford's *Our Village* (vi).

81. Early, 222–23.

82. Pratt terms this convention the "monarch-of-all-I-survey scene" (201).

83. Ibid., 213.

84. Ibid., 213.

85. Stevenson compares the irony employed in these headings to that of the chapter headings of Fielding (125).

86. In this case, Kingsley speaks of Herr von Lucke who helped in her progress and who had been getting some heat from his home office.

87. Kröller points out, in reference to a departure description, that Kingsley's rhetorical strategy involved using false starts to place her undertakings in "ironic brackets" while avoiding any questioning of her sincerity or the usefulness of her undertakings (96).

88. In this pairing of names, Kingsley very diplomatically avoids mentioning the nasty rivalry between Mann and Burton over who had first climbed the mountain. Edward Rice's biography of Richard Burton (*Captain Sir Richard Francis Burton* [New York: Scribner's, 1990]) describes this competition on pages 364–65. Kingsley comments on this rivalry later in a footnote on page 595. She also uses the names Big Cameroon and Little Cameroon for the two highest peaks, ignoring Burton's names of Victoria and Albert. Another major difference in their respective climbs is that Burton set up a whipping post after the climb to punish the natives he took with him, while Kingsley is preoccupied in caring for her bearers and guides.

89. Kingsley reports that a few weeks before the same climb had been made by two Germans. Blunt erroneously states that Kingsley claims to have been the first European to make a southeast ascent, page 73.

90. Interestingly, when Belinda Hollyer used material from *Travels* in her reading primer, *Mary Kingsley the Explorer*, Kingsley's statement that she could not see anything from the mountain top is simply ignored. Rather, Kingsley is shown looking outward with wind-whipped hair (and in a long skirt) over the statement that, "She could look out over many miles. She could see a lot of Africa" (24). The male explorer convention in maintained in establishing her as an explorer, even when it conflicts with her reporting.

91. J. A. Hobson's very influential text, *Imperialism: A Study* (1902), recognizes Kingsley's insight into the problems of British colonial governing and quotes from her *West African Studies* (121, 266) supporting the validity of her arguments (Ann Arbor: University of Michigan Press, 1965).

92. Frank, 285.

93. Quoted in Frank, 262.

94. Quoted in Stevenson, *Victorian* 145.

95. Quoted in Blunt, 137.

96. Blunt, 138.

97. Ibid., 138.

98. Ibid., 53.

99. Quoted in Blunt, 139.

100. Ibid., 127.

CHAPTER 6. CONCLUSION

1. Patricia Phillips, *The Scientific Lady: A Social History of Women's Scientific Interests, 1520–1918* (New York: St. Martin's, 1990), 252–54.

2. Ibid., 256.

3. Ibid., 257.

4. Philippa Levine, introduction to *Untrodden Peaks and Unfrequented Valleys: A Midsummer Ramble in the Dolomites* by Amelia Edwards, 1873 (London: Virago, 1986), xxv.

5. Bernard Lightman, "Constructing Victorian Heavens: Agnes Clerke and the 'New Astronomy,' " in *Natural Eloquence: Women Reinscribe Science,* ed. by Barbara T. Gates and Ann B. Shteir (Chicago: University of Chicago Press, 1998), 64.

6. Quoted in Lightman, 72.

7. Cynthia Irwin-Williams, "Women in the Field: The Role of Women in Archaeology before 1960," in *Women of Science: Righting the Record*, ed. by G. Farnes Kass-Simon and Patricia Farnes (Bloomington: Indiana University Press, 1990), 8.

8. Ibid., 2.

9. Ibid., 16.

10. Thomas S. Kuhn, *The Structure of Scientific Revolutions*, 2nd ed. (Chicago: University of Chicago Press, 1970), 10.

11. Donna Haraway, *Primate Visions: Gender, Race, and Nature in the World of Modern Science* (New York: Routledge, 1989), 150.

12. Ibid., 150.

13. Quoted in James Krasner," 'Ape Ladies' and Cultural Politics: Dian Fossey and Biruté Galdikas," in Gates and Shteir, 243; Harold T. P. Hayes, *The Dark Romance of Dian Fossey* (New York: Simon & Schuster, 1990), 217.

14. Sy Montgomery, *Walking with the Great Apes: Jane Goodall, Dian Fossey, Biruté Galdikas* (Boston: Houghton, 1991), 207.

15. Ibid., 130.

16. Krasner, 244–45. See Harold T. P. Hayes's *The Dark Romance of Dian Fossey*, for example.

17. Quoted in Montgomery, 217.

18. Krasner, 241.

19. Ibid., 242.

20. Montgomery, 175.

21. Krasner, 245–49.

22. Haraway, 158–59.

Works Cited

Abir-am, Pnina G., and Dorinda Outram, eds. *Uneasy Careers and Intimate Lives: Women in Science, 1789–1979.* New Brunswick, NJ: Rutgers University Press, 1987.

Abrams, M. H., ed. *Norton Anthology of English Literature.* 5th ed. New York: Norton, 1986.

Adams, Percy G. *Travel Literature and the Evolution of the Novel.* Lexington: University Press of Kentucky, 1983.

"The Admirals' Doom." *Punch* 17 June 1893, 285.

Alexander, Caroline. *One Dry Season: In the Footsteps of Mary Kingsley.* New York: Knopf, 1990.

Alic, Margaret. *Hypatia's Heritage: A History of Women in Science from Antiquity through the Nineteenth Century.* Boston: Beacon, 1986.

Allen, David Elliston. *The Naturalist in Britain: A Social History.* London: Allen Lane, 1976.

Anderson, Nancy Fix. *Woman Against Women in Victorian England: A Life of Eliza Lynn Linton.* Bloomington: Indiana University Press, 1987.

Arbuckle, Elisabeth Sanders, ed. *Harriet Martineau's Letters to Fanny Wedgwood.* Stanford, CA: Stanford University Press, 1983.

Austen, Jane. *Pride and Prejudice.* 1813. Edited by Tony Tanner. London: Penguin, 1972.

Barber, Lynn. *The Heyday of Natural History: 1820–1870.* Garden City, NY: Doubleday, 1980.

Barr, Pat. *A Curious Life for a Lady: The Story of Isabella Bird.* London: Macmillan, 1970.

———. Introduction. *Journeys in Persia and Kurdistan* by Isabella L. Bird. Vol. 1. London: Virago, 1988. v-xiii.

Barrett, Dorothea. *Vocation and Desire: George Eliot's Heroines.* London: Routledge, 1989.

Barton, H. Arnold. *Scandinavia in the Revolutionary Era, 1760–1815.* Minneapolis: University of Minnesota Press, 1986.

Basalla, George, William Coleman, and Robert H. Kargon. *Victorian Science: A Self-Portrait from the Presidential Addresses to the British Association for the Advancement of Science.* New York: Anchor-Doubleday, 1970.

Beer, Gillian. *Darwin's Plots: Evolutionary Narrative in Darwin, George Eliot and Nineteenth-Century Fiction.* London: Routledge, 1983.

———. "Darwin's Reading and the Fictions of Development." *The Darwinian Heritage.* Edited by David Kohn. Princeton: Princeton University Press, 1985. 543–607.

Behdad, Ali. *Belated Travelers: Orientalism in the Age of Colonial Dissolution.* Durham, NC: Duke University Press, 1994.

Benjamin, Marina. "Elbow Room: Women Writers on Science, 1790–1840." *Science and Sensibility: Gender and Scientific Enquiry, 1780–1945.* Edited by Marina Benjamin. Oxford: Blackwell, 1991.

Bird [Bishop], Isabella Lucy. *Among the Tibetans.* New York: Revell, 1894.

———. *The Golden Chersonese and the Way Thither.* 1883. Reprint, New York: Oxford University Press, 1967.

———. *Journeys in Persia and Kurdistan.* 2 vols. 1891. Reprint, London: Virago, 1988–1989.

———. *Korea and Her Neighbors.* 1897. Reprint, London: KPI, 1985.

———. *A Lady's Life in the Rocky Mountains.* 1879. Reprint, Sausalito, CA: Comstock, 1987.

———. *Six Months Among the Palm Groves, Coral Reefs and Volcanoes of the Sandwich Islands.* 7th ed. 1890. Reprint, Rutland, VT: Tuttle, 1974.

———. *The Yangtze Valley and Beyond: An Account of Journeys in China, Chiefly in the Province of Sze Chuan and Among the Man-Tze of the Somo Territory.* 1899. Reprint, Boston: Virago/Beacon Press, 1985.

Birkett, Dea. *Mary Kingsley: Imperial Adventuress.* London: Macmillan, 1992.

———. *Spinsters Abroad: Victorian Lady Explorers.* Oxford: Blackwell, 1989.

Blunt, Alison. *Travel, Gender and Imperialism: Mary Kingsley and West Africa.* Mappings: Society/Theory/Space: A Guilford Series. New York: Guilford, 1994.

———, and Gillian Rose, eds. *Writing Women and Space: Colonial and Postcolonial Geographies.* New York: Guilford, 1994.

Boorstin, Daniel J. Introduction. *A Lady's Life in the Rocky Mountains* by Isabella L. Bird. Norman: University of Oklahoma Press, 1960. xiii–xxi.

Bowerbank, Sylvia. "The Bastille of Nature: Wollstonecraft versus Malthus in Scandinavia." *Studies on Voltaire and the Eighteenth Century* 304 (1992): 826–27.

Bowler, Peter J. "Holding Your Head Up High: Degeneration and Orthogenesis in Theories of Human Evolution." *History, Humanity and Evolution: Essays for John Greene.* Edited by James R. Moore. Cambridge: Cambridge University Press, 1989. 329–53.

Browne, Edward Granville. *A Year Amongst the Persians: Impressions as to the Life, Character, and Thought of the People of Persia.* 1893. Reprint, London: Black, 1970.

Browne, Janet. *Charles Darwin: Voyaging.* New York: Knopf, 1995.

Buell, Lawrence. "American Pastoral Ideology Reappraised." *American Literary History* 1 (1989): 1–29.

Burton, Richard F. *The City of the Saints and Across the Rocky Mountains to California.* 1862. Reprint, New York: AMS, 1971.

———. *Two Trips to Gorilla Land and the Cataracts of the Congo.* London: Sampson Low, 1876. Reprint, New York: Johnson Reprint, 1967.

Buzard, James. *The Beaten Track: European Tourism, Literature, and the Ways to Culture, 1800–1918.* Oxford: Clarendon, 1993.

Byatt, A. S. "Morpho Eugenia." *Angels and Insects: Two Novellas.* New York: Random, 1992. 3–183.

Caine, Barbara. "Victorian Feminism and the Ghost of Mary Wollstonecraft." *Women's Writing* 4 (1997): 261–75.

Cameron, Kenneth Neill, ed. *Shelley and His Circle 1773–1822.* 4 vols. Cambridge: Harvard University Press, 1961.

Christiansen, Rupert. *Romantic Affinities: Portraits from an Age 1780–1830.* New York: Putnam's, 1988.

Christie, John Aldrich. *Thoreau As World Traveler.* New York: Columbia University Press, 1965.

Corfield, Penelope J. "The Case of *The Cabinet.*" *Times Literary Supplement* 21 March 1997, 11–12.

Cowie, Alexander. *The Rise of the American Novel.* New York: American Book, 1948.

de Crèvecoeur, J. Hector St. John. *Letters from an American Farmer and Sketches of Eighteenth-Century America.* Edited by Albert E. Stone. 1782. Reprint, New York: Penguin, 1981.

Curzon, George N. "Ladies and the Royal Geographical Society." Letter. *London Times* 31 May 1893, 11.

Darwin, Charles. *The Correspondence of Charles Darwin.* Vol. 4. 1847–1850. Cambridge: Cambridge University Press, 1988.

David, Deirdre. *Intellectual Women and Victorian Patriarchy: Harriet Martineau, Elizabeth Barrett Browning, George Eliot.* Ithaca: Cornell University Press, 1987.

Dent, Anthony Austen. *The Horse Through Fifty Centuries of Civilization.* New York: Holt, 1974.

Derry, T. K. *A History of Scandinavia: Norway, Sweden, Denmark, Finland and Iceland.* Minneapolis: University of Minnesota Press, 1979.

Dijkstra, Bram. *Idols of Perversity: Fantasies of Feminine Evil in Fin-de-Siécle Culture.* New York: Oxford University Press, 1986.

[Disraeli, Benjamin.] Review of *Society in America,* by Harriet Martineau. *Times of London* 30 May 1837, 5.

Dixie, Florence. *Across Patagonia.* New York: R. Worthington, 1881.

"Donna Quixote." *Punch* 28 April 1894, 194–95.

Early, Julie English. "The Spectacle of Science and Self: Mary Kingsley." *Natural Eloquence: Women Reinscribe Science.* Edited by Barbara Gates and Ann B. Shteir. Madison: University of Wisconsin Press, 1997. 215–36.

Edwards, Amelia. *Untrodden Peaks and Unfrequented Valleys: A Midsummer Ramble in the Dolomites.* 1873. Reprint, London: Virago, 1986.

Emerson, Oliver Farrar. "Notes on Gilbert Imlay, Early American Writer." *PMLA* 39 (1924): 406–39.

Ernstrom, Adele M. "The Afterlife of Mary Wollstonecraft and Anna Jameson's *Winter Studies and Summer Rambles in Canada.*" *Women's Writing* 4 (1997): 277–96.

Fairchild, Hoxie Neale. *The Noble Savage: A Study in Romantic Naturalism.* New York: Russell & Russell, 1961.

Ferguson, Moira. *Colonialism and Gender Relations from Mary Wollstonecraft to Jamaica Kincaid: East Caribbean Connections.* New York: Columbia University Press, 1993.

————, and Janet Todd. *Mary Wollstonecraft*. Boston: Twayne, 1984.

Flexner, Eleanor. *Mary Wollstonecraft: A Biography*. Baltimore: Penguin, 1972.

Foster, Shirley. *Across New Worlds: Nineteenth Century Women Travellers and their Writings*. Hemel Hampstead, England: Harvester, 1990.

Foucault, Michel. *The History of Sexuality: An Introduction: Volume 1*. Translated Robert Hurley. New York: Vintage-Random, 1990.

————. Introduction. *Herculine Barbin: Being the Recently Discovered Memoirs of a Nineteenth-Century French Hermaphrodite*. Translated by Richard McDougall. New York: Pantheon, 1980. vii–xvii.

————. *The Order of Things: An Archaeology of the Human Sciences*. New York: Vintage, 1970.

Frank, Katherine. *A Passage to Egypt: The Life of Lucie Duff Gordon*. Boston: Houghton, 1994.

————. *A Voyager Out: The Life of Mary Kingsley*. New York: Ballantine-Ivy, 1986.

Frawley, Maria H. "Harriet Martineau in America: Gender and the Discourse of Sociology." *The Victorian Newsletter* 81 (1992): 13–20.

————. *A Wider Range: Travel Writing by Women in Victorian England*. Rutherford, NJ: Fairleigh Dickinson University Press, 1994.

Fussell, Paul. *Abroad: British Literary Traveling Between the Wars*. Oxford: Oxford University Press, 1980.

Gates, Barbara T. *Kindred Nature: Victorian and Edwardian Women Embrace the Living World*. Chicago: University of Chicago Press, 1998.

————, and Ann B. Shteir, eds. *Natural Eloquence: Women Reinscribe Science*. Madison: University of Wisconsin Press, 1997.

Gilbert, Sandra M., and Susan Gubar. *The Madwoman in the Attic: The Woman Writer and the Nineteenth-Century Literary Imagination*. New Haven: Yale University Press, 1984.

Gilmour, Robin. *The Victorian Period: The Intellectual and Cultural Context of English Literature, 1830–1890*. London: Longman, 1993.

Godwin, William. "Memoirs of The Author of The Rights of Woman." In *A Short Residence in Sweden, Norway and Denmark by Mary Wollstonecraft and Memoirs of the Author of The Rights of Woman by William Godwin*. Edited by Richard Holmes. Harmondsworth, England: Penguin, 1987.

Gosse, Philip Henry. *The Romance of Natural History*. Boston: Gould & Lincoln, [1860].

Gould, Stephen Jay. *The Mismeasure of Man*. New York: Norton, 1981.

————, and Rosamond W. Purcell. *Finders, Keepers: Eight Collectors*. New York: Norton, 1992.

Gwynn, Stephen. *The Life of Mary Kingsley*. 2nd ed. London: Macmillan, 1933.

Haraway, Donna. *Primate Visions: Gender, Race, and Nature in the World of Modern Science*. New York: Routledge, 1989.

Hardy, Thomas. *Tess of the d'Urbervilles*. Edited by Scott Elledge. 1891. 2nd ed. New York: Norton, 1979.

Hare, Robert R. Introduction. *The Emigrants: Traditionally Ascribed to Gilbert Imlay But, More Probably, By Mary Wollstonecraft*. Gainesville, FL: Scholars' Facsimiles, 1964.

Hayes, Harold T. P. *The Dark Romance of Dian Fossey*. New York: Simon & Schuster, 1990.

Hill, Michael R. Introduction. *How to Observe Morals and Manners*. By Harriet Martineau. New Brunswick, NJ: Transaction, 1989. xi–lx.

Hobson, J. A. *Imperialism: A Study*. 1902. Reprint, Ann Arbor: University of Michigan Press, 1965.

Hoecker-Drysdale, Susan. *Harriet Martineau: First Woman Sociologist*. Oxford: Berg, 1992.

Hollyer, Belinda. *Mary Kingsley the Explorer*. London: MacDonald Educational, 1975.

Holmes, Richard. *Footsteps: Adventures of a Romantic Biographer*. New York: Viking, 1985.

————, ed. *A Short Residence in Sweden, Norway and Denmark by Mary Wollstonecraft and Memoirs of the Author of The Rights of Woman by William Godwin*. Harmondsworth, England: Penguin, 1987.

Imlay, Gilbert. *A Topographical Description of the Western Territory of North America . . . the Third Edition, with Great Additions*. 1797. Reprint, New York: Johnson Reprint, 1968.

Ingpen, Roger, ed. *The Love Letters of Mary Wollstonecraft to Gilbert Imlay, with a Prefatory Memoir*. London: Hutchinson, 1908.

Irwin-Williams, Cynthia. "Women in the Field: The Role of Women in Archaeology before 1960." *Women of Science: Righting the Record*. Edited by G. Kass-Simon and Patricia Farnes. Bloomington: Indiana University Press, 1–41.

Jameson, Anna. *The Diary of an Ennuyée*. 1826. Reprint, Boston: James R. Osgood, 1876.

Jordanova, Ludmilla. *Sexual Visions: Images of Gender in Science and Medicine Between the Eighteenth and Twentieth Centuries*. Madison: University of Wisconsin Press, 1989

Jung, C. G. *Aion: Researches into the Phenomenology of the Self*. Translated by R. F. C. Hull. 2nd ed. Bollingen Series 20. Princeton: Princeton University Press, 1968.

Kass-Simon, G. "Biology is Destiny." *Women of Science: Righting the Record*. Edited by G. Kass-Simm and Patricia Farnes. Bloomington: Indiana University Press, 215–67.

————, and Patricia Farnes, eds. *Women of Science: Righting the Record*. Bloomington: Indiana University Press, 1990.

Katz, Eve. "The Problem of the Environment in *Les Reveries du Promeneur Solitaire*." *Studies in Eighteenth-Century Culture* 4 (1975): 95–107.

Keller, Evelyn Fox. *A Feeling for the Organism: The Life and Work of Barbara McClintock*. New York: Freeman, 1983.

————. *Reflections on Gender and Science*. New Haven: Yale University Press, 1985.

Kelly, Gary. "Godwin, Wollstonecraft, and Rousseau." *Women and Literature* 3.2 (1975): 21–26.

King, Kathryn R. "Of Needles and Pens and Women's Work." *Tulsa Studies in Women's Literature* 14 (1995): 77–93.

Kingsley, Mary H. *Travels in West Africa: Congo Français, Corisco and Cameroons*. London: Macmillan, 1897.

————. *West African Studies.* 1899. 3rd ed. New York: Barnes, 1964.

Kipling, Rudyard. "Dirge of Dead Sisters." *The Complete Verse.* London: Kyle Cathie, 1990. 179–180.

Koerner, Lisbet. "Linnaeus' Floral Transplants." *Representations* 47 (1994): 144–69.

Krasner, James. " 'Ape Ladies' and Cultural Politics: Dian Fossey and Biruté Galdikas." *Natural Eloquence: Women Reinscribe Science.* Edited by Barbara Gates and Ann B. Shteir. Madison: University of Wisconsin Press, 1997. 237–51.

Kröller, Eva-Marie. "First Impressions: Rhetorical Strategies in Travel Writing by Victorian Women." *Ariel: A Review of International English Literature* 21 (1990): 87–99.

Kuhn, Thomas S. *The Structure of Scientific Revolutions.* 2nd ed. Chicago: University of Chicago Press, 1970.

Review of *A Lady's Life in the Rocky Mountains*, by Isabella L. Bird. *Times* 21 November 1879, 3.

Lane, Margaret. *The Tale of Beatrix Potter.* Rev. ed. Glasgow, Scotland: Fontana-Collins, 1968.

Laqueur, Thomas. *Making Sex: Body and Gender from the Greeks to Freud.* Cambridge: Harvard University Press, 1990.

Le Gassick, Trevor. Introduction. *Midaq Alley* by Naguib Mahfouz. New York: Doubleday, 1981. 3–9.

Levine, George. *Darwin and the Novelists: Patterns of Science in Victorian Fiction.* Cambridge: Harvard University Press, 1988.

Levine, Philippa. Introduction. *Untrodden Peaks and Unfrequented Valleys: A Midsummer Ramble in the Dolomites.* By Amelia Edwards. 1873. Reprint, London: Virago, 1986. xv–xxviii.

Lightman, Bernard. "Constructing Victorian Heavens: Agnes Clerke and the 'New Astronomy.' " *Natural Eloquence: Women Reinscribe Science.* Edited by Barbara T. Gates and Ann B. Shteir. Madison: University of Wisconsin Press, 1984. 61–75.

————, ed. *Victorian Science in Context.* Chicago: University of Chicago Press, 1997.

————. " 'The Voices of Nature': Popularizing Victorian Science." *Victorian Science in Context.* Edited by Bernard Lightman. Chicago: University of Chicago Press, 1997.

Lindsay, Debra. "Intimate Inmates: Wives, Households, and Science in Nineteenth-Century America. *Isis* 89 (1998): 631–52.

Livingstone, David. *Missionary Travels and Researches in South Africa.* 1858. Reprint, New York: Johnson Reprint, 1971.

Livingstone, David N. "Climate's Moral Economy: Science, Race and Place in Post-Darwinian British and American Geography." *Geography and Empire.* Edited by Anne Godlewska and Neil Smith. The Institute of British Geographers series no. 30. Oxford: Blackwell, 1994.

Lloyd, Clare. *The Travelling Naturalists.* Seattle: University of Washington Press, 1985.

Lovejoy, Arthur O. "Buffon and the Problem of Species." *Forerunners of Darwin: 1745–1859.* Edited by Bentley Glass, Owsei Temkin, and William L. Straus, Jr. Baltimore: Johns Hopkins Press, 1959. 84–113.

Lowes, John. *The Road to Xanadu: A Study in the Ways of the Imagination.* Rev. ed. Boston: Houghton, 1927.

Lyell, Charles. *Principles of Geology.* 2 vols. 1832. Reprint, Chicago: University of Chicago Press, 1990.

Mansfield, Peter. *The British in Egypt.* New York: Holt, 1971.

Martineau, Harriet. *Eastern Life: Present and Past.* 2nd ed. Boston: Roberts Brothers, 1876.

———. *Harriet Martineau's Autobiography.* 2 vols. Introduction by Gaby Weiner. 3rd ed. 1877. London: Virago, 1983.

———. *How to Observe Morals and Manners.* Introduction by Michael R. Hill. 1838. Reprint, New Brunswick, NJ: Transaction, 1989.

———. "On Female Education." *The Monthly Repository* 18 (1823): 77–81.

———. *Retrospect of Western Travel.* London: Saunders and Otley, 1838.

———. *Society in America.* 3 vol. 1837. Reprint, New York: AMS Press, 1966.

Mason, Nondita, and George Otte. *Writers' Roles: Enactments of the Process.* Fort Worth, TX: Harcourt, 1994.

McClintock, Anne. *Imperial Leather: Race, Gender and Sexuality in the Colonial Contest.* New York: Routledge, 1995.

McGuinn, Nicholas. "George Eliot and Mary Wollstonecraft." *The Nineteenth-Century Woman: Her Cultural and Physical World.* Edited by Sara Delamont and Lorna Duffin. London: Croom Helm, 1978. 188–205.

Mead, W. R. *An Historical Geography of Scandinavia.* London: Academic Press, 1981.

Melman, Billie. *Women's Orient: English Women and the Middle East, 1718–1918.* Ann Arbor: University of Michigan Press, 1992.

Merchant, Carolyn. *The Death of Nature: Women, Ecology and the Scientific Revolution.* 1980. Reprint, San Francisco: Harper, 1990.

Mermin, Dorothy. *Godiva's Ride: Women of Letters in England, 1830–1880.* Bloomington: Indiana University Press, 1993.

Merrill, Lynn L. *The Romance of Victorian Natural History.* New York: Oxford University Press, 1989.

Middleton, Dorothy. "Some Victorian Lady Travellers." *Geographical Journal* 139 (1973): 65–75.

———. *Victorian Lady Travellers.* New York: Dutton, 1965.

Miller, Luree. *On Top of the World: Five Women Explorers in Tibet.* 1976. Seattle: Mountaineers, 1984.

Millhauser, Milton. *Just Before Darwin: Robert Chambers and Vestiges.* Middletown, CT: Wesleyan University Press, 1959.

Mills, Sara. *Discourses of Difference: An Analysis of Women's Travel Writing and Colonialism.* London: Routledge, 1991.

Moi, Toril. *Sexual/Textual Politics: Feminist Literary Theory.* London: Methuen, 1985.

Montgomery, Sy. *Walking with the Great Apes: Jane Goodall, Dian Fossey, Biruté Galdikas.* Boston: Houghton, 1991.

Montrose, Louis. "The Work of Gender in the Discourse of Discovery." *Representations* 33 (1991): 1–41.

Morgan, Susan. Introduction. *Recollections of a Happy Life Being the Autobiogra-*

phy of Marianne North. Vol. 1. 1892. Reprint, Charlottesville: University Press of Virginia, 1993.

————. *Place Matters: Gendered Geography in Victorian Women's Travel Books about Southeast Asia.* New Brunswick, NJ: Rutgers University Press, 1996.

————. "Women, Wisdom, and Southeast Asia." *Victorian Sages and Cultural Discourse: Renegotiating Gender and Power.* Edited by Thaïs E. Morgan. New Brunswick, NJ: Rutgers University Press, 1990. 207–24.

Morrell, Jack, and Arnold Thackray. *Gentlemen of Science: Early Years of the British Association for the Advancement of Science.* Oxford: Clarendon, 1981.

Morris, Mary, ed. *Maiden Voyages: Writings of Women Travelers.* New York: Vintage, 1993.

Morris, R. J. *Cholera 1832: The Social Response to an Epidemic.* New York: Holmes & Meier, 1976.

Morton, Peter. *The Vital Science: Biology and the Literary Imagination, 1860–1900.* London: Allen, 1984.

Moss, Sidney P. *Charles Dickens' Quarrel with America.* Troy, NY: Whitston, 1984.

Mulvey, Christopher. *Anglo-American Landscapes: A Study of Nineteenth-Century Anglo-American Travel Literature.* Cambridge: Cambridge University Press, 1983.

Myers, Mitzi. "Mary Wollstonecraft's *Letters Written . . . in Sweden*: Toward Romantic Autobiography." *Studies in Eighteenth-Century Culture* 8 (1979): 165–85.

Nightingale, Florence. *Letters From Egypt: A Journey on the Nile 1849–1850.* Edited by Anthony Sattin. New York: Weidenfeld and Nicolson, 1987.

Noble, Mary. "Beatrix Potter and Charles McIntosh, Naturalists." *A Victorian Naturalist: Beatrix Potter's Drawings from the Armitt Collection.* By Eileen Jay, Mary Noble, and Anne Stevenson Hobbs. London: Warne, 1992. 55–135.

Nyström, Per. *Mary Wollstonecraft's Scandinavian Journey.* Acts of the Royal Society of Arts and Sciences of Gothenburg. Humaniora No. 17. Translated by George R. Otter. Göteborg, Sweden: Kungl. Vetenskaps-och Vitterhets-Samhället, 1980.

Ogilvie, Marilyn Bailey. "Marital Collaboration: An Approach to Science." *Uneasy Careers and Intimate Lives: Women in Science, 1789–1979.* Edited by Pnina G. Abir-am and Dorinda Outram. New Brunswick, NJ: Rutgers University Press, 1987. 104–25.

O'Hanlon, Redmond. *Into the Heart of Borneo.* New York: Vintage, 1987.

————. *In Trouble Again: A Journey Between the Orinoco and the Amazon.* New York: Vintage, 1990.

Paul, C[harles] Kegan, ed. *Mary Wollstonecraft: Letters to Imlay.* 1879. New York: Haskell, 1971.

————. "Memoir." *Mary Wollstonecraft: Letters to Imlay.* 1879. New York: Haskell, 1971. v–lxiii.

Peterson, Linda H. "Harriet Martineau: Masculine Discourse, Female Sage." *Victorian Sages and Cultural Discourse: Renegotiating Gender and Power.* Edited by Thaïs Morgan. New Brunswick, NJ: Rutgers University Press, 1990. 171–86.

Phillips, Patricia. *The Scientific Lady: A Social History of Women's Scientific Interests, 1520–1918.* New York: St. Martin's, 1990.

Pichanick, Valerie Kossew. *Harriet Martineau: The Woman and Her Work 1802–1876*. Ann Arbor: University of Michigan Press, 1980.

Poovey, Mary. *The Proper Lady and the Woman Writer: Ideology as Style in the Works of Mary Wollstonecraft, Mary Shelley, and Jane Austen*. Chicago: University of Chicago Press, 1984.

Poston, Carol H., ed. *A Vindication of the Rights of Woman* by Mary Wollstonecraft. New York: Norton, 1975.

Pratt, Mary Louise. "Fieldwork in Common Places." *Writing Culture: The Poetics and Politics of Ethnography*. Edited by James Clifford and George E. Marcus. Berkeley: University of California Press, 1986. 27–50.

———. *Imperial Eyes: Travel Writing and Transculturation*. London: Routledge, 1992.

Previté-Orton, C. W. "Political Writers and Speakers." *The Cambridge History of English Literature*. Vol. 11. New York: Putnam, 1914. 37–62.

Rice, Edward. *Captain Sir Richard Francis Burton*. New York: Scribner's, 1990.

Richards, Evellen. "Huxley and Woman's Place in Science: The 'Woman Question' and the Control of Victorian Anthropology." *History, Humanity, and Evolution: Essays for John C. Greene*. Edited by James R. Moore. Cambridge: Cambridge University Press, 1989. 253–84.

Richards, Thomas. *The Imperial Archive: Knowledge and the Fantasy of Empire*. London: Verso, 1993.

Ronald, Ann. Introduction. *A Lady's Life in the Rocky Mountains*. By Isabella Bishop. Sausalito, CA: Comstock, 1987. xi–xviii.

Rousseau, Jean-Jacques. *Reveries of the Solitary Walker*. Translated by Peter France. Harmondsworth, England: Penguin, 1979.

"The Royal Geographical Society and the Admission of Ladies." Letter. *London Times* 29 May 1893: 7.

Rusk, Ralph Leslie. "The Adventures of Gilbert Imlay." *Indiana University Studies* 10 (1923): 3–26.

Ryall, Anka. "A Vindication of Struggling Nature: Mary Wollstonecraft's Scandinavia." Conference Paper. Snapshots from Abroad: A Conference on American and British Travel Writers and Writing. University of Minnesota, Minneapolis. 16 November 1997.

Said, Edward W. *Culture and Imperialism*. New York: Knopf, 1993.

———. *Orientalism*. New York: Pantheon, 1978.

Sanders, Valerie. *Reason Over Passion: Harriet Martineau and the Victorian Novel*. New York: St. Martin's, 1986.

Sapiro, Virginia. *A Vindication of Political Virtue: The Political Theory of Mary Wollstonecraft*. Chicago: University of Chicago Press, 1992.

Sattin, Anthony. Introduction. *Letters From Egypt: A Journey on the Nile 1849–1850*. By Florence Nightingale. New York: Weidenfeld and Nicolson, 1987. 11–19.

Schiebinger, Londa. *The Mind Has No Sex?: Women in the Origins of Modern Science*. Cambridge: Harvard University Press, 1989.

Seelye, John. "The Jacobin Mode in Early American Fiction: Gilbert Imlay's *The Emigrants*." *Early American Literature* 21 (1986): 204–12.

Showalter, Elaine, ed. *Daughters of Decadence: Women Writers of the Fin-de-Siè-cle.* London: Virago, 1993.

———. "Smoking Room." *Times Literary Supplement* 16 June 1995: 12.

Shteir, Ann B. "Botany in the Breakfast Room: Women and Early Nineteenth-Century British Plant Study." *Uneasy Careers and Intimate Lives: Women in Science, 1789–1979.* Edited by Pnina G. Abir-am and Dorinda Outram. New Brunswick, NJ: Rutgers University Press, 1987. 19–43.

———. "Elegant Recreations?: Configuring Science Writing for Women." *Victorian Science In Context.* Edited by Bernard Lightman. Chicago: University of Chicago Press, 1997. 236–55.

Slater, Michael, ed. *The Dent Uniform Edition of Dickens' Journalism: Sketches by Boz and Other Early Papers, 1833–39.* Columbus: Ohio State University Press, 1994.

Smalley, Donald. Introduction. *Domestic Manners of the Americans.* By Frances Trollope. Gloucester, MA: Peter Smith, 1974. vii–lxxvi.

Smith, Amy Elizabeth. "Roles for Readers in Mary Wollstonecraft's *A Vindication of the Rights of Woman.*" *Studies in English Literature* 32.3 (1992): 555–70.

Smith, Charlotte [Turner]. *The Poems of Charlotte Smith.* Edited by Stuart Curran. New York: Oxford University Press, 1993.

Stein, Richard L. *Victoria's Year: English Literature and Culture, 1837–1838.* New York: Oxford University Press, 1987.

Stevenson, Catherine Barnes. "Female Anger and African Politics: The Case of Two Victorian 'Lady Travellers.' " *Turn-of-the-Century Woman* 2 (1985): 7–17.

———. *Victorian Women Travel Writers in Africa.* Twayne's English Authors Series 349. Boston: Twayne, 1982.

Stone, Albert E. Introduction. *Letters from an American Farmer and Sketches of Eighteenth-Century America* by J. Hector St. John de Crèvecoeur. 1782. Edited by Albert E. Stone. New York: Penguin, 1981. 7–25.

Sunstein, Emily W. *A Different Face: The Life of Mary Wollstonecraft.* New York: Harper, 1975.

Swindells, Julia. *Victorian Writing and Working Women: The Other Side of Silence.* Minneapolis: University of Minnesota Press, 1985.

Swinnerton, Frank. Introduction. *Cranford.* By Elizabeth Gaskell. London: Dent, 1977.

Thomas, Gillian. *Harriet Martineau.* Boston: G. K. Hall, 1985.

Tinling, Marion. *With Women's Eyes: Visitors to the New World 1775–1918.* Hamden, CT: Archon, 1993.

———. *Women into the Unknown: A Sourcebook on Women Explorers and Travelers.* New York: Greenwood Press, 1989.

"To the Royal Geographical Society." *Punch* 10 June 1893: 269.

Todd, Janet. *Gender, Art and Death.* New York: Continuum, 1993.

Tomalin, Claire. *The Life and Death of Mary Wollstonecraft.* 1979. New York: Meridian, 1983.

Torrens, Hugh. "Mary Anning (1799–1847) of Lyme; 'the Greatest Fossilist the World Ever Knew.' " *The British Journal for the History of Science* 28 (1995):257–84.

Tristan, Flora. *Flora Tristan; Utopian Feminist: Her Travel Diaries and Personal*

Crusade. Edited and translated by Doris Beik and Paul Beik. Bloomington: Indiana University Press, 1993.

Trollope, Anthony. "An Unprotected Female at the Pyramids." *Anthony Trollope: The Complete Short Stories: Tourists and Colonials*. Vol. 3. Edited by Betty Jane Slemp Breyer. Fort Worth: Texas Christian University Press, 1981. 57–85.

Trollope, Frances. *Domestic Manners of the Americans*. Edited by Donald Smalley. Gloucester, MA: Peter Smith, 1974.

Tweedie, Ethel. [Ethel B. Harley; Mrs. Alec Tweedie]. *A Girl's Ride in Iceland*. London: Griffith, Farran, Okeden & Welsh, 1889.

Vicinus, Martha. Review of *Spinsters Abroad: Victorian Lady Explorers*, by Dea Birkett. *Victorian Studies* 34 (1990): 123–24.

Wang, Orrin N. C. "The Other Reasons: Female Alterity and Enlightenment Discourse in Mary Wollstonecraft's *A Vindication of the Rights of Woman*. *Yale Journal of Criticism* 5.1 (1991): 129–49.

Wardle, Ralph M., ed. *Collected Letters of Mary Wollstonecraft*. Ithaca: Cornell University Press, 1979.

Webb, R. K. *Harriet Martineau: A Radical Victorian*. London: Heinemann, 1960.

White, Hayden. "The Fictions of Factual Representation." *Tropics of Discourse: Essays in Cultural Criticism*. Baltimore: Johns Hopkins University Press, 1978. 121–34.

Wollstonecraft, Mary. *"On Poetry," Contributions to the Analytical Review 1788–1797*. Edited by Janet Todd and Marilyn Butler. Vol. 7. New York: New York University Press, 1989. 7 vols.

———. *A Short Residence in Sweden, Norway and Denmark. A Short Residence . . . .* Edited by Richard Holmes. Harmondsworth, England: Penguin, 1987. 57–200.

———. *A Vindication of the Rights of Woman*. 1792. Edited by Miriam Brody. London: Penguin, 1992.

Woolf, Virginia. "Four Figures." *The Second Common Reader*. 1932. New York: Harcourt, 1960. 127–55.

———. *Three Guineas*. New York: Harcourt, 1938.

Yates, Gayle Graham, ed. *Harriet Martineau on Women*. New Brunswick, NJ: Rutgers University Press, 1985.

Yeo, Richard R. *Defining Science: William Whewell, Natural Knowledge, and Public Debate in Early Victorian Britain*. Cambridge: Cambridge University Press, 1993.

———. "Science and Intellectual Authority in Mid-Nineteenth-Century Britain: Robert Chambers and *Vestiges of the Natural History of Creation*." *Victorian Studies* 28 (1984): 5–31.

———. "Scientific Method and the Rhetoric of Science in Britain, 1830–1917." *The Politics and Rhetoric of Scientific Method: Historical Studies*. Edited by John A. Schuster and Richard R. Yeo. Dordrecht, The Netherlands: D. Reidel, 1986. 259–97.

Index

Abir-am, Pnina G., 13, 24, 244 n. 39
Adamson, Joy, 227
Addison, Joseph, 239 n. 60
"Admirals' Doom, The," 182
Agassiz, Louis, 13
Alexander, Caroline, 191, 256 n. 52
Alic, Margaret, 13, 243 n. 23
Allen, David Elliston, 20
Analytical Review, 40, 54
Anderson, Nancy Fix, 235 n. 53
Andrews, Stuart, 241 n. 85
Anning, Mary, 13, 233 n.10
Anthropological Institute, 21, 145
Anthropological Society of London, 34
Anthropologists, 176
Anthropology, 214, 227
Arbuckle, Elisabeth Sanders, 245 n. 50, 249 n. 106
Arrival trope, 67, 126
Atkins, Anna, 20
Austen, Jane, 194, 256 n. 55

Babbage, Charles, 96
Baird, Spencer, 13
Banks, Joseph, 23
Barber, Lynn, 20
Barr, Pat, 144, 147, 150, 165, 168, 250 nn. 27 and 29
Barrett, Dorothea 235 n. 51
Barton, H. Arnold, 79
Beche, Henry Thomas de la, 105
Beddoes, Thomas, 238 n. 44
Beer, Gillian, 235 n. 39
Behdad, Ali, 126, 245 n. 52, 248 n. 102
Benjamin, Marina, 48
Big game hunting, 207–11
Binomial nomenclature, 38
Bird Bishop, Isabella, 16, 22, 24, 25, 27, 29, 133–56, 158–74, 181, 205, 216, 226–31; *Among the Tibetans*, 144, 151, 173, 190, 194, 195–96, 251

n. 34; *Aspects of Religion in the United States*, 137, 146; *The English-woman in America*, 137, 146; *The Golden Chersonese*, 148, 162, 171; *Journeys in Persia and Kurdistan*, 134, 136, 140, 148, 151, 162–73; *Korea and Her Neighbors*, 148; *A Lady's Life in the Rocky Mountains*, 133, 136, 138, 139, 148, 149–50, 155–56, 158–61; *Six Months in the Sandwich Islands*, 139, 147, 154–55, 158; *Unbeaten Tracks in Japan*, 148, 235 n. 41, 253 n. 75; *The Yangtze Valley and Beyond*, 148–49, 164, 252 n. 64
Birkett, Dea, 145, 176, 183, 185, 234 n. 34, 250 n. 27, 253 n. 75, 254 n. 22, 255 n. 40
Bishop, John, 148
Blackburn, Jemima, 20
Blunt, Alison, 145, 176, 206, 250 n. 18, 255 nn. 39 and 40, 258 n. 89
Blunt, Lady Anne, 145
Bowerbank, Sylvia, 41
Bowler, Peter J., 236 n. 54
Brassey, Lady, 145
Brewster, David, 90, 243 n. 22
British Admiralty, 23
British Association for the Advance-
ment of Science (BAAS) , 21, 95–97, 244–45 n. 46
British Association of Anthropology, 224
British Museum, 142, 175, 186
Brontë, Charlotte, 54, 85, 192
Browne, Edward Granville, 102, 252 n. 64
Browne, Janet, 23, 233 n. 10
Bryce Commission, 222
Buell, Lawrence, 35
Buffon, Georges-Louis Leclerc, 19, 40, 42

271

Burke, Edmund, 54
Burton, Richard F., 101, 102, 191–92, 202, 206, 217, 248 n. 104, 258 n. 88
Buzard, James, 84–85, 104, 120, 126, 239 n. 60, 247 nn. 89 and 91
Byatt, A. S., 233 n. 10

Caine, Barbara, 89, 243 n. 17
Campbell, Bob, 229
Carlyle, Thomas, 117
Cary, Elizabeth, 13
Chambers, Robert, 20, 83, 84, 94, 103, 115, 124, 131, 242 n. 1
Chapman, Maria Weston, 88
Children's literature, 11, 180
Christie, Ella, 145
Christie, John, 234 n. 35
Churchill, Mary, 13
Clerke, Agnes, 223
Clodd, E., 220
Coleridge, Samuel Taylor, 46, 69, 72, 77–78, 234 n. 35, 239 n. 61, 241 n. 102
Collectors, 13, 19–20, 23, 207–10, 233 n.10
Colonial Nursing Association, 220
Comte, Auguste, 131, 225
Conrad, Joseph, 231
Cook, James, 23
Coprolites, 13
Corfield, Penelope J., 56, 238 n. 50
Cowie, Alexander, 72
Craik, George, 185
Crèvecoeur, St. John de, 63, 237 n. 19, 242 n. 102
Croker, John Wilson, 116
Curzon, Lord George, 133, 143–45, 181, 250 nn. 18 and 19, 254 n. 20

Daily Telegraph, 197
Darwin, Charles, 23, 29, 43, 44, 91, 94, 103, 207, 227, 233 n. 10, 237 n. 26, 242 n. 1, 245 n. 57
Darwin, Erasmus (brother of Charles), 18, 21, 103, 237 n. 26, 238 n. 44, 248 n. 93
Darwinism, 34, 236 n. 54. See also Evolution: paradigm of
David, Deirdre, 89, 92, 129, 243 n. 14
Davies, Emily, 222
Davy, Humphry, 243 n. 23

DeBrazza, Pierre, 202, 206
de Man, Paul, 238 n. 36
Dickens, Charles, 96, 97, 106, 244 n. 46, 246 n. 66, 247 n. 89
Dijkstra, Bram, 257 n. 62
Disraeli, Benjamin, 117, 247 n. 85
Dixie, Florence, 25, 136, 154, 162, 249 n. 6, 251 n. 50
Domestic imagery, 83, 93–94, 101, 106, 159–61, 177, 207, 211–15, 218, 226, 252 n. 65
"Donna Quixote," 156–57, 252 n. 53
Doyle, Richard, 247 n. 89
Dress, traveling, 156–59, 194–97, 252 nn. 56 and 63
Du Chaillu, Paul 202, 206, 208
Duff Gordon, Lucie, 125, 170, 248 n. 98
Durrell, Gerald, 255 n. 35

Early, Julie English, 176
Edgeworth, Maria, 238 n. 44
Edgeworth, R. L., 238 n. 44
Edwards, Amelia, 136, 151, 223
Egypt Exploration Fund, 223
Eliot, George, 42, 85, 100, 123, 235 n. 51, 245 n. 50, 248 n. 94
Emerson, Oliver Farrar, 72, 73, 241 n. 102
Enlightenment, 18, 19
Epistolary form, 48, 57–65, 71, 139, 239 n. 60
Ernstrom, Adele, 89
Erosion, 45
Ethnological Society, 34, 197
Ethnology, 227
Evolution: paradigm of, 83, 123–24; relationship to gender roles, 22, 175, 197–200, 236 n. 54; relationship to race, 176, 199–200
Explorer identity, 14, 164–68, 170, 172, 176, 193, 195, 202–3, 206–11, 226

Farnes, Patricia, 13, 244 n. 39
Fawcett, Millicent, 52
Female Spectator, The, 19
Feminine discourse, 211–14, 221
Ferguson, Moira, 238 n. 42, 247 n. 80
Fetishism, 191, 253–54 n. 8

Fish, 175, 177, 189, 202–3, 255 n. 36, 257 n. 63
Flaubert, Gustave, 248 n. 104
Flexner, Eleanor, 52, 53
Forbes, Anna, 25, 29, 235 n. 41
Forbes, Henry O., 233 n. 10, 235 n. 41
Forest ecosystem, 45–46
Forster, E. M., 247 n. 91
Fossey, Dian, 227–31
Foucault, Michel, 243 n. 8
Fox, William Johnson, 99
Frank, Katherine, 196, 248 n. 98, 253 n. 7, 255 n. 40
Frawley, Maria, 16, 24, 86, 104, 109, 136, 242 n. 2, 251 n. 50
Frazer, James, 22, 176, 248 n. 94
Frere, John, 224

Galdikas, Biruté, 227–31
Galton, Francis, 92
Gaskell, Elizabeth, 85, 212, 258 n. 80
Gates, Barbara, 15, 62, 91
Gatty, Margaret, 20
Gender blurring, 192–97
"Genius," 90
Gibson, Margaret Dunlop, 256 n. 44
Gilbert, Sandra, 257 n. 62
Girton College, 186, 222
Godwin, William, 60; *Memoirs of Wollstonecraft*, 43, 51–52, 240 n. 75
Goodall, Jane, 227–32
Gordon-Cummings, Constance, 136
Gosse, Emily Bowes, 20
Gosse, Philip Henry, 20, 42, 45
Gould, Elizabeth, 20
Gould, John, 20
Gould, Stephen Jay, 233 n. 10, 257 n. 62
Green, Alice Stopford, 220–21
Gregory, Richard A., 223
Grimstone, Mary Lemon, 89
Grove, Lilly, 145
Gubar, Susan, 257 n. 62
Guillemard, Henry, 188–90, 256 n. 46
Günther, Albert, 186, 195, 202, 257 n. 63

Hall, Basil, 106, 246 n. 67
Haraway, Donna, 229
Hardy, Thomas, 194
Hare, Robert R., 241 n. 99

Harems, 129
Haywood, Eliza, 19
Henslow, J. S., 12
Hershel, Caroline, 223
Hershel, John, 96, 105
Hill, Michael, 101
Hill, Octavia, 11
Hobson, J. A., 258 n. 91
Hoecker-Drysdale, Susan, 101, 131
Holloway, John, 29
Hollyer, Belinda, 258 n. 90
Holmes, Richard, 41, 55–56, 57, 58, 70–71, 236 n. 17, 238 n. 54
Hooker, Joseph Dalton, 12, 29
Hooker, W. J., 12
Horseback riding, 147, 152–59, 251 n. 45
Howard, Mary, 13
Huggins, Margaret Murray, 13, 223
Huggins, William, 13
Hunt, James, 34
Huxley, T. H., 34, 92, 94, 197–98, 257 n. 60

Imlay, Fanny, 56, 73
Imlay, Gilbert, 55–56, 70–77, 239 n. 57; *The Emigrants*, 55, 71–72; *A Topographical Description of the Western Territory*, 47, 55, 71–78, 239 n. 60, 241 nn. 92, 99, 100, and 102
Ingpen, Roger, 52
Innes, Emily, 252 n. 68

James, Henry, 51
Jameson, Anna, 18, 89, 240 n. 62
Jefferson, Thomas, 241 n. 100
Jeffreys, Lousia, 247 n. 87
Jellyfish, 44, 237 n. 27
Jerome, Jerome K., 194
Johnson, Hatty, 188
Johnson, Joseph, 54, 238 n. 44
Jolly, Alison, 227
Jordanova, Ludmilla, 198, 236 n. 8
Julian of Norwich, 98
Jung, C. G., 237 n. 27
Jungle description, 209–15

Kass-Simon, G., 13, 244 nn. 33 and 39
Keller, Evelyn Fox, 93, 95, 243 n. 4, 244, n. 33
Kelly, Gary, 240 n. 64

Keltie, John Scott, 145
Kempe, Margery, 28, 98
Kerr, H. Bellenden, 105
Kew Gardens, 11, 12
King, Kathryn R., 252 n. 65
Kingsley, Charles (brother of Mary), 186, 187–88
Kingsley, Charles (uncle of Mary), 177, 185
Kingsley, George (father of Mary), 185, 187, 255 n. 41
Kingsley, Henry (uncle of Mary), 185
Kingsley, Mary, 16, 22, 24, 25, 27, 31, 34, 58, 62, 63, 77, 135, 136, 138, 145, 169, 175–221, 223, 226–30, 233 n. 10; *Travels in West Africa*, 177, 188, 202–19; *West African Studies*, 177, 202
Kingsley, Mary Bailey (mother of Mary), 187
Kipling, Rudyard, 143, 179–80, 250 n. 13
Koerner, Lisbet, 37
Krasner, James, 229
Kröller, Eva-Marie, 178, 253 n. 75, 257 n. 68, 258 n. 87
Kuhn, Thomas S., 225

Labor: description of, 77–78
Ladies' Companion at Home and Abroad, The, 19
Ladies' Diary, The, 19
Lane, Edward William, 248 n. 100
Lane, Margaret, 233 n. 2
Laqueuer, Thomas, 198, 243 n. 8
Lavater, Johann Kaspar, 42, 237 n. 23
Leakey, Louis, 224, 227, 228
Leakey, Mary Nicol, 224
Lee, Sarah Bowdich, 20
Le Gassick, Trevor, 248 n. 100
Levin, George, 235 n. 39
Lewes, G. H., 245 n. 50
Lewis, Agnes Smith, 145, 188, 256 n. 44
Lightman, Bernard, 15, 223
Lindley, John, 20
Lindsay, Debra, 13
Linné, Elizabeth, 13
Linnean Society of London, 11, 187
Linneaus, 19, 37–38, 236 n. 2

Linton, Eliza Lynn, 34, 183, 200, 235 n. 53, 256–57 n. 60
Livingstone, David, 102, 202, 206
Lloyd, Clare, 175
Lockyer, Norman, 185
Logging, 46
London Missionary Society, 202
Loudon, Jane, 13, 19
Loudon, John Claudius, 13
Lowes, John, 59, 234 n. 35, 239 n. 61
Lubbock, John, 182
Lyall, Alfred, 176
Lyell, Charles, 20, 21, 84, 103, 114
Lysenko, Trofim, 236 n. 6

Macaulay, Catherine, 59, 239 n. 60
McClintock, Barbara, 93, 244 n. 33, 253 n. 8
MacDonald, Lady, 196, 200
McGuinn, Nicholas, 235 n. 51
McIntosh, Charles, 11
Macmillan, George, 193, 202
Malthus, Thomas, 41, 237 n. 26
Mann, Gustav, 217, 258 n. 88
Maple sugar making, 76
Marcet, Jane, 13, 18, 91, 92, 243 n. 23
Marsden, Kate, 143
Martineau, Harriet, 16, 20–21, 24, 25–26, 27, 51, 63, 77, 82–132, 135, 136, 169, 172–73, 190, 194, 195, 202, 215, 220, 225, 226, 227; deafness of, 109, 129; response to Trollope, 107–9, 111–14; compared to Wollstonecraft, 127; response to Wollstonecraft, 87–89, 237 n. 26; *Autobiography*, 104, 124; *Deerbrook*, 85; *Eastern Life: Past and Present*, 26, 83, 123–32, 138, 170; *How to Observe Morals and Manners*, 97, 101, 104, 105; *Illustrations of Political Economy*, 90–92, 99, 102, 103, 104, 110; "On Female Education," 87, 94; *Retrospect of Western Travel*, 83, 103, 104, 112–15, 118–23; *Society in America*, 83, 101, 103, 104, 115, 121
Massee, George, 11
Mazuchelli, Nina, 249 n. 6
Mead, Margaret, 227
Melman, Billie, 247 n. 92, 253 n. 77
Merchant, Carolyn, 243 n. 4

Mermin, Dorothy, 247 n. 90
Merrill, Lynn L., 20
Mesmerism, 42
Middleton, Dorothy, 28, 250 n. 27, 255 n. 39
Mill, J. S., 93
Miller, Hugh, 233 n. 10, 236 n. 12
Miller, Luree, 250 n. 27
Millhauser, Milton, 43, 237 n. 25
Mills, Sara, 30–32, 178, 235 n. 50, 249 n. 1
Milnes, Ricard, 125
Mining, 46
Monthly Repository, 99
Moon imagery, 69–70, 240–41 n. 83
Moore, Tom, 241 n. 102
Morgan, Lady, 89
Morgan, Susan, 29, 234 n. 30, 235 n. 41, 252 n. 68
Morris, Mary, 36, 251 n. 42
Morton, Peter, 235 n. 39
Moss, Cynthia, 227
Mountain climbing, 207, 215–19, 258 n. 88
Murray, John III, 145, 148, 150, 158, 247 n. 89, 250 n. 33
Murray, Margaret, 224

Nassau, Robert Hamill, 191, 209
Nathan, Matthew, 220
National Geographic, 229, 231
National Trust, 12
Natural history tradition, 15, 85, 226–27
Natural selection, 43
Nature, 223
Nature guides, 20
Needlework, 99, 101
Nerval, Gérard de, 248 n. 104
"New Woman" movement, 156–57, 178, 181, 197, 251–52 n. 52, 255 n. 44
Nightingale, Florence, 104, 180, 248 n. 100
Noble, Mary, 233 n. 1
North, Marianne, 25, 29, 138, 234 n. 30, 235 n. 41
Nugent, Jim, 169, 255 n. 41
Nyström, Per, 57

Oelsner, Elise, 244 n. 31
Ogilvie, Marilyn Baily, 13

Outram, Dorinda, 13, 24, 244 n. 39
Overpopulation and famine, fear of, 41

Paley, William, 19
Park, Mungo, 215
Paul, Charles Kegan, 52, 58, 239 n. 57
Pembroke, Earl of, 255 n. 41
Peterson, Linda H., 244 n. 29
Phillips, John, 96
Phillips, Patricia, 21–22, 222–23, 244 n. 39
Photographs, 164, 196–97, 229, 252 n. 64
Phrenology, 42, 237 n. 23
Pichanick, Valerie Kossew, 131, 245 n. 47, 253 n. 77
Pilgrimage discourse, 124, 129, 170–71
Pliny, 237 n. 27
Poole, Reginald, 223
Poovey, Mary, 60, 62–63
Popular education, 100, 135
Popularization in science, role of, 15, 140
Potter, Beatrix, 11–12, 222
Pratt, Mary Louise, 28, 30, 36, 37, 47, 58, 67, 206–7, 216, 235 nn. 37 and 50, 258 n. 82
Price, Richard, 53, 54
Priestley, Joseph, 238 n. 44
Primatology, 227–30
Professional scientific societies, formation of, 94, 141–142; women's membership in, 21, 82, 86, 95–97, 143–44, 163, 174, 175, 176, 186, 191, 198–99, 220–21, 222–26
Punch, 156–57, 181–83, 244–45 n. 46, 254–55 n. 23
Purcell, Rosamond, 233 n. 10

Rawnsley, Hardwiche, 11
Reid, Marion, 89
Rice, Edward, 258 n. 88
Richards, Evelleen, 34–35, 244 n. 39
Richards, Thomas, 142, 250 n. 13
Romanticism, 30, 31, 40, 54, 59, 120
Roscoe, Henry, 11
Rose, Gillian, 255 n. 39
Rousseau, Jean-Jacques, 19, 26, 47, 59–61, 68, 74, 236 n. 2
Rowing, 44, 113, 152, 193–94, 195
Roy, Violet Paget, 188, 256 n. 44

Royal African Society, 180, 221
Royal Asiatic Society, 21, 142, 145
Royal Astronomical Society, 223
Royal Geographical Society, 21, 22, 28, 133, 135, 142, 143–45, 180–83, 193, 197, 202
Royal Microscopic Society, 187
Royal Niger Company, 220
Royal Society, 142
Rush, Benjamin, 76
Rusk, Ralph Leslie, 72, 73
Ruskin, John, 120
Ryall, Anka, 40

Said, Edward, 71, 126, 248 n. 102
Sand, George, 100
Sanders, Valerie, 84, 253 n. 77
Sapiro, Virginia, 237 n. 34
Sattin, Anthony, 248 n. 100
Sawyer, Herbert, 137, 138, 141, 143, 164–67, 229
Schiebinger, Londa, 13, 86–87
Schoolcraft, Henry Rowe, 13
"Science:" meaning of, 12–15, 20, 85, 175, 200, 203, 224–25
Science: public rhetoric of, 33, 90, 94, 227
Scientific authority, 14, 94, 169–70, 208–9
Scientific biography: absence of women from, 12–17, 20
Scientific fieldwork: expectations for, 207–15, 227–30
Scientific histories, 23
Scottish Geographical Society, 143, 145
Sea monsters, 41–42
Sedgwick, Adam, 96
Seelye, John, 72
Separate spheres ideology, 197–200, 205–6, 212
Servants, 77–78
Sheepshanks, Anne, 223
Sheldon, May French, 143
Shelley, Mary Godwin Wollstonecraft, 49, 52, 239 n. 62
Shelley, Percy Bysshe, 59, 238 n. 36
Shore, Emily, 105
Showalter, Elaine, 252 nn. 52 and 53
Shteir, Ann B., 13, 15, 20
Skeat, Clara, 188

Sketchley, Arthur, 247 n. 89
Smalley, Donald, 246 n. 67
Smith, Amy Elizabeth, 240 n. 74
Smith, Charlotte Turner, 42, 240–41 n. 83
Smith, Lillian Zoe, 235 n. 50
Smith, Lucy Toulmin, 187, 256 nn. 44 and 50
Smollett, Tobias, 239 n. 60
Smyth, Warrington, 145
Society for the Diffusion of Useful Knowledge, 91
Sociology, 82–84, 97, 101, 106
Solitary narrative position, 14–17, 68, 138, 149–50, 177, 204, 228, 230
Solitary travel, difficulty for women, 17–18, 25, 26, 151–52, 192–93
Somerville, Mary, 13, 92, 223
Southey, Robert, 72, 77–78, 239 n. 61, 241 n. 102
Spencer, Herbert, 84, 92, 225
Stanley, Henry Morton, 206, 215
Steenstrup, Johannes Japetus, 44
Stein, Richard L., 85, 246 n. 70
Stevenson, Catherine Barnes, 211, 255 nn. 40 and 43, 258 n. 85
Stoddart, Anna M., 147
Strauss, David Friedrich, 123
Strindberg, August, 198
Strum, Shirley, 227
Sublime, 46, 62, 113–14, 204–5
Sunstein, Emily W., 238 n. 42
Surveillance convention, 215–19, 258 n. 82
Swindells, Julia, 33
Swinnerton, Frank, 258 n. 80
Sykes, Ella Constance, 153

Tait, William, 116
Talbort, D. Amaury, 149
Talleyrand, Charles Maurice de, 238 n. 52
Tennyson, Alfred, 42
Thiselton-Dyer, William T., 11
Thomas, Gillian, 26, 245 nn. 47, 53, and 77
Thoreau, Henry, 234 n. 35
Tinling, Marion, 234 n. 36, 250 n. 27
Tocqueville, Alexis de, 84, 109, 111, 115, 126, 246 n. 68

Todd, Janet, 53, 237 n. 35, 238 n. 42, 241 n. 88
Tomalin, Claire, 53, 55, 56, 68, 71, 238 n. 42
Tooley, Sarah, 197
"To the Royal Geographical Society," 181–83
Torrens, Hugh, 233 n. 10
Tourist traveling, avoidance of, 120, 123, 172, 247 n. 89
Trade language, 192
Tristan, Flora, 17–18
Trollope, Anthony, 246 n. 61
Trollope, Frances, 83, 106, 107–9, 118, 126, 127, 171, 188, 246 n. 67, 247 n. 89
Turner, Dawson, 12, 13
Turner, Mary, 13
Twain, Mark, 178, 194
Tweedie, Ethel Brilliana, 152, 154, 162, 249 n. 6, 251 n. 42, 252 n. 56

Volney, Constantin François de Chasseboeuf, 117, 247 n. 85

Wallace, Alfred Russel, 23, 29, 252 n. 69
Wang, Orrin N. C., 238 n. 36
Ward, Mrs. Humphrey, 183
Webb, R. K., 245 n. 47, n. 48
Wheatley, Phyllis, 71, 75
Whewell, William, 200, 244 n. 28
White, Gilbert, 209
Wilberforce, William, 146
Wilde, Oscar, 200
Wilkinson, John Gardner, 129, 248 nn. 94 and 100
Wollstonecraft, Eliza, 53

Wollstonecraft, Everina, 53, 54, 236 n. 15
Wollstonecraft, Mary, 16, 18, 19, 20, 24, 26, 31, 36–81, 84, 92, 100, 114, 135, 136, 139, 169, 195, 220, 224–31; *Female Reader*, 38; *Historical and Moral View of the French Revolution*, 56; *Letters to Imlay*, 52, 58; *Short Residence* 36–49, 53, 55–56, 57–70, 74, 76–81, 88, 89, 101, 115, 205, 238 n. 54, 239 n. 57; *Thoughts on the Education of Daughters*, 53; *Vindication of the Rights of Man*, 54, 238–39 n. 46; *Vindication of the Rights of Woman*, 40, 42, 44, 52, 54, 56, 62, 74, 86, 238 n. 54; and natural history, 40–49; compared to Martineau, 118–19
Women: access to government support, 23; education of, 21–22, 222; problems with biographical treatment of, 31, 49–53, 197, 229–32; role in colonialism, 32, 162–64, 176, 191, 220, 252 n. 68; vocation of, 32, 53–54, 178, 232
Women travelers: discomfort of, 171–72; economics of, 25; illness, 27, 147, 154, 168, 249 n. 4; narratives of, 24, 31, 110, 136, 151; physical engagement, 172–73, 193–94, 231; transportation, 195
Woolf, Virginia, 72, 168–69, 187, 241 n. 88, 255 n. 43
Wordsworth, William, 59, 69, 240 n. 69

Yeo, Richard R., 20, 33, 85, 242 n. 1, 243 n. 22, 244 n. 28
Young, Edward, 68
Young Woman, 197